Religion and Immigration

Immigration & Society series

Religion and Immigration

Migrant Faiths in North America and Western Europe

Peter Kivisto

polity

First published in 2014 by Polity Press

Polity Press
65 Bridge Street
Cambridge CB2 1UR, UK

Polity Press
350 Main Street
Malden, MA 02148, USA

ISBN-13: 978-0-7456-4169-0 (hardback)
ISBN-13: 978-0-7456-4170-6 (paperback)

A catalogue record for this book is available from the British Library.

Typeset in 11 on 13 pt Sabon by
Servis Filmsetting Ltd, Stockport, Cheshire
Printed and bound in Great Britain by TJ International, Padstow, Cornwall

The publisher has used its best endeavors to ensure that the URLs for external websites referred to in this book are correct and active at the time of going to press. However, the publisher has no responsibility for the websites and can make no guarantee that a site will remain live or that the content is or will remain appropriate.

Every effort has been made to trace all copyright holders, but if any have been inadvertently overlooked the publisher will be pleased to include any necessary credits in any subsequent reprint or edition.

For further information on Polity, visit our website: www.politybooks.com

Dedicated to the memory of Robert W. Nagle 1955–2014

Contents

Acknowledgments

The idea for this book originated in a conversation I had with Emma Longstaff in Montreal at the time she set out to launch the Immigration and Society series. I owe her a debt of gratitude for looking to me to write this particular volume for the series. In what is my first experience of publishing with Polity, I would like to extend my thanks to everyone I came into contact with, for in all instances they were a pleasure to work with. One person in particular deserves special recognition: Jonathan Skerrett. Although this is a relatively short book, it was a long time coming and during that time Jonathan proved to be the embodiment of patience, again and again revealing a remarkable capacity to remain (at least from my vantage) calm while waiting for the manuscript to land finally on his doorstep. He did gently nudge me along at various points, always expressing his continued support. I hope that he is pleased with the end result.

A number of people have helped me think through and frame the issues addressed herein, some very directly and others in a somewhat more indirect way. I would like to extend heartfelt thanks to Jeffrey C. Alexander, Paolo Boggani, Kevin Christiano, Phillip Connor, Thomas Faist, Margit Fauser, Nancy Foner, Inger Furseth, Doug Hartmann, Auvo Kostiainen, Peter Kraus, Feith Mansouri, Vince Marotta, Vanja La Vecchia-Mikkola, Peggy Levitt, Leo Lucassen, Tariq Modood, Tuomas Martikainen, Peter Marty, Ewa Morawska, Rubén Rumbaut, Pasi Saukkonen, Giuseppe Sciortino, Bill Swatos, Mari Toivanen, Östen Wahlbeck, R. Stephen Warner, and Rhys Williams.

Acknowledgments

For a different form of help, I would like to thank my children, Sarah and Aaron, and their respective partners, Bob and Katie. And, finally, there is one other person who knows something about patience, not to mention love and nurture: my wife Susan. I hope she enjoys this latest addition to our bookshelf.

1

Introduction: Religion on the Move

The Brick Lane Jamme Masjid is located in London's East End on the corner of Brick Lane and Fournier Street. A fifteen-minute walk from Liverpool Street Station, the mosque serves the large Bangladeshi population that began to flock into the surrounding neighborhood in the 1970s. The world these immigrants have created in this urban enclave was vividly depicted in Monica Ali's acclaimed and controversial novel, *Brick Lane* (2003). The listed Georgian building officially opened as a mosque in 1976 and since then a number of improvements to the interior and exterior of the building have been completed, including the construction of what has been described as a minaret-like public sculpture, a 90-foot-high, brightly lit stainless steel tower.

Reflecting the area's long history of ethnic succession, Jamme Masjid represents the fourth distinct religious identity of the building. Originally built in 1743, La Neuve Eglise served as a chapel for Huguenot refugees who fled persecution in France and soon became the dominant group in the silk-weaving industry of Spitalfields. By the early nineteenth century, considerable assimilation had occurred, along with a movement out of the neighborhood for more affluent parts of London. Very quickly, Huguenots were replaced by Jews. In 1809, Wesleyans leased the building with the idea of having it serve as the institutional hub of the London Society for Promoting Christianity. This was an evangelical group founded by Joseph Fry, a Jewish-born convert to Christianity, which was devoted to missionary work within the

Jewish community. This relatively short-lived and rather fruit-less effort was abandoned in 1819, when the facility became a Methodist Church whose outreach work no longer extended to Jews. It remained a Methodist house of worship until 1897, when a group of Orthodox Jews from Lithuania known as the Mahzikei Hadas (Strengtheners of the Faith) purchased the property and established the Spitalfields Great Synagogue, modeled after the major synagogues of Eastern Europe. With the arrival of large numbers of Jews from Eastern Europe in the early twentieth century, the congregation grew and thrived, becoming one of the most important institutions serving the needs of the immigrant population in East London.

As with the Huguenots earlier, Jews over time gained an economic foothold in the London economy, permitting over the course of the twentieth century the entry of many into the middle class. With upward mobility came geographic mobility. By World War II, large numbers of Jews had exited East London for more affluent London environs, such as Golders Green in North London. Attendance at the Great Synagogue declined precipi-tously in the post-war era, forcing the board to close operations in 1952. Some decades later, the Machzikei Hadath Synagogue was built in Golders Green. Meanwhile as Bangladeshis moved into the Brick Lane area, a group from within that community arranged to purchase the property and thus began the fourth and current reli-gious use of the structure 233 years after it had been built.

59 Brick Lane, the official address of the site, has thus been home to all three of what are increasingly referred to as the Abrahamic religions: Christianity, Judaism, and Islam. The first immigrants who were responsible for the building's construction were refugees fleeing religious persecution. Such was also true of Eastern European Jews, though political and religious oppression were mixed with economic factors in contributing to this infusion of newcomers. Finally, the postcolonial migrants from Bangladesh were a much clearer instance of labor migrants. Meanwhile the presence of a Methodist chapel for much of the nineteenth century is a reminder that ethnic enclaves usually contain a far more het-erogeneous population than is often appreciated, and this means

that immigrants invariably confront not only fellow ethnics, but also both members of other immigrant groups and members of the native-born population.

Not only did the three immigrant groups arrive in East London for somewhat different reasons, but arriving as they did at different historical moments, they entered a host society that was subject to profound and ongoing transformations brought about by the impact over time of industry and empire (Hobsbawm 1968). The Huguenots arrived before the Industrial Revolution had mechanized the textile industry. As silk weavers, they were part of a craft tradition that was under assault by the forces of technological transformation, leading to considerable conflict. This immigrant group was involved in militant actions that led to the passage of the Spitalfield Act of 1765, which for a time made silk weaving a protected industry with regulated wages. As the classic histories of the English working class make clear, these actions were incapable of stopping the juggernaut of industrial capitalism (Thompson 1963; Hobsbawm 1964).

Jews entered East London after capitalism's triumph and thus inhabited a different world of work. At the same time, they arrived when, beginning with the Chartist movement and extending to the creation of the Labour Party, the working class was acquiring a political voice and efforts were made to forge worker solidarity by overcoming ethnic divides within the ranks. This is not to overlook the fact that Jews confronted considerable anti-Semitic hostility during this time. That being said, the growing middle-class prosperity of the Jewish community over the course of the twentieth century took place during the creation and expansion of the British welfare state and the attempt to shape citizenship along the lines described by T.H. Marshall (1964) in which the status of citizenship and the three rights associated with it – civic, political, and social – in combination served to mitigate against the excessive inequality generated by an unbridled capitalism (see Kivisto and Faist 2007: 54–6 for a discussion of what Marshall refers to as "class abatement").

Finally, by the time Bangladeshis arrived in London, somewhat after their Indian and Pakistani counterparts from the Indian subcontinent, the era of postcolonialism was well underway and deindustrialization had begun to take hold with a vengeance. Instead of jobs in the manufacturing sector serving as transmission belts for upward mobility, newcomers entering Britain with low levels of human capital found themselves at a distinct disadvantage in the labor market. Timing played a role, for the large influx of approximately 330,000 Bangladeshis arrived at precisely that point when the British economy reached its nadir. As the Winter of Discontent gave way to the economic restructuring defined by the neoliberal policies of the Thatcher government, a new postindustrial society emerged. By the turn of the century, Bangladeshis had the highest unemployment level of any group in the UK, at nearly 20 percent. Reflective of a changing economy, only 12 percent found employment in the manufacturing sector, while 55 percent found work in the hotel and restaurant sector – as Brick Lane become a major tourist destination, akin to Chinatown.

Nevertheless, just before the economic crisis of 2008, the *Economist* magazine (2007) reported that there were measurable improvements in educational achievement of the second generation and that a growing number of workers were entering skilled and professional occupations. At the same time, as with Jews, the new immigrants experienced the hostile reaction of the receiving society, which was shaped in terms of both racial and religious otherness. This occurred, however, in a somewhat different context than earlier in the twentieth century, for despite limitations, British society today is more amenable to multiculturalism than it was only a few decades ago (Kivisto 2002: 138–54; Modood 2005, 2010). This is not to deny the backlash or the temptation toward what Paul Gilroy (2006) has called "postcolonial melancholia." Rather, it is to note that in the struggle over multiculturalism as a mode of incorporation, there are more proponents today than in the past (Alexander 2013).

From the eighteenth to the twenty-first century Brick Lane has experienced major economic changes. Its various immigrant populations have confronted different economic prospects and challenges, and with them an array of issues concerning their well-being such as housing conditions, health care, educational opportunities, and the prevalence of crime and other social problems in their environments. At the same time, they have had to deal with and confront obstacles that have prevented their political empowerment and stymied their efforts to become something other than second-class citizens. All of this takes place within social worlds shaped by gender, race, class, age, and generation. As anyone familiar with the already huge and ever-expanding literature on contemporary immigration to the developed nations can attest, social scientists have expended considerable time, energy, and resources addressing these issues. And increasingly, this has been done with an appreciation of the virtues of comparative analyses, be they comparisons between the past and present or between different contemporary contexts, or whether they are posed at the national or subnational level.

Brick Lane is, of course, a microcosm of a larger phenomenon. Although a paradigmatic example of neighborhoods characterized by the ethnic succession of ever-changing immigrant populations, one could find countless other examples from the cities of North America and Western Europe. Moreover, Brick Lane is a neighborhood located within the context of a larger urban conglomeration, which in turn is located in a region and ultimately a nation. Immigration research should of necessity concern itself with all of these levels, with an awareness of the dialectical relations between and among levels of analysis. Furthermore, as those who have advanced what has become known as a transnational optic have persuasively revealed, it is equally important to locate that which occurs within the containers of nation-states in terms of the larger parameters of transnational ties, networks, and fields (Glick Schiller 1997; Levitt and Jaworsky 2007).

For their part, the individuals who move across borders bring multiple aspects of their identities with them. Immigration studies concerned with the Great Migration to the United States between 1880 and 1924 have been particularly interested in the salience of ethnic identity as a factor contributing to the ease or difficulty of transition to a new environment. And reciprocally other studies have explored the varied reactions of the established residents of receiving societies to the presence of newcomers whose ethnic identities made them stand out from the larger national culture. Ultimately the two strands of research have in combination teased out the implications of the presence of newcomers in redefining what it means to be a member of a societal community. This has been a hallmark of scholarship from the Chicago School of Sociology to the work of social historians since the 1970s (Kivisto 1990). Although the significance of religion for these immigrants was not ignored, religion received considerably less attention than other aspects of ethnicity. This was particularly true of the major works produced by social historians, for a majority of them came to their topics from the vantage of class, race/ethnicity, and gender. Religion was not accorded anywhere near the same level of attention. A cursory examination of John Bodnar's *The Transplanted* (1985), the major work devoted to offering a synthetic account of the body of scholarship produced by social historians and historical sociologists, reflects this relative lack of attention.

At the same time that this work was being produced, social scientists were turning their attention to the new migratory wave flowing into all of the developing nations. Building on a tradition of research defined by the preceding major migratory wave, the empirical foci of the work on contemporary immigrants paralleled that devoted to the previous epoch. From the 1970s forward, a vast and ever-expanding body of research has been produced. Taking stock in the early 1990s of the portion of that work that was devoted to religion, I concluded that although one could point to a number of significant contributions to the topic, in fact overall religion as a topic of inquiry was characterized by relative neglect (Kivisto 1992). This neglect can be seen in Sylvia Pedraza-Bailey's conceptual map of immigration research published two years earlier. In her effort to summarize the major themes structuring what she called the recent "veritable boom in immigration research," religion does not appear as one of those themes, not even as – to use her metaphor – a blue highway, by which she means an unpaved road (Pedraza-Bailey 1990: 43).

Since the early 1990s, a lot has changed. A substantial body of research on religion and immigration has been published, with the

much has been done to redress the earlier mar-
religious factor in immigration studies (Warner
Ebaugh 2001; Cadge and Ecklund 2007; Massey
). Within sociology proper, within the sociology
ld, immigrant religion is today a hot topic, the
dy of new religious movements was two decades
while, many established sociologists of immigration
ot previously focused on religion are doing so (e.g.,
ad Alba 2008; Massey and Espinoza 2011), while younger
ues have picked up on the topic early in their careers. When
revised their best-selling *Immigrant America: A Portrait* for
rd edition, Alejandro Portes and Rubén Rumbaut (2006:
included a lengthy and in their word "overdue" chapter on
on. A relatively short time ago one could bemoan the lack of
attention paid to religion and immigration, and proffer possible
explanations for why this might be the case (e.g., the secular biases
of sociologists). Today one is left with the daunting task of sifting
through a very large body of research in order to: (1) discern
the lessons learned from it; (2) distill central themes shaping the
agenda; and (3) point to current shortcomings and lacunae. All
this would be essential if one wants to distill a synthetic account
of the state of the field.

Outline of Major Themes

The goal I have set out in this book is to provide such an account.
In so doing, I have identified four topics that can be found running
through the literature, sometimes intertwined, often not. Each
of these topics will be taken up in subsequent chapters, beginning with chapter 2, where we address whether or not religion
functions to promote immigrant adjustment. Here we are concerned with determining if, when, and how religion plays a role
in facilitating an individual immigrant's ability to come to terms
with his or her new home. Is religion a source of solace? Does it
offer spiritual compensation for earthly distress? Is it a vehicle for
incorporation? Is religious affiliation a means for making claims

directed at the receiving society about moral worthiness? On the other hand, do inherited religious traditions inhibit an immigrant's ability to become a full societal member? These and related questions concerning the impact of religious belief, practice, and affiliation on immigrants will be explored through an explication of the literature. An intriguing – though at this point rather speculative question – concerns differences in adjustment patterns between immigrants involved in institutional religion and those who are not.

Chapter 3 is concerned with institutional reframing. One aspect of reframing involves the form that religious organizations take in the new homeland. R. Stephen Warner (1994, 1998a) has argued that in the United States the religions of immigrants have tended to take on a congregational form, thereby adapting institutionally to the Christian – indeed, Protestant – character of American religion. This chapter investigates this phenomenon, paying particular attention to the implications of shifts in institutional structure on religious practice and levels of religious commitment. It also examines the extent to which institutional framing has facilitated civic engagement.

Another aspect of institutional reframing concerns relations between immigrant religious communities and the religious institutions of the receiving society. This would include such topics as ecumenical initiatives to foster at a minimum tolerance and maximally recognition and respect, denominational support of new immigrant religious bodies, and support for and resistance to the promotion of multi-ethnic institutions. Given that Warner's thesis can be read as being based at least implicitly on a version of American exceptionalism, this chapter offers fertile ground for comparative assessments of different national settings.

Chapter 4 analyzes the topic of religious transnationalism, which as a critical aspect of socio-cultural transnationalism has only in the past decade or so begun to receive the scholarly attention it merits. Using a distinction made by Peggy Levitt (2004), this chapter will address both what it means for individual immigrants to live transnational lives and the role of institutions representing the various major world religions in promoting the creation of transnational social spaces. The primary framework of this chapter will be on research that has employed the transnational optic to explore the interplay between origins and destinations in shaping the religious identities, beliefs, practices, and institutions of both migrants and non-migrants alike. The final topic introduced in the chapter concerns the role of religion in shaping homeland engagements, including in some instances promoting political agendas.

Contrary to postnationalist thinkers (Soysal 1994) and the influence of the postnationalist thesis on some theorists of transnationalism, recent research on the power of states to determine not only who gets in but on what terms calls for a need to bring the state back into the terms of analysis. Chapter 5 is devoted to precisely this topic, focusing on the role of receiving states in articulating and advancing top-down state policies concerning religion (Joppke and Torpey 2013). It also examines the place of religion in the public sphere and the role of collective actors in civil society in developing bottom-up, rather than top-down, responses to the expansion of religious diversity in liberal democracies. State and civil society are, of course, intertwined in a dialogical relationship. Thus, if public opinion suggests a repudiation of a government's integration policies, the state must take note.

While much of what is occurring in these interrelated spheres has proven to be uncontroversial, religion has not always insulated immigrants from hostility directed at them by members of the larger society, and in fact has sometimes been the central core of animus. This chapter analyzes the challenges to immigrant inclusion posed by prejudice and discrimination. Not surprisingly, since 9/11 and subsequent terrorist acts in places such as London, Madrid, and Bali, Muslims have been the objects of the greatest levels of antipathy. For that reason, though not the sole topic of this chapter, the growing presence of Islam in the West will receive the greatest amount of attention. In this regard, given the fact that there are differences in the levels of and forms taken by anti-Muslim sentiment in different countries, this chapter will offer the opportunity for comparative assessment.

Of course, immigrant religious adherents need not simply be

victims and innocents; they can also be advocates of violence, or promoters of what Mark Juergensmeyer (2003) refers to as "terror in the mind of God." Furthermore, conflict need not be violent, but can take various other more or less legitimate forms. It is clear that the fears associated with Islamophobia are disproportionate to the actual threat of jihadist violence. At the same time, the evidence in several nations with large Muslim populations points to troubling levels of social and economic marginalization. It is within this context that a climate of anxiety about the presumed failure of incorporative efforts plays out. When venturing into this topic, it becomes clear that one is dealing with a rapidly evolving topic and sociological analysis frequently gives way to the journalism of the moment.

Chapter 6, a brief epilogue, attempts to draw some admittedly circumspect conclusions based on the juxtaposition of the primary lessons to be drawn to date from each of the four topics. For instance, it will look at the question of whether immigrant religions over time will continue to prove to be bulwarks against secularization (admittedly entering into contested territory characterized by thorny debates over secularization theory), or whether the offspring of the immigrant generation, as they become more familiar with the receiving society and less familiar with the society of their parents, will as a consequence imbibe the secular culture of the new homeland. Or will they select religious options available in that homeland that are more consonant with its core values, in the process abandoning the religion of their parents? Or will they seek to revise, reform, or in some ways reshape their inherited religion to make it more fully conform to the cultural expectations of that homeland? Ultimately, these and related questions come down to the issue of how immigrants and non-immigrants alike confront what Robert Wuthnow (2005) has referred to as the "challenges of religious diversity."

The Religious Diversity of Immigrants

What do we know about the religious affiliations of contemporary migrants? The short answer is, considerably less than we wish we knew. In tracking the flows of migrants across international borders, the standard definitional unit is national origin, not religious affiliation. And the main tools of analysis, such as the passport, reinforce the idea that we define people by their national origins. Thus, one can obtain rather precise data on the number of legal (the undocumented are, of course, another story) immigrants who have entered the United States over a specified period of time from Mexico and various countries in Central and South America, and one can obtain similar data on the number of immigrants that have entered France legally from the nations of the Maghreb and from its former foreign territories. Similar data on religious affiliation have been, for the large part, lacking. This being said, there have been studies devoted to examining specific religious groups moving to particular destination countries, and there have been efforts to look at particular religions in differing national contexts (e.g., Foner and Alba 2008; Mooney 2009). However, such work has been rather limited in scope and none of it has provided a comprehensive global overview.

It is with this lack of crucial information in mind that the Pew-Templeton Global Religious Futures project – an effort jointly funded by The Pew Charitable Trusts and the John Templeton Foundation – has attempted to provide a broad overview of the movement of religions across borders along with the individuals that embrace them, in what is intended to be a baseline for further data-gathering efforts. Headed by primary researcher Phillip Connor, a report titled "Faith on the Move: The Religious Affiliation of International Migrants" appeared in March of 2012 and immediately received considerable media attention, as reflected, for example, in the headline of Tamara Audi's (2012) article that appeared in the *Wall Street Journal,* proclaiming "US Top Draw for Christians and Buddhists."

The United Nations estimates that in 2010 there were 214 million migrants globally, representing 3.1 percent of the total population of the world. Although the number of migrants had nearly tripled over the past half century, as a percentage of overall world population, the rise had only amounted to a 0.5 percent increase. At the same time, 214 million is a very large figure. In fact, there are only four countries in the world whose populations exceed that number. Given that immigrants often differ in significant demographic ways (such as age, gender composition, educational attainment, and the like) from those who stay behind and given that they constitute such a small slice of the global population, an immediate question arises concerning how well they are reflective of or differ from the primary religious affiliations of those who stay behind.

We will not concern ourselves here about the complexity of the project undertaken by the Pew Research Center, stitching together in order to obtain their estimates a substantial number of different censuses and surveys and complementing them with other data sources, such as the University of Sussex's Global Migrant Origin Database, when existing surveys or censuses did not suffice. Instead, we will concentrate on the main findings of the report, which while extremely valuable, should be seen for what they are: "a baseline look at the nominal affiliation of migrants, with no attempt to measure their levels of religious commitment" ("Faith on the Move" 2012: 8). In this project, it should be noted, researchers used the United Nations Population Division's definition of an immigrant as an individual who has lived for a year or more outside of the country in which he or she was born.

Table 1.1 provides a portrait of the religious composition of international migrants. As can be readily seen, Christians comprise by far the largest overall percentage, representing just under a half of all immigrants. Muslims are a distant second, their portion of the total being more than 20 percentage points lower than Christians. That being said, Muslims account for slightly over a quarter of all international migrants and comprise a far larger percentage than any of the other reported categories. Indeed, the next largest category, the unaffiliated, accounts for only 9 percent of the total, while in descending order, Hindus account for 5 percent, other religions for 4 percent (this includes such groups as

Table 1.1   Religious Composition of International Migrants

Religious affiliation	Number	Percentage
Christian	105,670,000	49
Muslim	58,580,000	27
Unaffiliated	19,330,000	9
Hindu	10,700,000	5
Other religions	9,110,000	4
Buddhist	7,310,000	3
Jewish	3,650,000	2

Data source: Pew Research Center's Forum on Religion and Public Life Global Religion and Migration Database 2010

Sikhs, Jains, Taoists, and members of various folk and traditional religions), Buddhists for 3 percent, and Jews for 2 percent (see table 1.1).

It is perhaps not surprising that Christians and Muslims are the two largest groups due to the fact that they are also the two largest world religions. That being said, given that at 2.3 billion adherents, Christians account for one-third of the world's population overall, their nearly 50 percent level among immigrants indicates that they are rather significantly overrepresented in the ranks of international movers. In the case of Muslims, the levels are closer, for whereas Islam's 1.6 billion adherents worldwide constitute 23 percent of the world's population, at 27 percent, the overall share of global migrants is only slightly higher. Jews, too, are overrepresented. By far the smallest of the world's major religions (indeed, there are somewhat more Sikhs than Jews in the world), at 0.2 percent, the 3,650,000 Jewish migrants amount to 2 percent of the total. All of the other categories reported are underrepresented in the ranks of immigrants, with Hindus being the most underrepresented. Looked at from a different angle, Jews offer evidence of being the classic diasporic people, for 25 percent of all Jews living today have migrated. This far exceeds the next highest figure, which is 5 percent for Christians. Muslims follow at 4 percent, the unaffiliated and Buddhists at 2 percent, and other and Hindus at 1 percent ("Faith on the Move" 2012: 11–12).

With this global perspective, we turn to an examination of specific regions and nations, both as points of origin and as destinations. The focus of this book is on immigrants to developed nations, or even more specifically to the nations of North America and Western Europe. However, it is useful to place those nations in comparative perspective. An examination of the top ten countries with the largest number of international migrants is instructive, for four of the ten are from outside those two regions. After the United States – the consummate nation of immigrants which with nearly 43 million immigrants is currently home to one-fifth of all international migrants – the country with the next largest number of migrants is the Russian Federation. Followed close behind is Germany, the only other nation with over 10 million immigrants. As table 1.2 indicates, the remaining seven nations contain between 5.2 and 7.2 million immigrants, interestingly with Saudi Arabia having a higher total than Canada, France, the United Kingdom, and Spain (United Nations Department of Economic and Social Affairs, Population Division, 2010).

Taking the Pew Center's seven religious categories, "Faith on the Move" identifies the country of origin providing the largest

Table 1.2 Top Ten Countries with the Largest Number of International Migrants

Country	Estimated number of international migrants
United States	42,813,000
Russian Federation	12,270,000
Germany	10,758,000
Saudi Arabia	7,289,000
France	6,685,000
United Kingdom	6,452,000
Spain	6,378,000
India	5,436,000
Ukraine	5,258,000

Data source: United Nations Department of Economic and Social Affairs, Population Division, Trends in International Migrant Stock: The 2008 Revision, UN database (New York: United Nations Department of Economic and Social Affairs, Population Division, 2009). Available at **http://esa.un.org/migration/index.asp?panel=1**

number of immigrants for each. In the case of Christians, the source country is Mexico, while for Muslims it is the Palestinian Territories. For Jews, it is Russia, for Hindus the country is India, and for Buddhists it is Vietnam. China is the top country for both other religions and the unaffiliated ("Faith on the Move" 2012: 15).

In terms of destination, the United States is the number one country for Christians, followed by Russia, Germany, Spain, Canada, Ukraine, the United Kingdom, Australia, France, and Italy. The United States is also the number one country for Buddhists, followed by Singapore, India, Hong Kong, Australia, Canada, Japan, Cambodia, Malaysia, and Germany. Finally, the United States is the main destination of the unaffiliated, followed by Russia, Germany, Canada, Australia, Hong Kong, the United Kingdom, Ukraine, Spain, and France. Israel is the main destination for Jews, followed by the United States, Canada, Australia, the United Kingdom, Germany, Russia, Spain, Brazil, and France. Saudi Arabia is the main destination country for Muslims, followed by Russia, Germany, France, Jordan, Pakistan, the United States, Iran, the United Arab Emirates, and Syria (of course, reflecting the period before the current rebellion). India is both the number one country of origin for Hindus and the number one destination country. As destination, it is followed by the United States, Bangladesh, Nepal, Saudi Arabia, the United Arab Emirates, Pakistan, the United Kingdom, Canada, and Sri Lanka. Meanwhile, the number one destination for those listed in the other religions grouping is Hong Kong, followed by the United States, Ivory Coast, Japan, the United Kingdom, India, Thailand, Canada, South Africa, and France ("Faith on the Move" 2012: 16–50).

In this detailed listing, two things are clear. Some countries, particularly the United States and Canada in North America and the large countries of Western Europe – Germany, France, Spain, and the United Kingdom – tend to appear over and over in the lists, reflecting their centrality as immigrant destinations at present. Many immigrants are prepared to travel substantial distances to arrive in these destinations. On the other hand, some countries appear only once in all the lists. For immigrants moving to these destinations, it appears that migration is defined in regional rather than global terms and involves one particular religion, as with the cases of Nepal and Sri Lanka for Hindus and Cambodia and Malaysia for Buddhists.

Near the end of the report, the authors turn their "spotlight" first on the United States and then on Europe, or more specifically the member states of the European Union. In addition to being the number one destination for Christians and Buddhists, as noted above, the United States is also the number two destination for Hindus and Jews. However, it ranks only seventh as a destination for Muslims. In terms of the overall religious composition of immigrants, 74 percent are Christian, with the unaffiliated at 10 percent constituting the next largest group. The remaining religious groups divide up the rest of the population, with Muslims at 5 percent, Buddhists at 4 percent, Hindus at 3 percent, other religions at 2 percent, and Jews at 1 percent ("Faith on the Move" 2012: 52).

To put these findings into perspective in terms of the larger patterns of religious affiliation, the percentage of immigrants who are Christian is only slightly less than the 78.4 percent Christian figure for the entire US population. The percentage of Jewish immigrants is actually slightly smaller than the 1.7 percent of the overall population that is Jewish. This is also true of the unaffiliated, for 16.1 percent of the total population reports being unaffiliated. On the other hand, in the case of the other three major world religions, the percentage of the immigrant population exceeds that of the overall population, where the respective percentages are 0.7 percent for Buddhists, 0.6 percent for Muslims, and 0.4 percent for Hindus (US Religious Landscape Survey 2008: 10). Given that the numbers for each of these three groups – both in terms of immigrants and citizens/permanent residents – are small, the increases have not resulted in dramatic reconfigurations of the nation's religious landscape, though clearly it has become more rather than less diverse over time.

Turning to Europe, the situation becomes more complicated. First, it is necessary to account for national differences in a number of crucial areas, such as but certainly not limited to differing groundings for citizenship and national identity (as with Brubaker's [1992] civic versus ethnic distinction), differing welfare state regimes (as with Esping-Andersen's [1990] three welfare state regimes: liberal, corporate, and social democratic), and differing types of church/state relations (analyzed by Joppke and Torpey [2013]). Second, the fact that the European Union is a unique trans-state entity and that with the passage of the Schengen Agreement in 1985 the citizens of its member states have the ability to move freely among the states, it is often necessary when speaking about immigrants to distinguish between movements across national borders by citizens of the EU in contrast to third-party nationals from outside the EU. Third, there are substantial differences in economic development and in the stability of democratic rule between the most developed Western members of the EU and the new ascension states of Eastern Europe.

With these factors in mind, the EU's current 27 members have a combined population of just over 500 million, making it considerably larger than the 312 million in the United States. This comparison is useful when observing that in contrast to the 43 million immigrants in the United States, the EU has 47 million, a larger number, but a smaller percentage of the overall population – about 14 percent compared to 9 percent. That being said, some of the member states have been impacted by immigration to a much greater extent than other member states. The report notes that many of the larger and most developed nations have immigrant populations that as a percentage of the overall population approximate that of the United States.

The religious composition of immigrants in the EU can be described in two ways, either by including migrants from within the EU or by excluding them. The comparison between the two is revealing insofar as it highlights the growing presence of Muslims from outside of the EU. The real issue is the relative percentage of Christians versus Muslims since all of the other groups reported in "Faith on the Move" not only constitute a small overall percentage of immigrants, but the differences between all immigrants versus only those outside the EU are minimal. Thus, the figure for Jews in both instances is a mere 1 percent and likewise for Hindus it is 2 percent. The figure for Buddhists increases from 2 percent for all immigrants to 3 percent for those outside the EU and comparably the figure for other religions increases from 3 percent to 4 percent. In contrast, the figure for the unaffiliated decreases slightly for immigrants from outside of the EU, dropping from 10 percent for all immigrants to 8 percent for those from non-EU countries.

With these contrasts as backdrop, if one considers all immigrants, Christians constitute 56 percent of the total. That figure drops substantially to 42 percent when looking only at immigrants from outside of the EU. At the same time, the Muslim figure of 27 percent for all immigrants rises significantly to 39 percent when excluding migration from within the EU. In other words, when considering migrants from outside the EU, the totals for Christians and Muslims are very similar, as the actual numbers indicate: 13,170,000 Christians versus 12,290,000 Muslims. One way of looking at this is to note that slightly more than half of Christian migrants come from within the EU (13,200,000), while this is true of only 620,000 Muslims.

Thus, despite the fact of free movement across the borders of EU states, in fact relatively few Muslims are making this internal migration. This is, no doubt, a reflection of the fact that Muslims from EU countries constitute a comparatively small percentage of the European religious mix. On the other hand, given that the dominant religion of EU member states is Christianity, it is not surprising that such a large number of internal migrants are Christian. The origins of Christians from outside the EU are varied. The largest numbers come from Russia and other former communist nations to the east, but the origins of Christian immigrants also include the United States, several Latin American countries, as well as several from sub-Saharan Africa ("Faith on the Move" 2012: 54–5).

Given that the Islamic presence in North America and even more so in Western Europe evokes anxiety (thus, we speak of Islamophobia, but not Hinduphobia and the like) and often overt hostility in a way that is not true for other major world religions, it is useful to consider what projections tell us about the likely demographic significance of Muslims in these countries as we proceed further into the twenty-first century. As will become evident in the chapter on religious inclusion and exclusion, Islam is more often perceived to be a problem in Western Europe than it is in North America. One very simple reason for the difference, which does not in and of itself offer a sufficient explanation for the differences in responses, but nonetheless does account in part for them, is that Muslims are and will continue to be a larger part of the overall population mix in Western Europe than in North America.

According to the projections of the Pew Research Center contained in their report, "The Future of the Global Muslim Population" (2011: 142), in terms of numerical increases, the Muslim population in North America will grow dramatically over the next two decades. In the United States, it will more than double, from 2.6 million in 2010 to 6.2 million in 2030. Similar growth is projected for Canada during the same time frame, rising from just under a million to 2.6 million. However, in both countries, they will continue to be a small minority of the overall population. Canada's Muslim minority is projected to increase from 2.8 percent in 2010 to 6.6 percent in 2030, while that in the United States will increase from 0.8 percent to only 1.7 percent.

In the case of Europe, the Pew Center's study observes that as a percentage of the world's total Muslim population, those living in Europe are and will continue to be a small percentage, rising to 3 percent by 2030. Most Muslims in Europe do and will continue to reside in countries in Eastern Europe, where rather than being recent immigrants, they have long historic roots. Kosovo and Albania are, in fact, Muslim majority nations and have been for centuries. They are projected to become over the next two decades respectively 93.5 percent and 83.2 percent Muslim. While the report breaks Europe into four regions – North, South, East, and West – for our purposes the countries of interest are the wealthiest ones.

Figure 1.1 examines these 17 countries. The first thing to note is that taking them as a whole, the current percentage of Muslims is 4.5, which is higher than that of North America, but still a relatively small figure. The projection calls for that to rise to 7.1

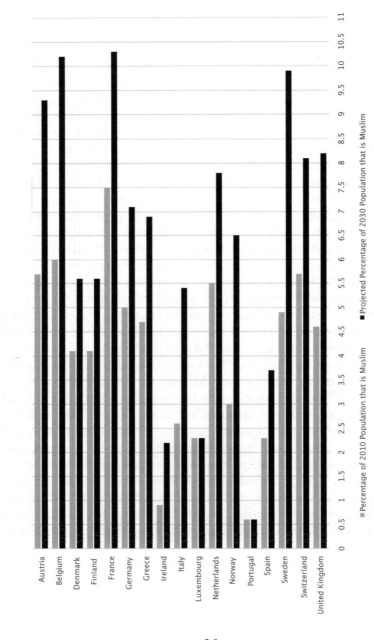

Figure 1.1 Muslims as a percentage of the total population in selected countries (estimated 2010 and projected 2030)

Data source: "The Future of the Global Muslim Population." 2011. Washington, DC: Pew Research Center.

percent by 2030. Second, there are rather pronounced differences among these nations. Some countries currently have very small Muslim populations and that will likely continue to be the case. Finland's 0.8 percent figure for 2010 will only rise to 1.9 percent (which, incidentally, almost exactly parallels the United States), and Ireland, Luxembourg (despite its very high level of immigrants overall), and Portugal will have percentages of Muslims under 3 percent. At the other end of the spectrum are the countries that have and will continue to have the highest percentages. Only two countries, France and Belgium, are projected to have Muslim population percentages over 10 percent. They are followed by Sweden and Austria, whose estimates are in the 9 percent range, and these in turn are followed by the United Kingdom and Switzerland, with projections in the 8 percent range, and Germany with slightly over 7 percent ("The Future" 2011: 124).

Why belabor the fact that Muslims comprise small percentages of the populations of all countries in North America and Western Europe? One reason is that it will help to put into perspective the realities on the ground when we turn to the topic of religious conflict in chapter 5, in which Islam will understandably be the focus of concern. Voices on the extreme right depict the movement of Muslims into the West as an invasion or an assault. Thus, the masthead of the Gates of Vienna website reads, "At the siege of Vienna in 1683 Islam seemed poised to overrun Christian Europe. We are in a new phase of a very old war" (http://gatesofvienna. blogspot.com). In making their conspiratorial case, such anti-Muslim extremists presume that the number of Muslims in the West is much higher than is actually the case. Such arguments are not confined to the fringe right, but can be found elsewhere too, as, for example, is evident in *Weekly Standard* editorial board member and *Financial Times* contributor Christopher Caldwell's (2009) claim that a demographic "revolution" brought about by mass immigration has resulted in an oversized Muslim population that is advancing an "adversary culture" to the detriment of European civilization. We will look more closely at his argument in chapter 5. Such thinking is also found within the public at large, including among those who are unsympathetic to the militant right, but nevertheless exhibit considerable anxiety about the presumed negative impact Muslim newcomers may be having on national identity and solidarity – on a way of life.

Setting the Stage

This era has been described by Stephen Castles and Mark Miller (2009) as an "age of migration," which, indeed, it is. As noted earlier, approximately 214 million immigrants today represent a larger number than the populations of all but four of the world's nations. On the other hand, this amounts to only 3.1 percent of the global population. Likewise, one can come to a similar conclusion after reviewing the Pew Center data on the religious diversity characteristic of contemporary immigrants, and in particular, the growth in the number of non-Christian religious adherents. The data are clear that the citizenry of both North America and Western Europe dwell in places that are today more religiously pluralistic than was true a half century ago. At the same time, as a percentage of the overall populations in the receiving nations, non-Christians remain rather small minorities.

With this in mind, many have been struck by the different responses to religious diversity in North America – and particularly the United States – and Western Europe. In the former case, religion is generally viewed in positive terms, as a source of overcoming marginalization and a major facilitator of integration, while in the latter case religion is seen as a problem, as an impediment to incorporation into the societal mainstream. Nancy Foner and Richard Alba (2008) have characterized this difference as one between a perspective evident in the United States that treats religion as a "bridge" to inclusion versus a counter view in Europe that treats religion as a "barrier" to inclusion. This claim will be examined in further detail in subsequent chapters.

Some would argue that the reason for these differing assessments of immigrant religion is a consequence of the different religious landscapes on either side of the Atlantic. In his influential "new paradigm" article, R. Stephen Warner (1993: 1080,

1058) has argued that as a result of its distinctive "combination of disestablishment and institutional vitality" the religious system of the United States has proven to be conducive to creating and maintaining a "social space for cultural pluralism." This stands in contrast to Western Europe where a long history of established state churches and a wide-scale retreat from involvements in institutional religion by large segments of the public have created a very different climate for immigrant religion. Complementing this distinction between establishment/disestablishment and high levels versus low levels of religiosity is the claim that Americans and Western Europeans differ in terms of how they value religion per se. Gustav Niebuhr (2007) contends that whereas people in the United States exhibit a positive view of religion, the same is not true of many Western Europeans. The implication to be drawn from this distinction is that whereas the religious engagement of immigrants in the United States will serve to facilitate inclusion, similar engagements on the part of immigrant counterparts in Western Europe will have the opposite effect. Whether or not this is the case will be addressed in the chapters to follow.

There are, of course, numerous other variables to consider, those concerning both the demographic or compositional characteristics of the immigrants and contextual issues other than those directly associated with the religious sphere (Van Tubergen and Sindradóttir 2011). In terms of the former, one can include issues concerning human capital such as educational attainment level, occupational background, and employment status, as well as factors such as age, gender, race, and national origin. In terms of the latter, factors would include the size and density of the immigrant community, patterns of social relations with members of the dominant society in the workplace, school, neighborhood and the like, the economic climate of the receiving society, levels of political participation, and so forth. To the extent that various of these factors prove to have explanatory power, the idea that the differences between the United States and Western Europe are due to differing institutional and cultural approaches to religion would have to be revised at least to the extent that where indicated the differences would be understood as the result of multiple causation.

This being said, it is also possible that there are more commonalities between North America and Western Europe than is fully appreciated, and that perhaps the processes of immigrant adjustment and incorporation are more alike than different. While the focus of research to date has been on exploring and explaining differences, a recent dissertation by Phillip Connor (2010) suggests that similar processes of immigrant *religious* adjustment and assimilation are at play. His findings also indicate that religious involvement appears to facilitate incorporation in some areas (such as having a positive impact on mental health) but not necessarily in others (for example, it does not appear to have an impact on employment or income).

As we proceed into the following four thematic chapters, they should be viewed as a whole as an attempt to refine our understanding of the significance of immigrant religion in either promoting or retarding inclusion. Thus, while the chapters can be read as discrete topics, they should also be seen as creating a cumulative picture that offers a more comprehensive vantage from which to begin to draw various conclusions. Each chapter is rooted in and will attempt to stay close to the existing literature on immigrant religion – chiefly that voluminous body of work produced during the past two decades since my initial survey of the research landscape in 1992.

One word of caution is in order. The state of the research field is such that one must draw conclusions circumspectly. While there is, in my estimation, ample evidence of robust theorizing and of high-quality empirical work, both qualitative and quantitative, there are – as scholars in the field are always the first to admit – gaps in research agendas and data shortcomings. This being said, the present is a particularly fertile moment for bringing together in productive ways the distinctive conceptual frameworks of sociologists of religion and immigration scholars.

2

Immigrant Identity Work and Religion

The Pew Research Center's "Faith on the Move" study attempts to trace the movement of religions across international borders, doing so by seeking to identify the religious affiliations – at least nominal – of individual immigrants. The study does not address the issue of religious conversion once those migrants have settled in the destination country. But conversions do occur, though we know relatively little about how frequently this happens, which immigrant groups are most likely to convert, what religions are embraced in the conversion experience, and what underlying factors can be identified that explain the phenomenon. What we know at present about the religious conversion of immigrants is quite limited, with the research to date largely being ethnographic. Fenggang Yang has been exploring the conversion of Chinese immigrants in the United States – particularly those from the People's Republic of China (PRC) – over the past two decades, studying Chinese churches and affiliated religious organizations in several regions of the country, and examining both immigrants who arrived as early as the 1950s and the post-Tiananmen Square generation who immigrated in the wake of the bloody suppression of the pro-democracy movement in 1989 (Yang 1998; Wang and Yang 2006).

One research site in which Yang and colleague Yuting Wang studied the latter group was located in Iowa City, a small Midwestern community that is home to the University of Iowa, the state's flagship public university. Because of its status as a university town, Iowa City is the current residence for a fairly substantial international student population. Indeed, over 10 percent of the student body was composed of around 3,000 international students when they conducted their study, including around 600 from the PRC. There were already Chinese immigrants residing in Iowa City before this influx, mainly from Taiwan and Hong Kong, and in addition to students, there was a small Chinese business community, not to mention researchers and visiting scholars. The longer-term Chinese residents who were not from mainland China contained enough Christians – some pre-migration converts, some post-migration – to found the Chinese Church (CC) in the early 1980s. When the number of PRC immigrants increased during the 1990s, the existing Chinese Christians sought to attract them, and did so chiefly through a student organization known as the Chinese Bible Study Group (CBSC), which met weekly. This organization would over time become the incubator for the creation of a second Chinese congregation, the Chinese Evangelical Church. Its members were almost entirely from the PRC. By the time they met the members of the CBSC, Wang and Yang found that around 130 students from the PRC were regular attendees, which amounted to over 20 percent of the PRC students enrolled at the university.

Virtually all of these students were non-Christians when they arrived. In fact, they were the products of a doctrinaire educational system in China that advanced an ideological brief on behalf of atheism and roundly condemned not only religious institutions, but religious belief. What prompted over a fifth of the PRC students at the University of Iowa to show up for the CBSC's weekly Friday night meetings? Was it a desire to socialize with fellow ethnics who had shared life experiences and thus whom one could relate to? Was it because there was something particularly attractive about the conservative theology being promoted by the existing group that resonated with the newcomers? Was it because they felt adrift in a seemingly meaningless world and sought a worldview that would offer them a sense of purpose and meaning, as well as solace?

One thing is clear: both the study group and the congregation were set up to facilitate conversion. The leaders of both organizations saw efforts devoted to evangelizing the nonbelievers as constituting a crucial aspect of their mission, and to that end they expended considerable time and energy working to make this happen. There were two specific events that marked major transitional events in the life of the convert. The first takes place when the individual makes a public declaration of belief (*jue zhi*) and the second occurs, usually months or even years later, by taking part in a full-immersion baptismal ceremony (*shou xi*). Wang and Yang (2006: 185) describe the typical first step in the conversion process in the following way:

> Most PRC converts "make the decision" after attending a moving lecture or series of lectures, which were often delivered by professionals or professionals-turned-pastors and evangelists. Some did it after watching the "Jesus" film [a docudrama produced by the Campus Crusade for Christ and widely used by its affiliates]. Usually, at the end of an evangelistic lecture, the speaker would ask the audience to get ready for a prayer by bowing their heads. The speaker would then say: "If you would like to receive Christ into your heart today, if you would like to receive God's blessings today please raise your hand." As some people raise their hands, the speaker would say loudly, "I have seen it, please put it down. I have seen it, thank the Lord. I have seen it, please put it down." After repeating the call a couple of times, the speaker would conclude the meeting with an elaborate prayer. Immediately following the lecture, the leaders would approach the people who raised their hands, congratulating them on their *jue zhi* as having become Christian and asking them to attend a catechism leading to baptism.

If this describes how conversion occurs, at least in Iowa City, left unanswered are questions about why these immigrants are prepared to embrace a religion that in most instances they knew little about not long before. In his earlier research on Chinese Christians in the Greater Washington, DC area who had arrived in the United States earlier in the second half of the past century, Yang (1998) wanted to determine not simply why people had converted to Christianity, but why the attraction appeared to be to conservative evangelical Christianity. He was convinced that although such factors were part of the equation, in fact joining churches for material advantage, in order to facilitate assimilation by appearing to be more American, or seeing in a Chinese church a place to socialize with fellow ethnics were not the major variables contributing to conversion.

Rather, he stressed the impact of China's turbulent modern history, one that sought to overthrow the vestiges of a feudal past in a dramatic and rapid revolutionary movement committed to making a radical break with the past in order to create a radiant future. Yang (1998: 250) writes that "Chinese cultural traditions have been mercilessly attacked, destroyed, and smashed into fragmentary pieces," including the Confucian core to traditional Chinese culture. Tradition was, in short, no longer an available resource. Those who remained in China and lived through tumultuous events such as the Cultural Revolution were subjected to the new rulers' version of Marxist ideology combined with the cult of Mao as the one and only permissible cultural alternative. For those who departed China and ended up in the highly religious United States, "alternative meaning systems" were now available and in the marketplace of religion, the Christian option was by far the most widely available (Yang 1998: 251).

Why opt for a theologically conservative version of Christianity? Yang (1998: 252) suggests that there are two reasons that account for this preference. First, like homegrown fundamentalists, these Chinese immigrants are searching for absolute truth and certainty in a world that is complex, diverse, and ambiguous. Mainline Protestants come across as too comfortable with relativism, uncertainty, and doubt. Moreover, their social justice concerns do not resonate. Second, these Christian converts see something of value in traditional Confucian culture, and they find a parallel between it and conservative Christianity in terms of such things as views regarding the family, an ascetic work ethic, and an authoritative source of moral principles. In the later research on post-1989 immigrants, Wang and Yang (2006: 179) observe that some of the most prominent leaders of the pro-democracy movement who ended up in exile in the United States converted to Christianity.

Their explanation echo
for meaning and certa
change.

What makes these newer immigra... ...om t.
arrived earlier is that they can return to ...a. In fact, with stud... ...
visas, most are expected to do so. Thus, they frame their attraction
to Christianity in reference to what they perceive their homeland
to be. A common characterization expressed by the Iowa City
converts is that China is too materialistic and, as corruption at all
levels attests, the nation is morally bankrupt. Moreover, they are
critical of the Chinese authority's general antipathy to religion.
Unlike the earlier arrivals, they are more critical of traditional
Chinese culture, which they see as shaping modern China more
than proponents of the revolution would be prepared to admit.
Nonetheless, they continue to believe that certain distinctly
Chinese values persist and should be nurtured, including "hard
work, frugality, temperance, filial piety to parents, respect to
elders, honesty, and trustworthiness to friends, etc." (Wang and
Yang 2006: 186).

If in his earlier research Yang stressed the idea that converts saw
an affinity between traditional Confucian culture and conservative
Christianity, an affinity that was less obvious when considering
liberal Protestantism, in the jointly authored study the attraction
to theologically conservative Christianity is qualified. It became
clear that these students actually knew very little about the range
of Christian expressions, and that a major factor in accounting
for their decision to become members of evangelical Christian
congregations has much to do with the religious ecology of the
university. Put simply, the conservatives were well organized and
assertive in their proselytizing efforts, while mainline denominations were not, leading the two researchers to conclude that if the
latter had been more active, they, too, might have been successful
in attracting these Chinese students into their ranks (Wang and
Yang 2006: 191).

The Dislocations of the Migratory Experience

The lyrics to Steve Earle's song, "What's a Simple Man to Do?" take the form of a letter being written late at night in a California jail. The individual penning the letter to Graciela, his wife or girlfriend, is a young Mexican who had been busted in San Diego for selling drugs. His sad and brief tale tells of someone who lost his job in the maquiladora and out of desperation got caught up in drug trafficking, which he sought to define as a short-term fix to his financial plight. His mournful plea is to be forgiven, asking Graciela to let his mother know his situation and to "light a candle for me. Pray that I'll come home someday." This is the story of a young undocumented migrant who is confused and feels that his life has spun out of control. Thus, he does something he otherwise would not have done – and the social controls that may have been operative in the past appear to have lost their efficacy.

One can find the theme of alienation – whether it is explicitly so defined or whether related terms are used – recurring frequently in contemporary fictional accounts of immigrants as well as in popular music. One can also find it in journalistic accounts. Thus, for example, it has been asserted in accounts in the British media that the British-born and -raised bombers of the London Underground and transit system on July 7, 2005 were alienated youth – alienated from the larger mainstream society and from their own parents. However, in terms of immigration studies, a review of the literature would lead one to conclude that alienation has to large extent dropped out of sociological research in recent decades. In this section, I will make two claims. First, the earliest sociological work on immigration was attentive to the alienating consequences of the immigration process, and second that contemporary sociology would benefit from reconsidering its efficacy in contemporary efforts to theorize the ways incorporation does or does not occur.

The earliest sociological research program on immigration was located at the Chicago School of sociology, chiefly under the influence of W.I. Thomas and in particular after his forced departure from the institution by Robert E. Park. With a certain amount of irony, I would claim that inquiry into the role alienation played in the immigrant experience began with the Chicago School – even though its members, to my knowledge, did not use the term alienation in their work.

Rather the operative term was disorganization. As Stow Persons (1987) has pointed out, this particular term was in evidence in American sociology as early as the first decade of the twentieth century. He cites Charles Horton Cooley's 1909 book *Social Organization* (1962) as perhaps marking the beginning of a concern with social organization and disorganization. With what reads today as a fairly heavy dose of middle-class moralism and the optimism of someone who identified with the progressive movement, the Janus-faced social organization-disorganization could, as Persons (1987: 49) notes, serve as a "convenient receptacle in which to store a full complement of moral judgments." Nonetheless, the idea could be employed in various institutional settings to examine the impacts of rapid social change both on the social psychology of individuals and on the capacity of institutions to adjust to rapid social change. In this regard, the parallel between this concept and Durkheim's anomie is clear. Both concepts as introduced at that time avoided linking anomie or disorganization to capitalism. Rather, the thrust of these two approaches was to emphasize the impacts of rapid social changes in industry, technology, communications, and the like. Social disorganization signaled the breakdown of effective social bonds, as seen especially in changes in the family and neighborhood, and in the eroding efficacy of traditional social controls.

W.I. Thomas and Florian Znaniecki structured their classic study of *The Polish Peasant in Europe and America* (1918/1920) around these concepts. However, this was not Thomas' first utilization of these terms. Rather, they figured prominently in his 1923 book *The Unadjusted Girl* (1967), a book that was to play a central role in subsequent sociological studies of deviance, concerned as it was with young women who engaged in delinquent or criminal behavior and were in various ways defined by the authorities and the public as in some sense maladjusted. What is not always appreciated is the fact that Thomas was making a sociological, as opposed to a psychological, argument. In doing so he was advancing a version of cultural sociology. Specifically, he was concerned with changes in the moral order that resulted in declines in the efficacy of various social institutions to function as they once did.

The European social theorist whose ideas most closely resembled those of Thomas was Georg Simmel, for both thought that the most salient characteristic of modern society can be seen in what Michael Parenti (1967: xvii) has described as "the individualization of choice and definition [of the situation]." He went on to claim that "incorporated into the collective definitions of a modern commercial society is the very expectation that collective definitions can be challenged by individualized definitions." As Thomas (1967: 42) himself put it, in contemporary society "there are rival definitions of the situations, and none of them is binding." It should be noted that disorganization is not perceived to be a necessarily negative phenomenon. Moreover, it is conceived not simply as a state of affairs, but often as a process, which when the conditions are optimal leads to reorganization.

With this general framework in mind and Znaniecki's treasure trove of Polish letters, *The Polish Peasant,* all 2,200+ pages appeared four years after *The Unadjusted Girl.* Organization-disorganization were treated as a continuum and served as ideal types, where neither existed in a situation free from the other and thus they never occurred in their pure form. Traditional social organizations, in premodern societies, were represented by groups in which the established conventions, attitudes, and values submerged the individual in the interests of the collectivity. The characteristic feature of disorganization in the modern world was that the individual began to compete with and/or take precedence over the collective. To the extent that this was occurring, traditional social organizations increasingly lost their efficacy. During the process of adjustment, before new cultural values took hold and new institutions emerged, on the one hand, there could be deleterious consequences for an individual sense of well-being, while on the other hand, it could be perceived as liberation from the constraints of premodern modes of social organization and control.

Such could be seen in the idea of the marginal man [sic], which would play a prominent role in the research endeavors of various figures associated with the Chicago School. As Park (1950) makes clear, the idea of the marginal man is indebted to Simmel's 1908 essay on the stranger, that type who, as he famously put it, "comes today and stays tomorrow" (Simmel 1971: 143; for a recent commentary on various views on the relationship between the marginal man and the stranger, see Marotta 2012). The stranger occupies an interstitial space between the detached wanderer and the attached inside member. The stranger is "inorganically" appended to the group, but nevertheless comes to be organically connected to the group. Simmel was not inclined to treat the stranger as a social problem, stressing instead what might be seen (he doesn't use the term) as the cosmopolitan character of this social type. In the hands of the Chicago School, more attuned to the issue of social problems and social reform, the marginal man has a dual-edged character. On the one hand, the social location of such people is perceived to contribute to high levels of creativity, objectivity, and sophistication – thus paralleling Simmel. He is, as Park (1950: 376) put it, "always relatively the more civilized human being." However, on the other hand the marginal man was depicted as experiencing personality problems associated with those who see themselves as caught between two worlds and not capable of feeling sufficiently a part of either.

The Chicago School did not dwell on those who remained solely attached to their traditional cultures and aloof from the larger culture of the host society, for they were perceived, not quite as an anomaly, but rather as the least common type of response to a new setting. This is the sort of person described by criminologist Thorsten Sellin (1938: 68) in his Social Science Research Council report, *Culture Conflict and Crime*, where he reports on the "absence of mental conflict" in the Sicilian immigrant in New Jersey who killed the seducer of his teenaged daughter and was stunned by his subsequent arrest because he defined his actions as necessary to restore the family's honor. As is the case today with honor killings within Muslim communities in Western Europe, such a lack of engagement with what Sellin called the "conduct norms" of the receiving society was an infrequent occurrence. The reason for this is that, as Park (1950: 376) succinctly put it, the marginal man is concerned "less . . . with a personality type than with a social process, the process of acculturation."

Before turning to the matter of acculturation, it is worth pointing out that a tradition of research emerging out of the Chicago School went on to shape criminological research, particularly as it was developed by Clifford Shaw and Henry McKay (1942). Locating social disorganization in terms of the natural urban areas described by Park and Burgess (the famous concentric zones familiar to every student of introductory sociology courses), Shaw and McKay found that delinquency rates in Chicago were linked to specific locales and not to specific ethnic groups. Thus, the zone nearest to the central city would persistently record the highest rates of delinquency while experiencing ethnic succession.

Though Oscar Handlin was not a product of the Chicago School, and indeed not even a sociologist, his Pulitzer prize-winning *The Uprooted* (1951) was perhaps the last major expression of the social disorganization model in immigration studies. There is no doubt that he was profoundly influenced by the work of Thomas and Park, though he preferred to use the language of alienation, much in vogue during the 1950s due to the impact of French existentialism and the work of mass society theorists. One of the book's chapters is titled "The Shock of Alienation." This was, in his view, the fate of a significant portion of the first generation, those who had left their homelands and with distance and the passage of time became increasingly alienated from it. At the same time, they found themselves in but not of the new society. Part of their inability to become incorporated into the new society had to do with nativist resistance to immigrants, while part of it was a consequence of the immigrants' critical stance toward their new environment. The key to overcoming this, which would begin to occur with the second generation, was assimilation. In this, Handlin's views explicitly paralleled those of the Chicago School.

He offered what has been described as a "dark view" of the immigration experience (Deaux 2006: 11). Such a view has been challenged in recent decades by social historians, sociologists, and social psychologists. However, it is worth noting that this position has not disappeared, though it is no longer linked to the Chicago School formulation or to the particularities of the US context. Pointing to one exemplary case, the title of the book of the late Algerian sociologist Abdelmalek Sayad says it all: *The Suffering of the Immigrant* (2004). Influenced by the theoretical orientation of Pierre Bourdieu, the book focuses on the painful transformation Algerian peasants have experienced since they began to enter France in large numbers after World War II. Sayad stresses the ambivalence of the immigrants' situation, captured well in the following passage:

> Torn between two "times," between two countries and between two conditions, an entire community lives as though it were "in transit." Being condemned to refer simultaneously to two societies, emigrants dream, without noticing the contradiction, of combining the incompatible advantages of two conflicting choices. At times, they idealize France and would like it to have, in addition to the advantages it gives them (a stable job, a wage, etc.), that other quality of being a "second" land of their birth – which would be enough to transfigure the relationship and to magically transform all the reasons for the dissatisfaction they experience in France. At other times, they idealize Algeria in their dreams after spending time there during their annual holidays. (Sayad 2004: 58)

Neil Smelser (1998) describes ambivalence as an affective state characterized by simultaneously holding two opposed emotions toward an object: attraction and repulsion; love and hate. While it would be a mistake to claim that all immigrants react ambivalently to their homeland and their new place of residence, there is abundant evidence not only in the work of social historians and sociologists but also in memoirs and fictional accounts of immigrant life, past and present, that ambivalence is a very common emotional reaction to migration – indeed, perhaps the most characteristic response. Borrowing from Albert Hirschman (1970), Smelser contends that there are three responses to ambivalence: exit (which stresses the negative side of ambivalence), loyalty (which represses the negative side), and voice (which seeks to steer a middle course between the positive and negative). These options are more complicated for immigrants given that they can feel ambivalent toward their place of origin, their destination, or both. Indeed, the migratory field is conducive to both types of ambivalence.

Elizabeth Aranda's (2007) research on contemporary Puerto Rican professionals who often move several times between the island and the mainland provides a telling example of the struggles involved in responding to ambivalence. That her subjects are not by most definitions true immigrants since they are US citizens is not relevant here; the fact that their ability to move freely back and forth offers a particularly telling instance of how difficult it can be for people attempting to sort out their emotional attachments and their prospects for reconfiguring a sense of belonging. Making explicit use of the Hirschman/Smelser framework, Peter Kivisto and Vanja La Vecchia-Mikkola (2013) have found among a sample of Iraqi immigrants in Helsinki and Rome ample evidence of ambivalence toward the homeland, and expressions of exit, loyalty, and voice. In a companion article, they analyze the salience of ambivalence towards the country of settlement to the identity work involved in reinscribing and reconstructing a sense of self (Kivisto and La Vecchia-Mikkola, forthcoming; for a comparable use of the idea of ambivalence, see Warner, Martel, and Dugan 2012).

The consensus among scholars today is that immigrants deal with ambivalence with more resources than scholars such as Thomas and Znaniecki, Handlin, and Sayad took into account. This consensus, while recognizing the fact that immigrants frequently confront nativist hostility, economic exploitation, and political and cultural marginalization, is predicated on the contention that they nonetheless have generally managed to be agents of their own lives. In other words, they play an active role in the process of adjustment and becoming a part of their new homeland. John Bodnar's *The Transplanted* (1985) presents a synthesis of the work of social historians and historical sociologists dating from the 1960s forward. As the title of his book suggests, it is meant to be in part a critique of Handlin's ideal typical portrait of an uprooted generation. While it is true that many immigrants opted for exit, returning to their origins (Wyman 1993), and others sought to express their loyalty by rejecting their roots in an effort to fit in, the typical immigrant in Bodnar's account exhibited voice, seeking to negotiate the terms of incorporation predicated on a selective embrace of the host society's institutions and values, while picking and choosing which aspects of their cultural heritage to transplant and which to abandon. They did so, he argued, with a *mentalité* that he characterizes as pragmatic.

Two central features of his work serve to distance it from the earlier generation of immigration scholarship. First, while his predecessors tended to either ignore the macro-context of migration or located it in terms of modernization theory, Bodnar stresses the specific linkages between the rise of industrial capitalism and immigration. Second, he treats the negotiation process as a group endeavor and not an individual initiative. In so doing, he focuses on the ethnic community as both resource and agent. Although he didn't use the language of networks, the affiliations made possible by a complex of ethnic institutions and social relationships that made up ethnic communities were seen as playing a profound role in the precise way that different groups ended up over time becoming incorporated into American society. The community served to buffer the difficulties immigrants inevitably encountered and in the process assisted in the process of becoming members of the wider society – a phenomenon that Barbara Ballis Lal (1990: 96) has referred to as the "ethnicity paradox." What she meant by this term is that ethnic communities, rather than retarding incorporation, actually were important for making incorporation possible.

Social psychologist Kay Deaux's (2006) recent work reinforces Bodnar's stress on the negotiated character of immigrant behavior. Focusing on contemporary immigrants in the world's liberal democracies, she finds that the vast majority of immigrants do not seek to remain separate from the wider society. Indeed, the only exception she reports is that of Turks in Germany who prefer separation to incorporation. I would point out that there is abundant evidence that challenges the view of Turks in Germany as an exception to the general inclination to seek inclusion. Whether the immigrants call it integration, incorporation, assimilation, or a colloquial expression for fitting in, the major conclusion to be drawn from her work is that voluntary labor migrants are prepared to some extent to be transformed in order to become part of the settlement society. That the preferred term, especially outside the United States, tends to be integration rather than assimilation is due to be fact that while the former is defined as permitting immigrants to maintain their cultural identity, assimilation is seen by many as entailing a loss of such identity (Deaux 2006: 60–1).

Of significance here is the fact that outcomes are dependent on several factors, including the obstacles to inclusion posed by the receiving society. Deaux pays particular attention to public opinion and the stereotypes and prejudices harbored by citizens toward newcomers. In addition, it is important to factor into the equation what immigrants bring to the table – motivations, skills, expectations, values, and needs – and what they encounter, which includes social networks, a particular opportunity structure, and a climate shaping interpersonal relationships. At the social psychological level, these factors serve to shape the varied ways immigrants negotiate their identity while at the level of social interaction they influence relationships with group members and with members of the wider society, which includes the sorts of collective action generated by the immigrant community.

A major lesson to be derived from both Bodnar and Deaux is that, for most immigrants, being an immigrant means being prepared to be transformed. However, this seldom means that immigrants think that the transformation in question calls for a complete repudiation – a forgetting – of the pre-immigration past. Rather, the process of becoming incorporated into the new setting requires a sifting and choosing of which aspects of one's cultural background to preserve and which social ties to maintain. This is an inherently complex undertaking, made even more complex when immigrants must reckon with their ambivalent feelings about both their homeland and the land of settlement.

It is at this point that the utility of alienation as a concept, or perhaps more specifically the concept complex of organization/disorganization/reorganization, ought to be reconsidered. The reason is that what is needed is an adequate theoretical account of the *processes* of incorporation. The Chicago School called for such an account and perhaps its members thought they had managed to provide it. If they did, it was essentially by seeing assimilation as a natural process that inevitably unfolded, provided that resistance from the larger society did not prevent it from occurring. This is clearly not very convincing, it being the product to large extent of the now widely discarded ecological perspective embraced in particular by Park (Matthews 1977: 137–43). Rather, what is needed is a model that adequately accounts for social psychological factors – of both immigrants and members of the mainstream society – and structural and cultural variables. I am aware of one explicit call for a return to rethink the Chicago School's legacy in criminological research, Robert Bursik's (2006) essay in a collection on *Immigration and Crime* edited by Ramiro Martinez, Jr, and Abel Valenzuela, Jr. Here and elsewhere Bursik has called for a new theory of social disorganization based on but going beyond that of the Chicago School. As a criminologist, his interest is clearly on the more deviant consequences of disorganization. However, it is not only the protagonist of Steve Earle's song that ought to concern the sociology of immigration. Rather, it is equally important to see the effects of organization/disorganization/reorganization in the cases of the vast majority of immigrants who are not involved in crime or deviant behaviors. The challenge is to begin to move from the static depiction of incorporative outcomes to understanding the processes that led to specific outcomes.

Religion and Identity

In their review essay on the current state of scholarship on immigration and religion, Wendy Cadge and Elaine Howard Ecklund (2007: 363) contend that identity – both individual and collective – has proven to be a "central theme" in the literature. I would expand on their assessment to suggest that under this rubric one can find at least three subthemes. The first, the one Cadge and Ecklund discuss, concerns the relationship between religion and other aspects of identity that are a part of the multiple identities assumed by people in the modern world and the different saliences attached to each: ethnicity, race, nationality, gender, class, age, educational background, profession, and so forth. Cadge and Ecklund concentrate on two of these relations, those between religious identity and, respectively, ethnicity and gender. Given that their article is designed to survey the current literature, one can assume that this particular subtheme has constituted the primary focus of recent scholarship. However, alongside this thematic focus are two additional ones. The second subtheme is concerned with the impact of religion on the psychological adjustment of immigrants to their new surroundings. The third subtheme involves examining the extent to which immigration can be seen as what historian Timothy L. Smith (1978: 1175) has referred to in an oft-cited article as a "theologizing experience." We turn to an examination of each of these themes in the following pages.

Remaking Identity in the Migratory Context

Individuals in the modern world are made up of a composite of multiple identities, some of those identities being mutually reinforcing, some related in a more or less cause-and-effect way, others being in conflict, and still others coexisting in an unsettled fashion in a fragmented self. Movers and stayers are alike in this regard. What makes the former – immigrants – different is that their identities need to be renegotiated and reconfigured in the migratory setting as they try to come to terms with both here and there, the receiving society and the homeland. One of the most consequential elements of identity is ethnicity, which speaks to a sense of peoplehood predicated on the perception of a shared history and culture, with the ethnic group being defined in Max Weber's (1978: 389) classic formulation as "those groups that entertain a subjective belief in their common descent because of similarities of physical type or of customs or both, or because of memories of colonization and migration." Contained in this pithy social constructionist account of ethnicity is the assertion that it can be predicated on race, religion (insofar as it can be seen as an aspect of culture), and memories of a shared history in various combinations. Weber's emphasis on the beliefs of the constituent members of the ethnic group needs to be complemented by the role played by those outside the boundaries of the group, particularly those who are more powerful and located in the center rather than the periphery of a society, for they have the capacity to play a major role in boundary setting and in the moral adjudication of the group – depicting them as more or less worthy of being included in the societal mainstream (for the most sustained attempt to advance theorizing about boundaries, see Wimmer 2008 and 2013).

Ethnicity and Religion

Ethnicity has proven to be a highly variable and complex phenomenon subject to historical transmutations and transformations, and it is this variability and complexity that lends itself to differing ways in which it is related to religion. In attempting to construct a typology aimed at capturing that diversity, the focus to date has been on the United States, but it is clear that the categories are also intended to be applicable elsewhere. Sociologists of ethnicity have long referred to some ethnic groups as "religio-ethnic." To fall into this category, a group would be defined in such a manner that its members' religious identity and ethnic affiliation are deeply embedded in each other, and in combination they serve to define the group (Abramson 1975). Whereas German immigrants to the United States would not be defined as a religio-ethnic group, Jews are often considered to be the paradigmatic instance of such a group. Other groups that would readily be included in this categorization are the Amish and Hutterites. However, this is a more complicated relationship than the term might suggest, as the Jewish case attests. Does being a Jew depend on being a religiously observant Jew, or can an atheist, freethinker, or convert to Christianity be a Jew? What about individuals who convert to Judaism? From Rogers Brubaker's (2004) perspective, which challenges both essentialism and what he calls "groupism," it would

be argued that the answer to the question depends entirely on the claims-making success of various actors, individual and collective, in the process of advancing alternative definitions of the situation in competition with other claims-makers. As such, any religio-ethnic label amounts to an ongoing accomplishment requiring persistent efforts aimed at maintaining the connection between religion and ethnicity. In other words, the label is always histori-cally contingent.

Harold Abramson (1980), in an entry on "Religion" in the *Harvard Encyclopedia of American Ethnic Groups,* made the fol-lowing assertion:

> Religion becomes a major and consequential reason for the develop-ment of ethnicity. The Armenian Orthodox, the Chinese Buddhists, the Finnish Lutherans, the German Jews, the Scottish Presbyterians, the Sephardic Jews, the Southern Baptists, the Spanish-speaking Catholics, and the Utah Mormons are only a few of the groups in which ethnicity and religion are inextricably linked.

Given what Abramson considers to be the rather broadly con-ceived linkage between religion and ethnicity in the American case – primarily a consequence of being a settler nation where a vast majority of the population is composed of immigrants and their offspring – he moves beyond the earlier singular notion of religio-ethnic as an adequate concept to capture that variability by postulating four types of relationship. The first type most closely approximates what the original term means. In this type, religion serves as the "major foundation" of ethnicity. The examples he cites are those already noted above: Jews, Hutterites, Amish, and Mormons (Abramson 1980: 869). Leave aside the fact that the Mormons are a suspect example, for it is not clear in what ways they ought to be treated as an ethnic group at all. What he appears to have in mind is a sense of ethnic peoplehood inextricably rooted in a particular religion.

In the second type, "a particular ethnic group may be grounded in a relatively unique religion, but one that has a more marked association with a distinct territory or homeland, a particular language, or an evolving sense of nationality" (Abramson 1980:

870). The examples cited include Dutch Reformed, the Church of England, the Serbian Orthodox, and Scottish Presbyterianism. Implied in the effort to distinguish this type from the preceding one is the assumption that the relationship between religion and ethnicity is more historically circumstantial than is the case for the previous type. In other words, the linkage is somewhat looser and more subject to change, particularly to erosion.

The third type is, according to Abramson, the most common. It refers to a situation in which a number of distinct ethnic groups share a common religious tradition. This would include the Nordic groups and Germans who shaped American Lutheranism, the Irish, Polish, Italian, Mexican, and other groups who are major constituent components of Roman Catholicism in the United States, black and white Baptists, and more recently the many nations that together form the composite Islamic population of the nation (Abramson 1980: 870). The final type is considered to represent the smallest of the four. Here the relationship is very loose, as religion plays a very small and insignificant part in the definition of an ethnic identity. The examples pointed to include the Romany, a tiny group in the United States that is both larger and more visible in Europe, and American Indians. The latter can be debated, but it is not clear if Abramson means the traditional religions of Indian tribal units or is thinking about the fact that a sizeable segment of the Native American population has over time converted to Christianity.

As is the case with such typologies, it is designed to offer a snapshot at a particular point in time. As such, there is a static quality to this schema. It is not capable of capturing or explaining the changes that have occurred over time. Given their derivation, such ideal types are necessarily historically variable, and as such when the gap between the ideal and real becomes too pronounced, it becomes necessary to revise or reformulate the type. Religious change during the last half of the past century has called into question the continuing utility of these types. Take, for instance, Lutherans. While it is certainly true that almost all Lutherans in the United States up to the first half of the twentieth century could trace their origins to one of the Nordic countries or to Germany, and even today one can detect the significance of the linkage between ethnic background and Lutheranism, in fact much has changed. First, outreach efforts to both African Americans and Hispanic and Asian immigrants have resulted in increasing the ethnic diversity of the denomination. However, far more significant has been the impact of intermarriage between Nordics or Germans and others of European ancestry. Thus, the typical Lutheran congregation today looks considerably more pan-European than in the past.

Adopting and modifying, rather than substantively revisiting, Abramson's typology, Phillip Hammond and Kee Warner (1993) attempted to take stock of the ways that the relationship between religion and ethnicity had been transformed by the end of the last century. As such they sought to link process to structure. They depicted two processes working in tandem to effect a progressive loosening of the ties that had heretofore linked religion to ethnicity: assimilation and secularization. Contending that both ethnicity and religion are "vulnerable to forces that diminish their social importance," they consider assimilation and secularization to be accurate characterizations of parallel declines in salience of these two aspects of identity, attributing both to the advance of individualism in the society at large (Hammond and Warner 1993: 56–7).

Within this general perspective, they turn to the Abramson typology, giving names to the three types they consider relevant to the American scene (the fourth type, the most inconsequential in the original formulation, is simply ignored). The type wherein religion is the major foundation of ethnicity is called "ethnic fusion." Such groups may succeed in maintaining the powerful linkage between religion and ethnicity. But they do so at a price, which is that the "very strength [of the bond] may keep such groups small and insulated" (Hammond and Warner 1993: 59; see the basic argument in the classic article by Granovetter 1973). If we exclude Mormons as an inappropriate group for this type, what is obvious about these groups (Hutterites, Amish, and Jews [or at least Ultra-Orthodox Jews]) is that they represent examples of non-proselytizing religions. As such, in their attempts to preserve bright boundaries between insiders and outsiders, they represent a side stream in the larger currents of American religion.

For this reason, Hammond and Warner focus on the other two types, which they defined as ethnic religion (e.g., Greek Orthodox and Dutch Reformed) and religious ethnicity (e.g., Irish, Italian, and Polish Catholics). They note that a crucial differentiating characteristic of ethnic versus religious identity is that the former is perceived to be invariably inheritable, while the latter is not. As they point out, although the salience of ethnicity might erode and even disappear, it is unlikely that people would engage in ethnic switching. Such, of course, is not the case with religious affiliation. Nonetheless, they contend that the evidence they bring to bear suggests that assimilation and secularization are mutually reinforcing processes. Moreover, they think that both are occurring in all of the groups they examined, though the rate of change varies based on whether or not the groups are the victims of discriminatory exclusion and marginalization. When groups are so victimized, the pace of both assimilation and secularization is slowed. Finally, they contend that in the future the connection between religion and ethnicity will erode, due chiefly to the fact that as religion increasingly becomes a matter of individual choice, "ethnicity, along with other background characteristics, will have a declining effect in determining religious identity" (Hammond and Warner 1993: 66).

A curious feature of this study is that, despite framing it in terms of the impacts of the dual processes of assimilation and secularization, in fact there is nothing in the data that are employed that would permit an examination of whether or not secularization is occurring. It does address standard measures of assimilation (evidence of mixed versus single ancestry, in-group or out-group marriage, and a measure of the level of subjective attachment to people from one's ancestral background). However, no similar measures are included that could be construed as measuring the relative social significance of religion for respondents. Thus, although the authors can make a case that the role of ethnicity in determining religious identity has declined, they cannot argue on the basis of the data that religious identity itself has eroded.

Will Herberg (1955), writing four decades earlier than Hammond and Warner, was uninterested in a typology designed to capture the different ways that religion and ethnicity might interact, but rather in describing the major historical trend and largely ignoring the minor exceptions to that trend. Relying on the work of pioneer of immigration history Marcus Lee Hansen's characterization of generational changes from the first to third generations, and having the benefit of hindsight as the third generation had come of age by the middle of the twentieth century, Herberg argued that while ethnicity and religion often were intimately interconnected for the immigrant generation, they began to be severed in succeeding generations. In his view, the ethnic factor – seen most explicitly in culture and language – began to erode with the second generation, but for it and subsequent generations the question of identity arose, specifically the question addressing national identity: what kind of Americans were they?

Herberg argued that by embracing but modifying the religion of their ancestors, those born in America could simultaneously define their place in the new homeland and maintain a distinctive group identity. He contended that, "Religious association now became the primary context of self-identification and social location for the third generation, as well as for the bulk of the second generation of America's immigrants, and that meant, by and large, for the American people" (Herberg 1955: 31). The assumption underlying this conclusion was that assimilation was resulting in the steady decline of the ethnic factor in American life, while the highly religious character of the country called into question the secularization thesis.

While it may be true that the ethnic factor declined, it did not disappear, as what Thomas Archdeacon (1990: 54) called an "ethnic hum" continued to "exist [perhaps] almost indefinitely as a motif in the society." This hum could manifest itself as "symbolic ethnicity" (Gans 1979) or in other ways afford "ethnic options" (Waters 1990; see also Alba 1990) to individuals as they selectively abandon and embrace elements of their ethnic heritage. At the same time, negative outsider attitudes could also continue to exist, making it difficult for marginalized groups to become fully incorporated into the society. In the current wave of immigration and in an era characterized by various "multicultural experiments" (Kymlicka 2010: 257), it is less clear whether the assimilatory path of the American past will repeat itself.

And if one wants to extrapolate these findings to other advanced industrial societies, it is even less clear. At the same time, Americans continue to be highly religious, while even those who have questioned the secularization thesis have tended to consider secular Europe as an exception (see, for example, Berger, Fokas, and Davie 2008; Torpey 2012). Thus, there are clearly challenges both to past/present comparisons and to cross-national comparisons. Given this situation, what can be distilled from recent research? Before answering that question, it is necessary to note both that most of the research to date has had an American focus and in all instances it is limited to the first and second generations since the latter has come of age only in the past few years and the succeeding generation either has not been born or is very young. Moreover, this research has tended to be ethnographic in nature, and thus one can reasonably question how much we can extrapolate from these findings in order to offer persuasive generalizations.

Research Findings

Based on a selective, but I think representative, sample of studies, we find on the one hand conclusions that suggest the mutual reinforcement of ethnic and religious identities and on the other those that see a growing gulf between the two. In terms of the former, one can point to studies by Carl Bankston III and Min Zhou (1995, 1996) and Rebecca Kim (2004, 2006). Bankston and Zhou's study of Vietnamese 1.5 and second-generation adolescents in New Orleans found that the Catholic congregations they belonged to provided a major source for defining themselves in ethnic terms. In their ethnic congregations, these young people were able to present themselves in ethnic terms while avoiding doing so in school and other arenas of everyday life. Rather than being an impediment to adjusting to the receiving society, they argued that ethnic religious involvements helped to facilitate fitting into the societal mainstream.

Kim's research begins with the observation that Asian students at elite universities such as Harvard, Yale, Stanford, and UCLA have come to constitute very large majorities of the memberships of evangelical Christian groups such as the Campus Crusade for Christ and Intervarsity Christian Fellowship. Her research has looked explicitly at Korean American students, who happen to have the largest Asian presence in such organizations. Having been raised in racially mixed neighborhoods and been educated in predominantly white schools, she asks what attracts Koreans to what are now largely ethnic organizations rather than joining multi-ethnic organizations and churches.

What she discovered is that many of these youth are reacting against their parents' religious practices, opting for practices and rituals that are embraced by their white generational counterparts. This makes the decision to opt for a linking of ethnicity and religion all the more puzzling. Kim contends that there are three reasons that account for this ethnic option. First, there are sufficient numbers of Korean Americans at elite institutions to make viable distinctly ethnic organizations. Second, she subscribes to the idea of homophily and thinks that the linking of the ethnic and religious congruently functions to reinforce that desire. Third, while these students are ambitious and successful and expect to enter into rewarding careers, the reality of racial marginalization makes associating with fellow ethnics appealing (Kim 2006: 87). This may amount to a transitional situation, for once they leave universities and find themselves in social settings with fewer Koreans, these current students will have to renegotiate their affiliations.

In an insightful comparative study, Prema Kurien (2001) contrasts Hindu and Muslim Indians residing in the United States. As will be discussed in greater depth in chapter 4 on transnationalism, Hindu nationalists sympathetic to the Hindutva movement that ties Indian national identity tightly to Hinduism, in effect assert the fusion of ethnic/national identity and religious identity. In contrast, Muslims from India, both at home and abroad, seek to portray their homeland as a religiously pluralistic society, thereby delinking to a considerable degree religion from national identity. Given that Islam is a global religion, Indian Muslims can attempt to define the religious aspect of their identity as tied to a worldwide Muslim community – the Ummah – and not only to the nation of India. In contrast, although Hindu communities exist outside of India, it is nevertheless a religion whose members are overwhelmingly Indian. Here we have in one case two religious traditions from the same nation with distinctive ways of defining the relationship between ethnicity and religion.

In a different type of comparison, Pyong Gap Min (2010) has sought to explore how two groups have attempted to preserve ethnicity through religion: Korean Protestants and Indian Hindus. His ethnographic research at the Korean Shin Kwang Church and the Indian Ganesh Temple, both located in New York City, was complemented by surveys and interviews from the first, 1.5, and second generations. His findings regarding the Hindu community, which reinforce Kurien's conclusions, reveal that because temple practices play a lesser role in religious life than congregational activities among Korean Protestants do, a key locus for the transmission of both ethnic and religious identities is the home, where routinized prayers at family shrines and other domestic ritual practices are crucial. The result is a fusion of the ethnic and the religious – for what it means to be Indian is to be Hindu and vice versa.

Although Shin Kwang Church is ethnic and one can see it as a vehicle for transmitting Korean culture, Min contends that the linkage between religion and ethnicity is more tenuous. For one thing, Korean Christians have options to join non-Korean churches. Secondly, given that Korean culture is not Christian, the connection is not the same. When the ethnic is emphasized in congregational activities, it typically takes on a Confucian character, as can be seen in activities promoting reverence for ancestors. Nevertheless, the members have sought to preserve the ethnic character of their church. This is a finding supported by Sharon Kim's (2010) ethnographic study of 22 Korean American congregations in the Los Angeles area.

In contrast to Bankston and Zhou's Vietnamese, Kim's Koreans, and Kurien and Min's Hindu Indians, other researchers have pointed to indications of a separation of ethnic and religious identities and a recalibration of their respective saliences. Pawan Dhingra's (2004) ethnographic research at three Korean Protestant congregations in the Dallas area illustrates a generational shift in which members of the second generation express a willingness to uncouple their ethnicity and their religious identity. The institutional pressure to do so will be discussed in the following chapter, an illustration of the fact that the analytical distinction between the psychological and the institutional aspects of adaptation are intertwined in ways that are often difficult to unravel.

The research reviewed here and similar studies are suggestive when attempting to determine if a similar pattern is emerging that parallels the experience of the immigrants from the Great Migration. One needs to be cautious in drawing conclusions given the relatively limited number of studies and the fact that almost all offer ethnographic snapshots of a particular congregation at a specific moment in time. At this point, data are lacking that address change over time and across generations. And given that Herberg included in his account of historical process the third generation, it is premature to conclude where the new immigrants might end up given that the third generation has to large extent not yet come of age.

Nevertheless, with these caveats in mind, it is likely that for the vast majority what Raymond Breton (2012: 49) describes as the progressive "disassociation of religion and ethnicity" is likely to occur, whereby individuals "come to see them as two distinct bases for their individual identities and for the identity of their community." There will be exceptions, with Jews being a prime example given that they are a paradigmatic case of Abramson's religio-ethnic group and Hammond and Warner's ethnic fusion model. However, the general trend is likely to parallel what Kurien (2012: 447) in a recent study of members of the Malankara Orthodox Syrian Church from the Indian state of Kerala now living in the USA describes – lending support to Breton's assessment – as the "decoupling of religion and ethnicity."

Gender, Ethnicity, and Religion

Deeply implicated in the ethnicity and religion nexus is gender, for the respective roles of immigrant men and women, authority structures in the household, locating roles within the public/private spheres, and so forth have been shaped by the ethnic culture and the religious tradition. In the pre-migration context, the two often operated more or less seamlessly in defining the often taken-for-granted character of patriarchy and the gendered division of labor both in general and in the home. But in the migratory context, a variety of factors can contribute to a reconfiguration of gender relations, which can include those related to the respective locations of men and women in the labor force, a growing familiarity with the host society's more egalitarian views, generational tensions within the home over homeland versus the receiving society's views on gender relations, and sometimes pragmatic considerations about the role of women in religious organizations. Cadge and Ecklund (2007: 365) contend that a shortcoming with the state of current research on the role of gender in the construction of immigrant religious identities has been that most research has focused on what happens within religious organizations at the expense of examining how what is happening in other realms of social life impacts what is going on within the religious sphere.

Among the notable exceptions to this focus, one can point to studies by Sheba George (1998, 2005), Orlando Tizon (1999, 2000), and Prema Kurien (1999). George explored the gender dynamics of immigrant Christians from the Indian state of Kerala – the same group that was the research site for Kurien's recent research. Christians from that Indian state are distinctive because it is a place that has had a Christian presence since the first centuries of the Common Era, when tradition has it that St. Thomas landed on the coast of Kerala. The immigrants in George's ethnography of a congregation in "Central City" were atypical insofar as women, mainly nurses who found professional opportunities in the United States, migrated while the remainder of the family remained beyond until a later date (George's mother was one such individual). When fathers and children ultimately followed, the fathers often had difficulty establishing themselves in similarly successful careers, despite the fact that many had been white-collar professionals in India. Thus, what this group experienced was gender role reversal linked to the loss of status of males. One way that this dynamic played out was that men began to compensate for their economic position by asserting a prime role as leaders in the church. In addition to finding ways of redefining gender relations in the household, both men and women had to confront stigmatization by other Indians who were critical of the men for their failure to maintain patriarchal authority and the women for being too independent.

Orlando Tizon's (2000) ethnographic research of a congregation he calls "Philippians," a Filipino Protestant congregation in Chicago, found a rather similar gender dynamic, though not quite as dramatic because women had generally not migrated prior to the arrival of men. In many respects, gender relations within the congregation follow the received cultural tradition. Women are involved in many aspects of the church, but Tizon finds that they are in particular assigned to do "emotion work," which entails counseling, caregiving, and social service projects. At the same time, at 72.3 percent Filipinas have a higher labor force participation rate than both the general population and other Asian groups. Many have careers in health professions (nurses, laboratory technicians, pharmacists, and so forth), while their husbands – like the men from Kerala – have experienced a loss of status as it is common for Filipinas to earn more than their husbands. As a consequence, women – particularly younger ones – have set an agenda calling for rejecting traditional gender relations by placing on the table the need to address "issues that challenge the core values of the traditional family and the church": divorce, premarital sex, and single-motherhood (Tizon 2000: 391).

Kurien's (1999) California-based fieldwork explored gender relations in three aspects of everyday life: the household, the local Indian community, and pan-Indian organizations. In this case, while a majority of women have entered the workforce, the downward mobility men experienced in the preceding two studies was not evident here. Noting that previous research was divided over whether the migratory setting had led to the empowerment of women or to even greater inegalitarian and restrictive conditions, she concludes that each offers accurate but partial accounts. On the one hand, the taken-for-granted character of "Indianness" in the homeland, where people simply "breathe in the values of Hindu life" (Fenton 1988: 127) no longer suffices in the receiving country, where women have acquired the primary role of socializing children and serving as "cultural custodians" (Kurien 1999: 650). This role provides the opportunity to redefine gender relations in ways that are favorable to women:

> The idealized family based on traditional gender images from Hindu religion is a central icon in the construction of an American Hinduism. Because women are the primary transmitters of religious and cultural traditions within the household and local associations, at these levels they are also able to reinterpret the patriarchal images more in their favor and construct a model of gender that emphasizes the importance of male responsibilities. (Kurien 1999: 650)

At the same time, pan-Indian organizations, both secular and religious, remain heavily male-dominated. These organizations function to project a specific public image of the Indian community, and much effort is expended to insure that they are seen as a "model minority." Part of that image revolves around depicting the Hindu woman as an exemplar of tradition who is "a virtuous and self-sacrificing homemaker, enabling the professional success of her husband and the academic achievements of her children through her unselfish actions on their behalf" (Kurien 1999: 650). In their research on 13 congregations in the Houston area, Helen Rose Ebaugh and Janet Chafetz (1999: 585) arrived at a similar conclusion. Where women's lay roles grew in number and significance and their resources similarly expanded, they were ironically accorded the role of "reproducing traditional ethnic culture."

Finally, as a broad generalization it is fair to say that immigrants come from societies that are more patriarchal than those of Western nations that have in recent decades become increasingly committed, in principle if not always in practice, to gender equity.

But as one study has revealed, one can find instances in which patriarchy is preserved by adapting to the new setting. Antony Alumkal's (1999) ethnography of a conservative Protestant Korean congregation in the New York metropolitan area found that the second-generation members provided evidence of abandoning a Korean cultural justification of a male-dominated gender hierarchy in favor of a conservative evangelical Christian justification. This suggests something about the varieties of reciprocal ways that gender and religious identities can play out. At the same time, Alumkal's study supports Breton's dissociation of ethnic culture and religion thesis.

Immigrant Adjustment

Charles Hirschman (2004: 1228) contends that the "centrality of religion to immigrant communities can be summarized as the search for three R's: "refuge, respectability, and resources" (a pithy formulation he attributes to Alejandro Portes). We address this trio here. Beginning with the first, the idea of religion as refuge is rooted in the view seen in Thomas, Handlin, Herberg, and others that immigration is an inherently disorienting, alienating experience. Religion, to the extent that it can provide refuge for immigrants, helps to overcome that experience.

As a research focus, refuge is generally translated into a concern with psychological well-being (Mahalingam 2006). As such, this aspect of immigrant adjustment can be seen as a subset of a more general research tradition devoted to exploring the implications of religious belief and involvement on self-image and coping capabilities. The John Templeton Foundation has been particularly interested in funding research addressing the role of spiritual and religious life on psychological health. For example, the Faith Matters survey conducted in 2006–7, was funded by the foundation. Researchers involved in the project found that religious people in general were more satisfied with their lives than people who were not actively involved in congregational life. Chaeyoon Lim and Robert Putnam (2010) concluded that this higher level of satisfaction was a product of attendance at religious services where social networks were created and sustained.

When concentrating on immigrants, much of the research to date is based on relatively small sample sizes and the results have been varied. However, it appears that the majority of studies confirm the idea that religion serves as a source of psychological well-being. Kyoung Ok Seol and Richard M. Lee (2012) offer a recent example of this sort of work. They studied 155 Korean American adolescents and concluded that those who manifested strong religious identities had far fewer behavioral problems and felt more integrated into American society than those with weak religious identities.

A more limited body of research has made use of larger data sets. One that has examined the impact of religion on the positive development of immigrant youth relied on two studies, the Longitudinal Immigrant Student Adaptation Study and the Role of Spiritual Development in Growth of Purpose, Generosity, and Psychological Health in Adolescence. The project was funded by the John Templeton Foundation, and as the title to the second data set suggests, there is a guiding assumption that religion can have a psychologically beneficial impact on immigrant youth. The authors of this particular study conclude that this may well be the case, but are careful not to draw unwarranted conclusions, contending instead that there is a need to engage in further research on the topic (Suárez-Orozco, Singh, Abo-Zena, Du, and Roeser 2012).

Perhaps the most expansive and significant study to date is contained in an article by Phillip Connor titled "Balm for the Soul: Immigrant Religion and Emotional Well-Being" (2012). He offers a comparative study of the United States, Western Europe, and Australia, making use of data for each of these regions respectively from the New Immigrant Survey, the European Social Survey, and the Longitudinal Survey of Immigrants to Australia. Connor found that in all three geographic locales, regular religious participation contributed to positive emotional/mental health outcomes. Moreover, he found that such positive outcomes did not occur as a result of membership in other types of organizational life, such as ethnic associations, leisure groups, or workplace groups. This led him to suggest "that religion has a unique relationship with immigrant emotional well-being" (Connor 2012: 130).

Turning to respectability, immigrants confront the challenge of not simply being tolerated, but being embraced with their differences valorized while being seen as an equal. The intertwined concepts of respect and recognition have complex theoretical lineages (Taylor 1992; Alexander 2006; Honneth 2007). Here we look to work that gets at this phenomenon in the more grounded terms required of empirical research. One approach would be to see to what extent immigrants come to view themselves as fully members of the nation, sharing an identity with native-born citizens, and in turn being seen by those long-term residents as truly part of the nation. And, more specifically, we are interested in knowing to what extent religion might play a facilitating role in this process.

A good illustration can be found in Carolyn Chen's (2008, 2006, 2002) research on Taiwanese immigrants in southern California, wherein she provides insights into how religion has assisted these newcomers in the process of Americanization. In her comparative ethnographic study of members of an immigrant Buddhist temple and an evangelical Christian church, she notes at the outset that whether opting for the dominant religion from the homeland or converting to the dominant religion of the receiving country, in both instances it appears that her subjects had become more religious as a result of the migration experience. From there she proceeds to argue that in both cases, what one sees unfold over time is a mutually reinforcing relationship develop between religiosity and Americanization.

While it may have appeared that those immigrants who opted to convert to Christianity were more intent on becoming American than their Buddhist counterparts, Chen's portraits suggest two parallel routes to Americanization. She found it puzzling that the presumably more "other-worldly" Buddhists were actually more publicly engaged than the "inner-worldly" Christians. In speculating about why this might be the case, she concluded that what each group found was a distinctive route to forging an identity with the receiving society. In the case of the Buddhists, they found that a devotion to charity constituted a form of civic engagement in accord with the republican tradition that has historically shaped in part the nation's "habits of the heart" (Bellah, Madsen, Sullivan, Swidler, and Tipton 1985). In contrast, the Christian converts embraced the individualistic notions of social reform deeply embedded in conservative Protestantism, where the emphasis is on saving individuals one by one rather than on transforming a fallen world. For both groups, religious participation proved to be a means of identifying with significant but selective aspects of the national culture of America.

Elaine Ecklund's (2006) ethnographic research on second-generation Korean Americans, some of whom are members of an ethnic church and others who are part of a multi-ethnic church (both of which would be defined as conservative and evangelical), describes interviewees that resemble Chen's Taiwanese Christian converts. Thus, when they engage in community service, the emphasis is on using such activities as "a means of living and spreading Christianity" (Ecklund 2006: 52). While they appear to embrace the political views of their native-born Christian right counterparts on issues such as abortion and same-sex relations, they are little inclined to be actively involved in political engagements. The main conclusion is that given the pluralism characteristic of American society writ large, what these immigrants have managed to do is to find in religious participation a vehicle for being accepted into the mainstream – or at least into one of the various currents of that mainstream.

In terms of religion as a resource, R. Stephen Warner (2007) has pointed to the need to factor religion into the process of segmented assimilation. What he has in mind is the way that religion can serve as a bridge between the culture of the homeland and that of the new setting, assisting immigrants to adjust to their new setting. In this he implicitly concurs with Lal's (1990) "ethnicity paradox," seeing in ethnic religious institutions a means of adjusting and fitting into new surroundings. Depicting religious affiliation as a source of both cultural and social capital, case studies have sought to determine to what extent it has played a role in enhancing educational attainment and occupational success.

Margarita Mooney's (2009) study of Haitians in Montreal, Paris, and Miami concluded that the Catholic Church in the United States had proven to have a positive impact in terms of obtaining needed social services and achieving employment success. However, such was not the case in either Canada or (especially) France, due to particular church/state regulations that prevented the Church from operating as freely as in the United States in offering services to its congregants. Making use of data derived from the New Immigrant Survey, Connor (2011) found little support for the idea that religious participation contributes to positive economic outcomes in terms of employment, occupational status, and earnings. The exception to this finding involves non-Protestant immigrants, for the religiously active among them do appear to benefit economically. What these findings point to is the need for further research, not only in terms of religion as resource, but also as refuge and source of respectability. Simply put, the research to date constitutes a promising beginning, but the limitations of this body of work make it necessary to draw conclusions circumspectly.

Is Migration a "Theologizing Experience"?

Are immigrants more religious than their counterparts who remain in the homeland? In other words, do the dislocations brought about by migration lead people to seek out religion? As is evident in the examples cited in the preceding pages of this chapter, much of contemporary research either explicitly points to an intensification of religious identification and involvement or implicitly assumes it is happening. In an oft-cited article, historian Timothy Smith (1978: 1175) argued that this was true of the Great Migration in America – and in his opinion all periods of American history. Concurring with Handlin's "uprooted" portrait of the alienating consequences of migration, Smith contended that as a result, "migration was often a theologizing experience." The individual migrant was forced to reckon with the fact that "[e]verything was new" from architecture to technology to language to everyday patterns of social exchange. Immigrants had to grapple with a situation in which they had been freed from the "moral constraints that village culture had imposed in matters monetary, recreational, occupational, alcoholic, educational, and sexual." In the face of this freedom, it was necessary "to determine how to act in these new circumstances by reference not simply to the dominant 'host' culture, but to a dozen competing subcultures."

Smith failed to offer a succinct account of what he meant by theologizing experience, but it appears that what he had in mind was more than religious participation, for it also implied a reflective quality. In other words, he believes that at least in the past immigrants tended to become more religious than they were in the homeland, and appears to think that their engagement with religion is self-reflective, rather than being the product of habit. That being said, contemporary scholars have been inclined to treat the idea of theologizing experience as being little more than a fancy way of describing heightened religiosity.

Chen's claim about the Taiwanese Buddhists and Christians she studied is representative of many studies which conclude that their subjects became more religious after migration. This raises the inevitable question that is asked about all ethnographic research, namely, how representative is it of immigrants in general. The problem is compounded in the study of religious belief, affiliation, and practice insofar as most research to date has focused on active members in religious organizations – congregations, temples, mosques, gurdwaras, and so forth. Missing from such research are immigrants who have opted not to become members of such organizations.

This lacuna has been addressed in the New Immigrant Survey, a panel survey of a nationally representative sample of new legal immigrants, conducted in 2003 under the direction of Guillermina Jasso, Douglas S. Massey, Mark R. Rosenzweig, and James P. Smith. An early book chapter by the principal figures did not address the matter of whether or not migration led to increased religious involvement. Instead, it offered a descriptive overview of the findings, stressing the growing religious pluralism in the nation resulting from contemporary immigration (Jasso, Massey,

Rosenzweig, and Smith 2003). The first effort to address religiosity, by Cadge and Ecklund (2006), actually made use of the smaller sample from the NIS's pilot study conducted in 1996, in which there were only two questions about religion included in the survey (about affiliation and attendance). They concluded that immigrants who were less integrated into the receiving society were more inclined to attend religious services regularly than was true of those who were more integrated.

Two recent studies have made use of the 2003 survey. The first, by Ilana Redstone Akresh (2011), picks up on an implication of the Cadge and Ecklund study, which is that as immigrants become more integrated into American society they will become less religiously active. Akresh does not focus on the contrast between pre-migration and post-migration, but instead on what happens to religious attendance over time in the post-migration context. She concludes that "there is a tendency towards greater attendance with increased time in the US and no evidence of a decline" (Akresh 2011: 657).

The second study, by Douglas S. Massey and Monica Espinoza Higgins (2011) explicitly addresses – indeed, challenges – Smith's "theologizing experience" thesis. Noting that most studies that advance Smith's hypothesis have used qualitative methods, they point to one quantitative study of Quebec, not the United States, that calls it into question (Connor 2008). Making use of the NIS data, Massey and Higgins note an overall dramatic decline in religious attendance after migration. The decline is more pronounced for Christians than non-Christians and within the ranks of Christians, the decline is greatest for Catholics. All other major religions also experience decline, though it is not as pronounced as for Christians, probably because adherents to these other faiths participated less in the pre-migration context than their Christian counterparts. This is reflected in the fact that Protestants exhibit higher levels of congregational membership than any other religious group. The study paints a complex portrait reflective of both the religious diversity of the immigrant population and the diversity of national origins. To cite one example of what this means, when looking at Christian patterns of membership, the range is broad, with only 10 percent of Salvadorans reporting membership in a church in contrast to 76 percent for Koreans (Massey and Higgins 2011: 1383).

Massey and Higgins (2011: 1387) conclude that rather than supporting Smith's theologizing hypothesis, their findings "are more consistent with what might be called an alienating hypothesis." They point out that immigrants must adjust in ways large and small to their new setting, and that the process of adjustment is time-consuming. Religion, thus, competes for time with the demands of jobs, schooling, language acquisition, and a host of other aspects of life that also require time commitments. Their second point is that immigrants that are not part of the Judeo-Christian tradition enter a religious sphere where their faith tradition may be institutionally thin. While these are no doubt factors contributing to a lessening of religious participation, it is less obvious why this situation should be seen as necessarily a matter of alienation. However, it does point to the fact that belief and participation must be located in a larger context. In particular, as Tubergen and Sindradóttir (2011) concluded in their comparative analysis of European nations, findings from the European Social Survey indicated that immigrants exhibited higher levels of religiosity in more highly religious countries (such as Poland) than in more secular ones (such as Sweden). Given that the United States ranks high on this measure, this contextual reality must be taken into account.

While Massey and Higgins (2011: 1387) are right that a focus on congregation-based samples can distort the picture of the larger immigrant religious landscape, it is also true that to more fully understand the religious experiences of the "highly selected and unrepresentative" members of congregations, it is important to explore changes taking place not simply at the level of the individual, but also the institutional level. It is this latter topic that we take up in the next chapter.

3

Reframing Religious Organizations and Practices

On February 10, 2010, a British appeals court overturned a lower court ruling and found in favor of Hindu spiritual leader Davender Kumar Ghai, who had sought permission to have his body cremated on an open-air pyre upon his death. The lower court had ruled that outdoor cremations violated the 1902 Cremation Act, which, in the course of legalizing cremation as a viable alternative to burial, stipulated that cremations would take place in purpose-built crematoriums. Ghai, who resides in a suburb of Newcastle-upon-Tyne, was also the founder and head of the Anglo-Asian Friendship Society, a registered charity that its website claims is the "largest multi-faith charity in Britain" (www. Anglo-Asian.org). In addition to peace missions and multi-faith pilgrimages, the website reveals that one of the organization's primary engagements concerns gaining permission to conduct traditional outdoor cremations in Britain.

Given that over 70 percent of Britain's dead are cremated rather than buried, the issue is not whether or not cremation is an option. The real issue revolves around why Ghai and his supporters reject the idea of turning to the local crematorium for their funerals. They do so because it is their conviction that the objective of the funeral ceremony is to permit the soul to be detached from the body and burning the body in the open air is the most propitious way to insure this result. Interviewing Ghai, Jerome Taylor (2010), writing for the *Independent*, wrote that "orthodox families believe a covered electric crematorium fails to do this, allowing the soul to

mingle with other souls and condemning the deceased to an inaus-
picious death that hampers them in the next life."

Acting on this conviction, Ghai had argued that open-air cremations did not necessarily violate the law. He pointed to the
open-air cremations near Brighton of Hindu and Sikh soldiers
who fought and died fighting for Britain in World War I, and the
1934 outdoor cremation near Surrey of the wife of the Nepalese
ambassador to the United Kingdom. In 2006 Ghai and his allies
conducted an outdoor funeral for Rajpal Mehat, a 31-year-old
undocumented immigrant from India whose body was found in a
canal near Slough. His cause of death was never determined, but
his family made clear their desire to have a traditional cremation
for him and Baba Ghai entered the picture. With the assistance of
a local funeral director, he arranged for an outdoor cremation at a
secret location in Northumberland. Although the authorities had
questions about the legality of the funeral, they allowed it to go
ahead. It was after this event that Ghai began his legal battle to be
permitted an outdoor cremation when he died.

Public opinion both outside of and within the Hindu and Sikh
communities was divided. Moreover, during the initial stage of his
campaign, Ghai was unable to elicit much enthusiasm from those
who were generally sympathetic to his cause. Indeed, some within
the leadership stratum of the Hindu community, such as the heads
of the Hindu Academy, contended that such funeral rites constituted an "antiquated practice." This opposition from within the
community reversed course with the intervention of the sensitivity-
challenged former Justice Minister Jack Straw, who contended
in an interview with a journalist that the British public would
likely "find it abhorrent that human remains were being burned
in this way." The result was that, "From then on all the major
Hindu community organisations including the Hindu Forum and
the Hindu Council, as well as a small body of Sikh gurudwaras
(temples), began backing Mr Ghai's bid" (Taylor 2010).

It was within this climate of public opinion that the appeals
court's ruling was issued. It declared that open-air cremations
did not violate the 1902 Act and did not necessarily raise public
health and safety concerns. This being said, the ruling also set

certain conditions. For one thing, cremations could not take place near roads or homes. In addition, traditional cremations on a pyre must be conducted in an enclosed structure, though the structure need not have a roof. This decision represented a negotiated settlement that was designed to appease both critics and proponents. By requiring a structure, funerals would be private rather than public events insofar as those not directly involved in the funeral would not be witness to the event. On the other hand, since direct access to the sky was of fundamental importance to proponents, the ruling made this possible. The ruling legitimated a traditional fire as opposed to the mechanical fire of modern crematoria and made possible the sun's rays falling on the dead body. Ghai proclaimed himself satisfied with the ruling, stating that, "I always maintained that I wanted to clarify the law, not disobey or disrespect it. My request was often misinterpreted, leading many to believe I wanted a funeral pyre cremation in an open field, whereas I always accepted that buildings and permanent structures would be appropriate. Now I may go in peace" (Taylor 2010).

At the time of this writing, Baba Ghai remains alive and the issue of outdoor cremations has received no further national press coverage. In the years before the court ruling, some predicted that should he prevail in his legal battle, the vast majority of Hindus in Britain, along with sizeable numbers of Sikhs and Jains, would opt for traditional outdoor funeral pyres. There is no evidence to date to support this claim. And, indeed, Ghai seemed to be aware of the fact that his quest would serve only a minority of like-minded believers, and he was comfortable with this situation. He told a BBC reporter while the court was considering his case that, "I fully respect that many Hindu-origin people will prefer the speed and convenience of crematoria, but for practicing Hindus like me, receiving last rites is quite literally a matter of life and death" (Kleiderman 2009). This view was echoed by Chandu Tailor, the manager of one of the largest chains of Asian-owned funeral homes in the country, who contended that, "Most people are perfectly happy with the normal crematoria. What they really want most are proper facilities to be able to prepare the body according to religious rituals" (Taylor 2010). And to that end, a cursory search of British funeral directors websites reveals that many firms, both Asian and non-Asian, have made very explicit appeals in their advertising to cater to this particular clientele.

Just as the vast majority of Hindu, Sikh, and Jain adherents have been prepared to revise traditional funeral practices in the migratory context in terms of cremation rites, so too have they revised practices related to the scattering of ashes. A survey of videos on the Asian-American Friendship Society website inevitably ends with members of the family transporting the urn containing their loved one's ashes to India, where a religious ceremony is conducted on the banks of the Ganges. Not only is this not speedy and convenient, but it involves substantial costs. It is not surprising, therefore, that an increasing number of people are opting to scatter ashes in British rivers, with, as one might have surmised, the Thames being the most commonly used.

Whereas the preceding chapter was primarily concerned with the psychological adjustments of individual immigrants and with the issue of religious identity, this one addresses the varied ways in which immigrant communities adapt and adjust to a new setting in religious belief and practices and in the organizational structure of religious institutions. We turn first to the latter, which has received considerable attention in the literature.

Organizational Adaptation

As immigrants settle into the receiving society and, in particular, after the second generation comes of age one can find a variety of responses to religious belief and practice. As the preceding chapter indicates, at the individual level this can mean one of three possibilities: (1) an effort expended at preserving homeland religion in as pristine a form as possible; (2) a revising of religious practice with the aim of assimilating into the religious landscape of the new homeland; or (3) an abandonment of religion (Mullins 1988). Those who seek to maintain a connection to religious organizational life in either the first or second of these options discover that a transformation in organizational structure is generally necessary and often beneficial (Breton 2012: 107–10).

Warner's de Facto Congregationalism Thesis

The most sustained attempts to analyze a general pattern of organizational adaptation have focused explicitly on the United States, with a string of publications by R. Stephen Warner (1993, 1994, 1997, 1998a, 1998b, 2000) on "de facto congregationalism" constituting the touchstone for this work. The idea of de facto congregationalism was first articulated in Warner's (1993) seminal essay on a "new paradigm for the sociological study of religion in the United States," where it represents one of the elements of the paradigm. The argument he advanced was that there was ample evidence of a new way of viewing religion in the United States emerging in the sociological literature, and that it marked a distinct contrast to the older, heretofore dominant model that had taken shape with (Western) European societies as the main referents (Berger 1969). Underlying the contrast between Europe and the United States as conceptual referents was the commonplace observation that whereas religious observance was on the decline in Europe, it remains robust in the United States. Warner points to an explanation of this difference in terms of the open religious market in the latter case versus the state monopoly in the former.

In this his view is reminiscent of the religious economy perspective advanced by Roger Finke and Rodney Stark (1992), though he stresses that, "The new paradigm is not *defined* by economic imagery, [. . .] but by the idea that disestablishment is the norm" (Warner 1993: 1053). In a detailed schematic comparison of the two paradigms, Warner offers the following contrast. The old paradigm presupposed a situation in which a particular faith tradition possessed a monopoly on legitimate institutionalized religion, and thus could readily make taken-for-granted claims to being a universal church with ascription being the primary basis for religious identity. The new paradigm is distinctive insofar as it envisions a competitive environment in which religious identities are contested and fluid, making way for entrepreneurial leaders – rather than prebendary officials – who must actively recruit members. The hallmark of this religious field is, thus, one characterized by cultural pluralism (Warner 1993: 1052, 1058). Primary attention throughout the article is directed to a reframing of the way in which we look at religious change. Specifically, the paradigm casts into doubt the old paradigm's assumptions concerning the secularization of modern societies, an assumption that was forced to treat the American case as an anomaly. In the old paradigm, the questions often posed tended to revolve around identifying what were presumed to be the sources of American exceptionalism. In the new paradigm, the unresolved questions concern European exceptionalism.

In subsequent publications, Warner outlined his understanding of the United States' religious field. First, he contends that Americans are "elective parochials," and religion in the nation is aptly characterized as being "profoundly associational and voluntaristic" (Warner 1998b: 124–5). Furthermore, he concurs with Morris Janowitz's contention that "American communities tend to be 'communities of limited liability'." Finally, while noting that there is no monolithic religious culture shared by all Americans, but rather a number of cultures, he contends that "religion mediates difference." It is, in his opinion, "the institutional area where US culture has best tolerated difference" (Warner 1997: 219).

Our interest here is in one facet of the model, which concerns organizational structure. Drawing on H. Richard Niebuhr's classic work, *The Social Sources of Denominationalism* (1929), Warner views the denomination in its American setting as a structural innovation made appropriate in a context characterized by disestablishment and its consequent facilitation of religious pluralism. This was true even during the earliest phase of the nation's history, when it was an overwhelmingly Protestant country, but one in which Protestantism was divided into an array of discrete religious bodies whose boundaries were based on such factors as theological differences, ethnicity, language, and the national origin of members. Secondly, Warner (1993: 1065) contends, "Another pervasive American pattern is the congregational model of local church organization, whether or not sanctioned by the hierarchy." Calling this pattern "de facto congregationalism," he goes on to spell out what this means. The term serves to label

> ... an institutionalized bias of American religious life toward affectively significant associations under local and lay control, beginning with observations of differences between congregations within the same denomination. ... De facto congregationalism implies that the local religious community is in fact constituted by those who assemble together (which is the etymological root of "congregation") rather than by the geographic units into which higher church authorities divide their constituents, which is what "parishes" historically are. (Warner 1993: 1066–7)

There is little question but that congregationalism has been a hallmark of American Protestantism in a nation that at its founding rejected the idea of a state church in favor of creating a wall of separation between church and state. But is this organizational pattern relevant to other religions, as well? Warner thinks it is, and in considering earlier waves of migration points to Catholic church historian Jay Dolan's (1985) assessment that whereas Vatican II pushed Catholic laity into a considerably more prominent role of leadership, evidence of their significance in establishing and developing churches should be dated to a far earlier time in the history of Catholic America. In the case of Judaism, Warner (1993: 1067) states that its "normative congregationalism ... has long facilitated adaptability ..."

He also contends that a similar tendency is at play among post-1965 immigrant religious groups. He cites as an example trends among Muslim immigrants in the United States. Whereas in the pre-migration setting the mosque was solely a place of prayer and the imam's role that of prayer leader, in the American context the functions of the mosque have expanded to include education and socializing, while the imam is tasked to engage in such activities as counseling, visitations to the sick and homebound, conducting marriages and funerals, and serving as a representative of the mosque to the larger society. In short, Warner (1993: 1067; see also 1998a: 209) writes, the imam becomes a "religious professional" who models his role along the lines of "pastors, priests, and rabbis." The findings of the New Ethnic and Immigrant Congregations Project (NEICP), which Warner directed with funding from the Lilly Endowment and the Pew Charitable Trusts, reinforced his conviction of de facto congregationalism. Admittedly, the project focused explicitly on congregations, and not on private religious practice nor on the operations of larger regional, national, or international religious bodies. Nevertheless, he saw similar patterns, be it among Rastafarians or various ethnic Christian churches in different cities across the country (Warner and Wittner 1998).

The second major research project on religion and the new immigrants, the Religion, Ethnicity, and New Immigrant Research (RENIR) project, was conducted in Houston under the leadership of Helen Rose Ebaugh and again funded by the Pew Charitable Trusts. The research team identified 793 immigrant congregations in the greater Houston metropolitan region. Many of these congregations had fleeting existences and the team determined that they would concentrate on the 413 congregations that appeared to have a more stable institutional presence. Data were collected on 60 percent of them, complemented by more intensive work with eight focus groups and in-depth field research at thirteen selected sites. The researchers' findings, based on the ethnographic component of the study, supported Warner's thesis: congregationalism constitutes one of the primary structural adaptations of immigrant religious institutions.

Although Warner subsumed the provision of various needed resources to its members under the congregational model, the researchers distinguished the congregational model from the community center model. Some congregations, particularly the smallest with the most limited resource bases (such as the Zoroastrian Center, did not fit the mold of the community center model, while most did to greater or lesser extent. In short, the RENIR researchers concluded that while de facto congregationalism is in fact the norm, it varies, not unexpectedly, in terms of how close particular congregations are to the ideal typical model (Ebaugh and Chafetz 2000: 49–62).

Warner (2000: 277–8) summarized the "congregational form" as it applied to immigrant religious institutions, a summary account of which includes the following:

- a voluntary membership association defined by choice rather than proximity;
- lay leadership taking form as boards of directors, trustees, deacons, and so forth;
- incorporation for tax purposes as a not-for-profit organization;
- it may be truly independent or may be part of a larger denominational organization;
- clergy tend to be viewed as professionals hired by the lay leaders;
- an exclusivity of membership based on ethnicity or national origin;
- a multifunctional organization that besides its religious function serves one or more other functions, which he specifies as including "educational, cultural, political, and social service activities";
- a tendency to conduct religious services and other activities on Sunday, paralleling Christian practices in America.

Fenggang Yang and Ebaugh (2001), making primary use of the RENIR findings, concur with Warner's de facto congregationalism in analyzing what they describe as the "transformations in new immigrant religions," though they do so with one significant revision. Actually, they depict three transformations. Besides adopting the congregational form, they also discuss what they see as a return to theological foundations and a reaching beyond traditional ethnic and religious boundaries to include other people. We will address both of these topics later in this chapter. Suffice it to note here that the third tendency toward greater inclusivity contrasts with Warner's emphasis on exclusivity.

Their discussion echoes Warner when they point to the prevalence of the congregational structure for Christian and non-Christian religions alike, for the centrality of the voluntary character of membership, the salience of lay leadership, the expansion of organizational functions – both religious and secular – and with this expansion, the expanded role of an increasingly professionalized clergy (Yang and Ebaugh 2001: 273–6). Unlike Warner, they observe the emergence of larger organizational networks that tend to resemble Protestant denominations, and rather than seeing congregations as being divided into the independent and those linked to larger institutions, they see the latter as characteristic of a general – though not universal – trend. In discussing ritual practices, they concur with Warner's claim about the shift to Sunday worship.

They add that in other ways immigrant congregations come to resemble Protestant churches. They note that whereas in traditional Buddhist temples the people sit on cushions on the floor, at the His Nan Temple in Houston pews have been installed and traditional chanting has been replaced by hymns, some of which have borrowed melodies from Protestant hymnals. Finally, they note that language is a fraught issue, particularly insofar as it reflects generational differences in acculturation to American society. Whereas the immigrant generation tend to want to maintain their homeland language, a shift towards English usage is evident, with a bilingual phase often setting the stage for a shift to English-only usage. In panethnic congregations, the move to English often occurs more quickly because of the need to find a common language (Yang and Ebaugh 2001: 277–8).

Studies that have made use of the de facto congregationalism model have tended to take it as a given and apply it to the particular case study being explored, adapting or adding features along the way. A representative example can be found in the work of Carl Bankston III and Min Zhou (2000; see also Bankston 1997 and Bankston and Zhou 1995). Their comparative research, which examined a Vietnamese Catholic congregation in New Orleans and a Laotian Buddhist temple in New Iberia, Louisiana, lends support to Warner's thesis. At the same time, they note a certain irony in this organizational adaptation insofar as a major impetus for founding immigrant religious institutions is to insure the "perpetuation of cultural traditions" (Bankston and Zhou 2000: 455). What they concluded in both cases was that efforts expended at promoting cultural preservation had the unintended consequence of assisting members in their effort to gain a socioeconomic foothold and to fit into the receiving society's public sphere.

Critique

Wendy Cage (2008) has provided the one instance of a sustained critical analysis of de facto congregationalism, calling for a revision of the original thesis. Her assessment builds on Manual Vásquez's (2005; see also Vásquez and Marquardt 2003: 224–7) brief but direct attack on de facto congregationalism, which he locates as an aspect of his broader criticism of Warner's new paradigm, which in turn is treated as an instance of an even more far-ranging challenge to Western intellectual elitism in the realm of religious studies, particularly as it gets refracted in modernization theory, dependency theory, American exceptionalism, and so forth. In his account, the new paradigm is described as "a cluster of 'provincial' theories" that reflects the American religious scene as it seeks to "universalize the US model." Meanwhile, lurking behind the de facto congregationalism model is a "crypto-normativism" (Vásquez 2005: 229–30). He raises the following specific problems: (1) the congregational thesis presumes that sending societies are homogeneous, thus denying that they are both institutionally differentiated and religiously pluralistic; (2) it is inattentive to the reality of transnationalism; (3) it ignores the dynamics of power within congregations; and (4) at the methodological level, a preoccupation with congregations blinds researchers to manifestations of religiosity in other facets of everyday life (Vásquez 2005: 231–3).

Vásquez suggests that some immigrants have been involved in congregational life in the pre-migration context – as with base communities shaped by liberation theology in Latin America. This is meant to dispute the idea that the congregational model is inherently rooted in the distinctive religious field of the United States. He also points to the case of undocumented agricultural workers in rural Florida who because of the insecurity of their lives and the lack of resources have failed to produce a "robust congregational life." In this example, he raises a question about whether there is an urban bias in research on immigrant religion and goes on to write that "we cannot deny the impact of funding agencies like the Lilly Endowment and Pew Charitable Trusts, which in generously supporting our research, have shaped our agendas" (Vásquez 2005: 233–4). With this broadside against de facto congregationalism, one might assume that Vásquez is prepared to assign it to the scrapheap of failed conceptual models. He doesn't. Instead, he suggests that:

> If it is relativized and stripped of normative and teleological assumptions, as the secularization and the assimilation paradigms have been, the congregational approach will likely continue to yield valuable insights into the ways in which religious organizations mediate the formation of collective identities among immigrants. (Vásquez 2005: 234)

It is here that Cadge picks up the critique. She begins her brief by contending that despite its apparent modesty, the hypothesis "touches on profound and central themes as regards the meaning of modernity and the changing nature of religious institutions in the modern world," and she points in particular to José Casanova's (1994) widely cited book on the return of public religion as a touchstone for her position (Cadge 2008: 346). She points to his concept of "denominization" as reflecting the differentiation of modern societies into discrete spheres of influence – a theme, it should be noted, that was central to both Talcott Parsons and Niklas Luhmann, though they do not factor into the analysis. Differentiation assumes concrete form when religious disestablishment takes hold. Cadge does not distinguish differentiation from pluralism, but she has in mind contexts that are characterized by the interplay of the two – though she does not pose it as such. She proceeds to locate congregationalism as a more local manifestation of Casanova's "more global vision" (Cadge 2008: 247).

She concurs with Vásquez that the de facto congregationalism thesis ignores transnationalism, treats the United States as a universal model, and contains both an unwarranted normative and teleological underpinning. Moreover, it fails to define, to use the language of Bourdieu, the proper organizational field and as such does not adequately account for variation in organizational forms or the precise social processes that account for the development of those forms. By treating congregationalism as a natural and desirable organizational form, the thesis fails to step back to determine when and in what circumstances the congregational model is most likely to emerge (Cadge 2008: 347).

The crux of her critique revolves around two charges. First, by failing to define the organizational field, Warner and those who embrace his thesis presume the existence of a unified field rather than considering the possibility of multiple and diverse religious fields. The second charge concerns the presumed failure to offer an adequate account of the processes by which one or another type of religious organization emerges. Here Cadge turns to the influential work of Paul DiMaggio and Walter Powell (1991) on institutional isomorphism, which specifies three ideal types of isomorphism: coercive, mimetic, and normative. She contends that Warner and those who have followed his lead have assumed, without stating so explicitly, that congregationalism is to large extent the result of the interplay of coercive and mimetic isomorphism.

Identifying these presumed shortcomings of Warner's thesis, Cadge offers a revised approach that hinges on the idea that it is necessary to speak about multiple organizational fields rather than a unitary organizational field. Her empirical case is Buddhist immigrants from Thailand. She argues that their temples across the United States engage one another in a sustained way both at the informal level and through the work of two umbrella organizations, the Council of Thai Bhikkhus and the Dhammayut Order in the United States. As such, she contends that they constitute one particular organizational field in the much larger arena of multiple religious organizational fields in the nation.

With this framing, she divides Warner's thesis into eight elements and offers her assessment of whether or not the Buddhist temples fit the model. She concludes that on four of the items they very clearly and uniformly do fit: (1) they are characterized by voluntary membership (2) in which people identify with the temple based on a sense of connection to fellow members rather than predicated on territorial proximity; (3) members undertake sys-tematic fund-raising efforts to insure the economic viability of the organization; and (4) they gather together regularly for worship and fellowship on Sundays.

For three of the items she finds what she refers to as variations. First, in terms of clergy being hired as professional employees, she observes that precisely how monks are selected differs somewhat among temples, as do the specifics of the job requirements and the amount of power and autonomy they are granted. While monks are called to temples by lay members, they are not paid salaries the way professional clergy are in Warner's model. The calling aspect clearly fits the model. Given that Cadge does not provide information about how monks are compensated, it is impossible to assess if their economic relationship to the temple departs sig-nificantly from the model. Furthermore, although the monks come from Thailand and are quite unfamiliar with American culture, the resultant intercultural strains and their implications for insti-tutional functioning are not addressed. As an earlier analysis of the "organizational dilemmas" created by cultural tensions between homeland and receiving country, Mullins' (1988) study of Japanese Buddhists in Canada is instructive, as is the more recent study also from outside of the United States of so-called "EasyJet priests," Polish priests serving Catholic Poles living in Britain (Trzebiatowska 2010).

Second, in terms of multifunctionality, she notes variations in what temples actually do, but notes that the "vast majority of Thai temples in the United States are multifunctional, including at least one educational, cultural, political, or social service activity in addition to their religious activities" (Cadge 2008: 360). That most temples provide such services to members would appear to validate Warner's position. The variations discussed by Cadge simply involve differences in the precise services performed and the extent to which they are. Larger temples with more extensive resource bases, not surprisingly, tend to offer a greater array of services. But in this regard, they do not differ from non-immigrant Protestant congregations, as Mark Chaves (2009, 2004) has shown in his research on American congregational life. He notes that, "The reality is that virtually all congregations do something that might be called social service, but much of this activity is very small-scale and informal and focused on short-term, emergency needs for food, clothing, and shelter" (Chaves 2009: 71).

Third, Cadge's study found that only a minority of temples were ethnically exclusive. Although she does not provide details about the heterogeneity of temples, she does point to the widespread presence of Laotians in the Thai temples and in smaller numbers of other Asian groups, including Cambodians, Vietnamese, Koreans, and Sri Lankans. In addition, slightly more than one in three temples has some non-Asian members. One of the consequences of this tendency is that English frequently becomes the lingua franca (Cadge 2008: 358).

The one element in Warner's model that Cadge did not test was the role of the laity in temple functions, because of both data limitations and some of the distinctive features of Thai Buddhist temples. However, what she has to say on the subject appears to lend credence to de facto congregationalism. Thus, she observes that "lay people have taken on more temple leadership roles through administrative work, the education of children, meditation teaching in some contexts, and other functions" (Cadge 2008: 355). Her article concludes by calling for a revised version of the de facto congregationalism thesis, one that is more attentive to heterogeneity and variability and which offers an account of process by utilizing the insights of the new institutionalism.

Assessing the Critiques

How convincing are the critiques? I would contend not very. In the case of Vásquez, the striking thing about his challenge to the new paradigm and in particular to the de facto congregationalism thesis is how far removed from Warner's account his discussion is. He treats Warner's work as being tainted with ideological biases that make it suspect, but never actually grounds his analysis in the textual evidence itself. He imputes normative and teleological inflections without offering exegetical evidence to support this charge. When Cadge picks up the gauntlet, she, too, conceptually inflates what Warner actually had in mind when he introduced the idea of de facto congregationalism, tying it to broad notions of modernization writ large.

I would suggest that, contrary to Cadge, his thesis is and was intended to be a rather more modest proposition. It's predicated on two main assumptions. First, the congregational model is an ideal type, and as such in the real world we can expect to find organizations that more or less resemble it on a scale – as well as finding some that don't seem to bear a resemblance to the type. Second, when it comes to immigrant religious organizations, the claim is that there is a *tendency* to take on the congregational form. This suggests that not all such religious bodies will assume this form. Moreover, those that do will not necessarily do so in ways that make them identical to the traditional Protestant congregation. And as to why such a tendency exists, Warner does not rely on theoretical appeals to modernity or to Bourdieu-inspired ideas about religious fields, but rather offers a far more grounded analysis based on such things as the quest for tax-exempt status and the pragmatic considerations that go into deciding to use Sunday as the primary worship and social gathering day of the week.

Why spend so much time with these critiques of Warner's position? I think better than offering a summary of those researchers who have taken the thesis at face value and applied it to particular cases, an examination of a sustained attempt to, if not deconstruct, revamp in significantly new ways the original thesis provides invaluable insights into the utility of the concept. As it turns out, I would argue that Cadge's case study serves to illustrate, not the problems of the original thesis, but rather its robustness.

This being said, there are two issues that are not adequately addressed by Warner. The one is a consequence of his focus on the settlement nation and not on the sending country and the potential interplay between the two. Vásquez called for the need to employ a transnational optic, something that quite clearly Warner does not promote. Concurring with the need to do so, I would note that the following chapter is devoted to precisely that topic. The second issue is less a conceptual one and more a question of whether or not there is empirical support for one of Warner's assumptions, namely that immigrant congregations will tend to be ethnically exclusive. Cadge's Thai Buddhist temples are multi-ethnic and it is reasonable to wonder whether this might be the more typical pattern. This particular topic will be addressed in the last section of this chapter as we examine what Yang and Ebaugh (2001) consider to be the third major transformation in immigrant religions. But before that, we turn to their second transformation in the next section.

Returning to Theological Foundations

In the preceding chapter, we took up the topic of whether or not the immigrant experience at the individual level can be aptly characterized as a theologizing experience. Here we address a related topic at the organizational level, one that looks at what Yang and Ebaugh (2001) depict as a "returning to theological foundations." This particular topic, of course, skirts the question of the level of religiosity among immigrants in general, being concerned with the nature of religious belief and practice for those who are institutionally affiliated.

Yang and Ebaugh (2001: 281) stress that a returning to theological foundations is not necessarily the same thing as a turn to fundamentalism, writing that whereas fundamentalists see "modern culture as a threat," they found that sometimes for their subjects "reaching toward foundations among immigrant religions can generate liberal or liberating ideas and actions – liberating followers of a religion from stifling cultural traditions and sectarian limitations." In their portrait, the tendency to return to theological foundations is driven in no small part by the need of religious minorities to transcend ethnic and national-origin boundaries in order to develop a critical mass sufficient for success in organizing a sustainable religious community.

Although they note that the return can be to either the actual origins or the imagined origins, it is my sense that the significance of the imagined or constructed nature of origins is understated in their formulation. That being said, what return entails is what Raymond Breton (2012: 113) calls a process of "pristinization," which amounts to an attempt to separate religion from culture in a "search for the 'universal' since the theological foundations must be common to all members, whatever their national or ethnic backgrounds."

Yang and Ebaugh (2001: 280) present a simple illustration of one of the less controversial ways this plays out. Noting that Pakistani Muslim immigrant men pray with caps, while Arab men do not, the former were forced to ponder whether there was a scriptural basis for the practice of cap wearing or if it was simply an artifact of their particular ethnic culture. Yang and Ebaugh do not address in any detail the larger sectarian divide between Shi'ites and Sunnis that characterizes Islam globally, but observe that umbrella organizations such as the Islamic Society of North America make an effort to stress the commonalities shared by all Muslims while downplaying differences. Breton frames the issue as follows:

> This may entail distinctions between what is fundamental and what is less so. In Islam, the fundamentals include the belief in one god, the existence of the prophet Mohammed, and salvation (for Shi'ites, there are five fundamentals). In addition, there are five pillars: the profession of faith, praying five times a day, almsgiving, annual fasting, and a pilgrimage to Mecca for all those able to make the journey. Muslims will still be considered Muslim if they do *not* practice the five pillars, but not if they disagree with any of the three basic principles. (Breton 2012: 114; see also Sutton and Vertigans 2005: 201)

Yang and Ebaugh report findings from the Houston study that indicate this tendency within Islam can also be seen in other non-Christian religions. Thus, Buddhists in the metropolitan area have sought to forge a consensus within the religion that overcomes traditional differences between Mahayana and Theravada Buddhists. Similarly, efforts are underway, spearheaded by leaders of an organization known as the World Hindu Council (Vishwa Hindu Parishad of America), to identify those concepts and practices that are shared by all Hindus. The Eastern Orthodox community has likewise sought to transcend national differences in constructing a unified Orthodox Church in America (Yang and Ebaugh 2001: 279–80).

These examples are intended to reflect a general trend, as the adherents of immigrant religions create a space for themselves in a pluralistic religious landscape, adapting and adjusting their beliefs and practices in the process. This was aptly described as the result of an effort to separate religion from culture. Another way of putting it is to describe it as an effort to separate religion from ethnicity. Of course, not all groups attempt to make this separation, instead working hard to define religion and ethnicity in such a way that the two are mutually reinforcing. Min's (2010) study of Indian Hindus and Korean Protestants in the New York City metropolitan area discussed in the preceding chapter reveals two groups that make just such an effort. He is particularly concerned with exploring the ways in which religion is or is not utilized to preserve ethnic identity. He discovered that Koreans were less successful in maintaining the religion/ethnicity linkage, due to large extent to a generational shift in which the children of immigrants distanced themselves from their Korean background as they assertively defined themselves as Christian in a manner that distances themselves from the particularities of being a Korean Christian. In contrast, for Hindus, from both the first and second generations, religion was an important vehicle for maintaining a sense of being Indian.

Min explains the difference in terms of differing levels of "dogmatic authority" in each belief system. Among Korean adherents to evangelical Christianity was a firmly rooted conviction that their religion was the one true religion, whereas among Indian Hindus, an embrace of religious pluralism and of mutual toleration of different religions leads to a lower level of dogmatic authority. The net result is that Korean Christians find that they do not need their ethnic background to reinforce their religious identity while Indian Hindus do (Prema Kurien's discussion in the following chapter complicates this picture by suggesting that Hindu immigrants may have differing levels of dogmatic authority depending on whether the geographical referent is India or the United States).

There are two main points to be made about this line of research. First, all of the studies to date capture small case studies in various locales throughout the country. They constitute a snapshot at a particular point in time, which is a relatively early one, given that these groups have not been in the receiving nation for more than a few decades and the second generation has only recently come of age. If we look back to the last major migratory wave in the United States, we see that from the third generation and beyond, the tendency has been to sever the earlier linkages between religion and ethnicity. While minority religious communities – such as the Amish and Hasidic Jews – have managed to keep the linkage intact, they remain very much outside of the mainstream currents (Kivisto 2007).

The general trend has been for ethnic churches to merge into larger bodies and, by so doing, relegating the ethnic character of the church to the realm of nostalgia. A major contributing factor for this shift was widespread intermarriage and with it religious switching. It is too early to determine if this general pattern will repeat itself. It is worth observing that past immigrants were overwhelmingly of European origin, and whether they were white on arrival or became white over time (Guglielmo 2003; Roediger 2005), by the time that the third generation came of age, race did not constitute a factor shaping marital choices – provided, of course, that marriages occurred between fellow Europeans/ Americans.

This leads to the second point. It is important to note that the vast majority of these past immigrants were Christian, whereas today's immigrants find representation from all of the major world religions and from many minor ones. That being said, as was made clear in the first chapter, Christians still constitute a substantial majority of the new immigrants. At issue is whether the ways in which immigrants respond to their respective religious traditions differ depending on whether the religion in question is Christian or non-Christian. For the former, a place at the table has already been set. Indeed, given the varieties of Christian expression in the nation, a number of places at the table have been set and they are free to sit where they please. In contrast, non-Christians are confronted with the task of finding a place at that pluralist table (Kurien 2007).

Returning to Cadge's idea of a religious field, I would take issue with her attempt to treat each religious tradition, in effect, as occupying its own field detached from other fields, including the dominant or majority field. Rather, I would contend that one should locate immigrant religions in terms of an overarching religious field that can be viewed as a dome covering all of the various manifestations of religious expression in a particular large-scale societal space such as a nation. To not do so makes it difficult to understand precisely what immigrant religions are responding to and how they are framing their presentation of collective self to the outside world and to members within the religious community. Immigrant Christians discover that Protestant Christianity in the United States is divided between two expressions that have lived in acrimonious relationship to each other since the nineteenth century. David Hollinger has chosen to distinguish the two versions of Protestantism as "ecumenical" and "evangelical." Synonyms for the former include liberal, mainline, and cosmopolitan, while for the latter they include conservative, fundamentalist, and parochial. He succinctly distinguishes the two by writing that, "While the ecumenists increasingly defined themselves through a sympathetic exploration of wider worlds, the evangelicals consolidated 'home truths' and sought to spread them throughout the globe" (Hollinger 2013: 21).

Since the 1960s, sociologists of religion have speculated about why ecumenical denominations have been losing numbers – or as the advocates of a rational choice perspective on religion would have it, market share – while evangelical churches (sometimes treated as "strict" churches in the literature) have witnessed dramatic growth until recently (Iannaccone 1994; Finke and Stark 1992). Given this reality, immigrants would appear to have a choice of opting for denominations in decline or denominations exhibiting vibrancy. And it is evident that many immigrants, particularly Asian immigrants but also Latinos attracted to Pentecostalism, have opted to affiliate with evangelical churches, whether they are part of larger denominational structures or among the substantial body of nondenominational churches.

But these institutional options are only part of the religious field, for immigrants also enter a landscape characterized by a set of cultural values that serve to frame how religion in general and particular religious expressions are to be recognized and what sorts of interreligious relations are to be encouraged and which discouraged. N.J. Demerath III (1995: 458) finds something paradoxical at play, for he argues that the decline of liberal Protestantism should be seen, not as having occurred because it watered down its doctrines as some have suggested, but as a consequence of its "cultural triumph on behalf of such values as individualism, freedom, pluralism, tolerance, democracy, and intellectual inquiry." Hollinger cites this argument favorably, adding the caveat that liberal Protestantism was not alone in shaping this general cultural milieu, but was aided and abetted by other sectors of American society with similar inclinations, including liberal Catholics, cosmopolitan Jews, and secularists. The point for our purposes here is that when immigration scholars contrast the climate of opinion regarding newcomers in the past versus the present, there is a general consensus that today's immigrants enter a more receptive society than did their earlier counterparts. And this is, ironically, due in no small part to the efforts of that sector of American Protestantism that is least likely to attract contemporary immigrants into their denominational life.

Immigrant Religions as Inclusive

This cultural shift points to the third major transformation identified by Yang and Ebaugh (2001: 281–3; see also Breton 2012: 114–15): "including other peoples." As noted earlier, it is on this point that the Houston findings diverge most explicitly from the conclusions Warner draws from the NEICP. Whereas Warner saw a growing exclusivity within immigrant religious institutions, Yang and Ebaugh contend that just the opposite appears to be occurring. Indeed, they make the following unqualified assertion:

"Immigrant religious communities are generally moving from particularism to greater universalism in membership" (Yang and Ebaugh 2001: 281). Whereas Warner considered greater ethnic inclusiveness likely in those instances when a particular ethnic group simply did not have a critical mass of members to establish a viable congregation, they see this as a general pattern regardless of the size of the religious community.

There are two ways in which inclusiveness plays out. On the one hand, there are many examples of shifting from an ethnic or national-origin church, such as an Assemblies of God congregation initially composed of Hong Kong Chinese becoming over time a pan-Asian congregation as not only Chinese from Taiwan and the mainland become members, but so, too, do immigrants from Southeast Asia. Russell Jeung's *Faithful Generations: Race and New Asian American Churches* (2005) explores the attempts of a number of both evangelical and mainline Protestant churches in the San Francisco area that were once defined either as Chinese or Japanese to transform themselves into multiracial congregations. He discovered that a redefinition was underway, but it was not into a truly color-blind sort of inclusiveness, but rather one in which race loomed large. What were once Chinese or Japanese congregations had become or were becoming pan-Asian congregations. A similar pattern can be observed fairly frequently among Latinos coming from different nations in the Western hemisphere.

They had succeeded in becoming more inclusive, but only within the parameters of what David Hollinger (1995) referred to as the nation's "ethnoracial pentagon." A panethnic group can also be imposed by authorities rather than being consciously chosen, as Peggy Levitt's (2001: 168) study of Dominicans in Boston illustrates. The local Catholic archdiocese viewed other, longer-established Latinos as the "proximal hosts" who shared a language and broad regional identity. As she pointed out, all of these groups "brought different practices, affinities toward particular saints, and distinct understandings of the relationship between religion and society" which had to give way to a "least-common-denominator Catholicism."

A second pattern involves proselytizing. Yang and Ebaugh cite the case of Zoroastrianism, a small monotheistic religion (perhaps the world's oldest), rooted in Persia and with a base in India, that has historically discouraged proselytizing, deeming it to be a sinful act. In all places, it has witnessed declining numbers, in part a reflection of the demographic reality of an economically successful group that limits family size. It is also due to the fact that a significant percentage of Zoroastrians in the diaspora marry out of the group, which historically has been opposed to conversion, seeing the faith as connected to ancestry. Concerned about the faith's future, some leaders of the Houston congregation that represent the approximately 400 Zoroastrians in the area have begun a dialogue about the possibility of encouraging conversion, a topic that divides traditionalists and reformers (Rustomji 2000). But conversion need not be linked to intermarriage. Indeed, Yang and Ebaugh (2001: 282) contend that "almost all immigrant religions have gained converts of native-born Americans, including whites and blacks," including not only major world religions such as Christianity, Islam, and Buddhism, but even Sikhism and Jainism.

The data to date do not permit us to determine with any precision just how extensive inclusiveness actually is. For example, just how many native-born Americans have converted to Jainism? It is reasonable to assume that the numbers are very low. Islam in the United States is a special case insofar as the Nation of Islam has had a presence among African Americans before the post-1965 immigrants began to arrive, while the appeal of Buddhism is often connected to an interest in meditation and to a more general countercultural sensibility with roots dating to the 1960s.

An examination of case studies from outside the NEICP and RENIR yields mixed results. On the one hand, one can find results that support Warner's exclusiveness hypothesis, while on the other one can find results confirming the inclusiveness hypothesis emerging from RENIR. An example of the former is Rebecca Kim's (2006, 2004) study of second-generation Korean American evangelicals on American university campuses that we discussed in the preceding chapter. Korean immigrants constitute the largest component of Asian evangelicals in the nation, and their presence on elite university campuses such as Harvard, Yale, and Stanford as well as prominent West Coast public universities such as UC Berkeley and UCLA means that they are a major membership core for a variety of conservative Christian groups on those elite campuses. Having grown up in multi-ethnic middle-class neighborhoods and resisting a distinctive ethnic approach to worship, it may have been assumed that these young people would opt to join inclusive multi-ethnic evangelical groups and congregations.

However, such is not the case, as they tend to prefer separate ethnic ministries. Kim attributes this to a desire to preserve the familiar in a novel context and a source of protection from racial marginalization. She contends that in this case ethnicity and religion have proven to be mutually reinforcing (Kim 2006: 140). At the same time, they have opted for affiliating themselves with umbrella organizations such as the Campus Crusade and Intervarsity that are part of the evangelical mainstream rather than remaining independent ethnic organizations. At the institutional level, this pattern has the potential for persisting as long as large numbers of upwardly mobile Asian Americans enter these and similar universities, and by maintaining connections outside of the ethnic community, it may make possible a smooth later transition to non-Korean churches once they leave university and enter the workforce.

Pawan Dhingra's (2004) study of three Korean American churches in the Dallas-Fort Worth area that primarily serve the second generation and as such use English rather than Korean in worship services, provides a counterpoint to Kim's research. He noted that there were about 130 Korean congregations in the area during the period in which he conducted his research, but only four were English-language congregations catering chiefly to the second generation, three of them representing his research sites. All three congregations are small, averaging 50 members. Concern about their long-term viability has led the pastors of each congregation to promote plans aimed at transforming their respective congregations into multicultural ones. The dilemma arises as attempts to downplay the distinctly Korean character of the church may erode ethnic solidarity, and with it a commitment to the congregation. Dhingra captured these congregations at a moment when it was difficult to predict what might happen, but he made clear that the challenges to creating a new multiracial identity were rather daunting.

The hurdles are not unique to immigrant congregations. In fact, for decades both ecumenical and evangelical churches have actively sought to bring racial minorities into their churches, with rather limited success. Michael Emerson (2006) reports that there are approximately 300,000 Christian congregations in the United States and the vast majority of them are so racially homogeneous that they warrant being designated hypersegregated. Defining a multiracial church as one in which no more than 80 percent of its members are from one racial group and making use of the National Congregations Survey, he estimates that 7 percent of congregations nationwide are multiracial (5 percent Protestant and 15 percent Catholic). Although the percentage is small, this means that there are about 21,000 multiracial congregations, which is not an unsubstantial number.

Based on the findings of in-depth analyses of 22 multiracial congregations, Emerson (2006: 52–61) identified three underlying reasons that congregations initiate changes that are intended to lead to ethnic diversity: mission, resource calculation, and the imposition of external authority. The first entails a proactive decision to promote multiculturalism. It can be due to a value commitment to achieve the dream of a beloved community where integration and equality prevail. Or it can reflect a decision to remain committed to a neighborhood in transition. Or it can be a combination of the two. The second represents a reactive decision based on what is perceived to be a threat to the existing congregation's viability – due to such factors as a declining and aging population, demographic changes in the church's immediate neighborhood, and so forth. The third depicts situations in which decisions are not made by congregational members, but rather are imposed by a third party. Given that Catholic churches diverge from the congregational model insofar as bishops have the ultimate authority to determine if churches close, remain open, or merge, one can reasonably assume that many congregations that arise as a result of the third reason are Catholic, and may account for the fact that there is a larger percentage of multiracial

Catholic churches than Protestant ones. This is unfortunate for the prospects of multiracial congregations, for Emerson contends that mandated congregations are the least likely to succeed over the longer term.

One of the churches Emerson (2006: 140) studied was Mosaic, a multi-ethnic evangelical mega-church in the Los Angeles area that attracts 1,400 people to Sunday services, the majority being young adults in their twenties who work in the Hollywood entertainment industry. While African Americans are not well represented among the membership, it has proven to be attractive to Anglos, Asians, and Latinos. This particular church, sometimes characterized as one of the nation's most diverse churches, was the subject of sociologist of religion Gerardo Marti's (2005) ethnographic study (he served as an assistant pastor during his research). Marti stresses that ethnic diversity is not a goal of Mosaic, but rather a means to fulfilling the church's mission. Even though ethnicity is one of the "havens," or niches, that members can gravitate to in order to find like-minded individuals – the others being theological, artistic, innovator, and age – he contends that the net result of involvement in one of the ethnic havens is to "render ethnic differences inconsequential" (Marti 2005: 3). This is possible because the members come into the congregation with what are already weak ethnic affiliations and a desire to escape the boundaries of their ethnic backgrounds. Given this reality, why church leaders decided to create an ethnic niche in the first place is unclear. Equally puzzling is why members would opt for this niche if they have weak ethnic affiliations to begin with.

Emerson, Marti, and others who have studied multi-ethnic congregations understand the difficulties and pitfalls associated with achieving diversity in ways that result in new forms of solidarity. Any number of issues needs to be reckoned with. Language is often a critical one. How, for example, should a Catholic congregation composed of an old Anglo membership and a new Latino membership define the vernacular? Should the newcomers be expected to accept English as the lingua franca, should separate masses be conducted in English and Spanish, or should both languages be incorporated into the fabric of the worship service?

Or consider culturally specific traditions. Should the veneration of Our Lady of Guadalupe simply be considered something appropriate for Mexicans or should others in the congregation – which might mean other Latinos or Anglos – also be expected to embrace a version of the Virgin intimately connected to Mexico? In what ways should a congregation use particular musical forms to appeal to the congregation and to potential members? While contemporary Christian rock works at Mosaic because the twenty-somethings regardless of ethnic background are rooted in rock music, it will not work in other places. If music reflects the identity of the church, rather than being a mere add-on feature, then it is not surprising that another Los Angeles area evangelical congregation called Oasis that appeals to both whites and blacks is defined by gospel, funk, soul, and rhythm and blues (Marti 2012).

What is clear in these studies is that if an ethnically diverse congregation is to succeed – whether it be the product of an immigrant congregation looking to become more inclusive or of congregations from the dominant society seeking to attract newcomers – it must engage in a complex and ongoing process of negotiation that touches on shared beliefs and collective religious practices. What is less clear is what happens in the process to various theological traditions. Are they maintained, abandoned, revised, redefined, or decentered?

One intriguing issue not explored by Emerson or Marti concerns the different challenges multiculturalism raises for ecumenical churches versus evangelical ones. It is the latter that they have studied. The former may confront a unique challenge due to their positions on hot button issues related to sexuality, especially same-sex marriage and abortion. The irony is that perhaps those mainline congregations most attuned to the broadest type of inclusivity, in particular by also including LGBT issues in their ambit, have a more difficult time achieving it because they are prepared to include people in their midst that some of the potential immigrant newcomers would not want to be associated with. To what extent this is true is difficult to determine, but Robert Putnam and David Campbell (2010: 295–6) did find that in a modest but nonetheless statistically significant way evangelical churches were more likely to be diverse than ecumenical ones.

Gender Roles in Immigrant Religious Institutions

In the preceding chapter we addressed the topic of gender roles and relations, doing so with a focus on the implications for the actors themselves – for their sense of personal identity and their under-standing of the dynamics of power in gender relations. We briefly connect that discussion to the impact of gender on immigrant religious institutions. While the literature is somewhat mixed as to whether patriarchy is reinforced by immigrant religious institu-tions or undermined by them (see, for example Ai Ra Kim 1996; Jung Ha Kim 1996; Alumkal 1999; Kurien 1999; Ebaugh and Chafetz 1999), there is a uniform message – explicitly or implicitly advanced – that without the active involvement of women in the operation of congregations, the expanded repertoire of functions performed by the institutions would be impossible.

While some of those activities appear to have quickly developed into particular women's niches – especially in religious educa-tion programs and more broadly in terms of preserving cultural traditions – in a number of instances women have also achieved leadership positions that locate them as equals, or near equals, to men. Moreover, Michael Foley and Dean Hogue (2007: 155) dis-covered, in their Washington, DC-based study involving a survey of 200 congregations and in-depth analyses of 20 of them, that "both lay men and women in immigrant worship communities are more likely to enjoy leadership roles in the performance of worship than lay people in the population as a whole."

Lois Ann Lorentzen's (2005) study of a Spanish-speaking Pentecostal church in San Francisco's Mission District can serve as an illustration of what is happening in many immigrant con-gregations regardless of the religion. She found that over time the patriarchal character shaping this particular religious community in various ways eroded. Patriarchy did not disappear. Nor was there a concerted conscious effort to challenge it. Instead, through any number of small changes, often occurring below the surface of immediate awareness, a transformation of gender relationships was underway from an early moment in time. It occurred both in the church and in the home. Thus, men assumed greater responsibilities for domestic chores as women entered the paid labor force and families had to juggle schedules as they tried to manage the time bind.

At the same time, as was the case with the congregations Foley and Hogue studied in Washington, DC, women in this Mission District church also assumed roles in the congregation that would have been unavailable to them earlier, in the pre-migration setting. This typifies the general proposition of Warner (1998b: 130) that, "Religious institutions will be the site of protracted renegotiation of relations between genders." He adds to this something not always captured in the research to date: this renegotiation takes on a generational dimension as a more Americanized second generation comes to these institutions as young adults with attitudes and values – including those related to gender – shaped by the receiving society to a greater extent than their parents'.

Civic Engagement

As noted in the discussion of the congregational thesis, immigrant religious institutions tend to become involved in various types of social services. Some of these services are inward-looking, designed to meet the various economic, cultural, social, and psychological needs of members. Others are more outward-directed, focusing variously on the local neighborhood, the city, the region, the nation, or globally. These activities require contact with other institutions and groups. Sometimes this entails working with or seeking to counter politicians, bureaucrats, business owners, and so forth. Sometimes it involves actions requiring the development of coalitions, including religious coalitions, but not limited to them.

In short, these sorts of activities provide immigrants with opportunities for civic engagement, thereby serving as a training ground for citizenship. Foley and Hogue (2007: 151–79) refer to this process as "building civic skills." Their conclusion that this is a rather widespread phenomenon in the congregations they studied is reinforced by the findings of two other multi-congregation metropolitan studies. Fred Kniss and Paul Numrich's (2007) study of sixteen congregations in the Chicago metropolitan area found civic engagement evident in all of them but, as one might expect, to differing degrees and in different ways. They offered a model that locates each congregation in terms of three variables – sectarianism, moral authority, and moral projects – and sought to account for the observable differences.

Alex Stepick, Terry Rey, and Sarah Mahler (2009) directed a Pew Charitable Trusts-funded Gateway Cities Initiative project in Miami that was influenced by the theoretical framework developed by Kniss and Numrich. The research team conducted ethnographic studies in immigrant churches of a number of Caribbean and Latin American immigrant groups and drew conclusions similar to the Washington, DC and Chicago studies. Of particular note with this city, perhaps not surprisingly given its proximity to Cuba and Haiti, was the prominence of transnational civic engagements.

The assumption of these researchers – often implicit – is that civic engagement is a means for making possible immigrant incorporation. As such, to borrow from Robert Putnam's (2000: 22–4) distinction, if much else in immigrant congregations is about bonding, civic engagement provides an ability to do bridging work, and insofar as this happens, it has the potential for enhancing immigrants' social capital by locating them within wider webs of group affiliation. And, it should be added, this has implications both for individual immigrants and for their religious institutions. In the case of the former, such engagements constitute a training ground for citizenship, while for the latter, it makes possible integration into the broader religious community and into the public sphere.

Turning from the Inside to the Outside

This chapter has been concerned with immigrant religious organizations, and as such has had a decidedly inward focus. The focus on the congregation – not simply a synonym for organization, but a distinct type of religious organization – has opened up certain vistas while remaining relatively inattentive to others. This is a reflection of the way a research agenda first developed in the early 1990s in the form of Warner's NEICP project and subsequently took off, the result being a robust body of research findings. Readers will note the obvious about this agenda: it has a decidedly American cast to it. Insofar as it was initially informed by the new paradigm, with its distinct American focus, this was inevitable.

It is not that research on congregations elsewhere has not occurred. It has, but not nearly to the same extent and not designed with the new paradigm in mind. This is particularly true of research conducted in Western Europe. These studies do not speak very directly to comparative questions that seek to determine the differences and similarities found in the United States and Western Europe. Given that Canada is often depicted as straddling a middle ground between the two, Breton's (2012) recent book is instructive. Although its focus is on Canada, much of the literature he cites derives from south of the 49th parallel. There is, however, a large enough body of research focusing specifically on Canada for him to pattern his analysis along the lines of American researchers. He concludes that trends in Canada to great extent parallel those of its much larger continental neighbor.

The general "take-away" from this large and growing body is that Foner and Alba (2008) are onto something when they contend that religion in America (and Canada) has proven to be a bridge to inclusion. The unanswered question is whether they are right in asserting that, in contrast, religion tends to be a barrier to inclusion in Europe. It is precisely this topic that we turn to in chapter 5, where we examine state–church relations and the place of religion in the public sphere. We do so after first turning in the following chapter to an analysis of transnationalism, which, as critics have pointed out, did not factor in an appreciable way into the congregational research agenda. We turn to this topic first since it has implications regarding if and how inclusion into receiving societies occurs.

Scholarship on immigrant religion in Western Europe has been far more inclined to look at the context of reception rather than the ways in which immigrants adapt and adjust to new circumstances. In particular, it has focused on state actions and on the attitudes and actions of the public at large. Moreover, it has been keenly interested in one particular religion: Islam. When religion is articulated as a problem, it is almost inevitably concerned with Islam, which, as we saw in chapter 1, has had a greater impact demographically in Europe than in the United States. Thus, when we turn to the state and public sphere in chapter 5, we will also be preoccupied with Muslim immigrants, seeking to assess to what extent this particular religion has proven to be a barrier to inclusion.

4

Immigrants and Transnational Religious Networks

A church service is underway in Ishpeming, a small iron-mining town in Michigan's Upper Peninsula, a remote, sparsely populated region settled by immigrants in the nineteenth century as two extractive industries took hold: mining and logging. One of the original settler populations in this place that the novelist Jim Harrison (2005) has described as "true North" originated in Finland, and today the region contains the largest concentration of people of Finnish ancestry in the nation. The church service reflects this fact. The signboard outside the austere structure built in the 1980s identifies the place as a Laestadian Lutheran Church. The parking lot is full, with a large number of the vehicles being either pick-up trucks or mini-vans. The church, too, is full, and it is quite clear that a number of families present have four or more children. The interior of the building is simple. A plain wooden cross stands over the altar, which has four burning candles on it. Just outside of the communion rail, right in front of the altar, is a pulpit.

The service, which will run between two to three hours long, has a very simple format consisting of the singing of hymns, readings from the Bible, readings from sermons by Lars Levi Laestadius, the congregation's namesake, and sermons by lay preachers. Although it is evident that all of those in attendance speak English, and the basic language of the service is English, nevertheless some of the hymns are sung in Finnish. This being a Lutheran church, congregants receive communion, though this is done only once

95

a month. The assembled are not immigrants. On the contrary, they are largely the third-generation and beyond offspring of the Finnish settler generation that made the region their home during the late nineteenth and early twentieth centuries.

On Finland's west coast, the Ostrobothnian city of Vaasa is home to one of the nearly 200 congregations affiliated with the Central Committee of Conservative Laestadian Congregations (*Suomen Rauhanyhdistysten Keskusyhdistys ry*). Church services there are not unlike those across the Atlantic, though there is a clearer identification with revivalism here. The church building is somewhat less austere than the one in Ishpeming. There is an altar painting of Jesus, an altar rack for votive candles, and off to the side a small altar, making room in the center for a substantial pulpit. The structure of the service would be familiar to an American Laestadian.

What links these two congregations is a shared history. Many of the Finnish immigrants in the Upper Peninsula came from Ostrobothnia, and, in fact, Ishpeming was described by Armas Holmio (2001 [1967]: 442) as "the great Ostrobothnian center in the Upper Peninsula." Their migration took place at around the time that Laestadianism was taking root in northern Finland and to a lesser extent in Sweden and Norway among the peoples of those countries with Finnish ethnic roots, such as the Kven in Norway. The movement is named after its founder, Lars Levi Laestadius (1800–61), a Swedish botanist who was also an ordained pastor in the Church of Sweden. Working in the northern region of Sweden around the Tornio River in the 1840s, he met a Sami woman who in recounting her spiritual awakening, triggered in him a similar spiritual experience that he thought transformed his life and defined his calling, which was to embark on a revival movement. To that end, he spent the rest of his life advancing his idea of Lutheran pietism, focusing his energies on marginalized groups in the northernmost regions of the Nordic countries, such as the Sami and Kven. The movement did not take off in his home country of Sweden, but it did appeal to many Finns, particularly in Ostrobothnia. Laestadius did not want his followers to call themselves Laestadians, preferring either simply the designation

"Christian" or calling on them to embrace their Lutheran identity. Although the movement is sufficiently Lutheran to accept the idea of an ordained clergy, from the beginning its spread was due in no small part to the work of lay preachers. This was true both in Finland and in the United States, where some lay preachers joined other labor migrants in seeking employment in the copper and iron mines of the Upper Midwest.

From the beginning on both sides of the Atlantic the movement took on a sectarian cast, defining a bright divide between insiders and outsiders and taking steps to insure that the former were not tainted by the latter. Given the reliance on untrained lay preachers and the fact that authority rested primarily in congregations, the stage was set for the persistence of internal conflicts leading to splits between various competing factions, a process that extended throughout most of the past century. While this happened in Finland and the United States, it did so in contexts characterized by differing church–state relations. The Evangelical Lutheran Church of Finland is the official state church that operates as a big tent with room for self-professed Lutherans from a wide range of theological perspectives.

In this setting, Laestadians have remained a part of the state church, and in some instances have exhibited real influence, such as having one from their ranks serve as the Bishop of Oulu in recent years. In contrast, in the disestablishment setting of the United States, Laestadians were never a part of the Suomi Synod, the American church body modeled after the Finnish state church, or the smaller National Lutheran Church. Preserving a strong link between ethnicity and religion has distinguished Laestadians from their Finnish American counterparts who created two larger denominations, both of which promoted assimilation into the religious mainstream. The Suomi Synod, the largest, eventually became part of the Evangelical Lutheran Church in America and the National Church a part of the Lutheran Church, Missouri Synod.

The Laestadian Lutheran Church, founded in 1973 after internal strife led to yet another split, serves as an umbrella organization for 29 congregations in the United States and Canada. In recent years it has more intentionally enhanced connections with Laestadians in Finland, specifically establishing an alliance with the Central Committee of Conservative Laestadian Congregations. The two have created similar alliances with associations in Estonia and Sweden. Throughout the history of this oft-divided and conflict-ridden movement contacts between Finland and the United States, and even more broadly between the Nordic countries and North America, have been preserved.

Preachers, lay and ordained alike, have moved back and forth or made extended visits. Some young men in the United States have opted to receive theological training in Finland, and lay people have visited abroad, often as part of congregation-sponsored trips. These and related connections have intensified in recent decades due to the use of new communications technologies. Not only do the parent organizations have fairly sophisticated websites, but so too do most of the individual congregations. It is difficult to know how many adherents of this tradition exist in the world today, in no small part due to poor record keeping at the congregational level. The highest estimates suggest a figure of around 200,000, but many would contend that a more accurate number would be in the 100,000 to 150,000 range. Whatever the case, it is clear that the largest population resides in Finland (estimates suggest 70,000 to 80,000), followed by the United States and then Canada. In part due to Finnish settlements elsewhere around the globe and in part due to missionary activity, there is a Laestadian presence in over 20 countries.

Despite claiming to adhere to the basics of Lutheran theology, Laestadians seek to keep their distance from "the world," which includes self-proclaimed Christians with more liberal ideas about moral issues. Although there is no official list of prohibited activities, and decisions are made at the congregational level, to a great extent the majority of Laestadians are opposed to premarital sex, birth control, abortion, alcohol consumption, television, movies, dancing, card-playing, swearing, popular music, and extracurricular activities at school such as sports and theater (in Finland, Conservative Laestadians seek exemptions from class excursions to theatrical productions). Life is structured around church activities, the purpose of which is to minimize contact with outsiders who might lead members astray. What is clear is that the persistent efforts of these conservative religious believers to keep their distance from "the world" have been accomplished throughout its history by creating and sustaining networks with fellow believers at home and abroad for over a century. And it appears that because their transnational religious connections have become more pronounced in recent years, the faith community has been reinvigorated.

Transnational Immigration and Transmigrants

Before looking specifically at transnational religious connections, we begin with an analysis of the evolution of the concept transnationalism more generally, for it is a contested term that is frequently used without a shared understanding of what the term entails (for a more sustained analysis, see Faist, Fauser, and Reisenauer 2013). The concept of transnationalism came into usage in research on contemporary migrants during the 1990s, in the first instance at a 1990 conference organized by Nina Glick Schiller, Linda Basch, and Cristina Szanton Blanc and co-sponsored by the New York Academy of Sciences, the Wenner-Gren Foundation, and the Institute for the Study of Man. The publication of the conference proceedings two years later marked a watershed event in the subsequent evolution of the concept (Schiller, Basch, and Blanc 1992; see also Basch, Schiller, and Blanc 1994 and Schiller 1997).

The only earlier use of the term that specifically addressed the topic of immigration was social critic Randolph Bourne's (1916) famous essay on "trans-national America." What Bourne had in mind was quite different from this new formulation, for his concern was with the role that immigrants might play in revitalizing a national culture that he feared had grown anemic. Between that usage and that of Schiller and her colleagues, one can find instances of it used to describe economic and political transformations. Thus, some economists in the 1920s depicted a "transnational economy," by which they meant an international economy, the two terms being essentially synonyms. Similarly, during the 1970s political scientists Robert Keohane and Joseph Nye (1977) used the idea of transnational relations to emphasize the increased saliency of the international interdependency of nations. In short, what Schiller and her colleagues had in mind was a novel concept that was in fundamental ways unconnected to these earlier uses of the term.

In the earliest articulation of transnational immigration, the phenomenon was depicted as something new that had arisen during the latter part of the past century, a type of migration that was to be seen as distinct from earlier migrations. In particular, the proponents of this new concept contended that immigrants who settled in the United States during the Great Migration that began around 1880 were not to be considered transnational migrants. Rather, they were viewed as immigrants who had left their home-lands with the full expectation of making a clean break from their respective nations of origin, which was in turn reinforced by the receiving society's assimilative expectations and demands. In stark contrast, contemporary immigrants were depicted as illustrating a powerful desire to establish new social relations in the receiving country while simultaneously maintaining ties to their country of origin. With this distinction between past and present in mind, these early advocates of transnationalism distinguished yesterday's immigrants from today's transmigrants (Schiller, Basch, and Blanc 1992: 1 and Schiller 1997: 158). Whereas immigrants were people for whom geographic mobility across borders was seen as a sin-gular event in a life course characterized primarily by permanent settlement, first there and later here, transmigrants are prepared to be permanently mobile.

Transnational migration was to be located in the larger context of what Saskia Sassen (1996: 6) has described as the "global foot-looseness of corporate capital." Just as capitalism, with the rise of the transnational capitalist class (Sklair 2001), is less and less bounded by the constraints of nation-states, so too are transmi-grants. In other words, transnationalism from above is countered by transnationalism from below, whereby the fluid character of transmigrant identities should be viewed as a form of resistance to "the global political and economic situations that engulf" contemporary international movers (Schiller, Basch, and Blanc 1992: 11).

In identifying causal factors contributing to this shift in the character of global migration, two were deemed to be of primary importance: developments in communications and transportation technologies. In terms of the former, the letter from the Great Migration was replaced by telephone calls, e-mail, and more recently by Skype and Facebook, while for the latter the steamship was replaced by jet airliners. Thus, in contrast to what was described as the progressive attenuation of contact with the place of origin for immigrants in the past, today's migrants are in a position to take advantage of technological advances that make possible the perpetuation of a variety of networks – economic, political, religious, cultural, and kinship – across the boundaries of nation-states.

This, in turn, was seen as an indication that transnationalism could be considered an alternative to assimilation as a mode of incorporation, a view echoed in Stephen Castles' (2002: 1158) speculation that, "It is possible that transnational affiliations and consciousness will become the predominant form of migrant belonging in the future." Integrally linked to this sense that transnationalism was a novel form of inclusion was the postnationalist idea that nation-states were becoming less consequential and capable of enforcing a singular ideal of national identity in the face of challenges to received notions of citizenship (particularly the Hague Convention's aversion to multiple citizenship).

During the ensuing two decades, transnationalism has become very much a part of the vocabulary of immigration research (see Vertovec 2009 and Faist, Fauser, and Reisenauer 2013 for broad overviews). At the same time, a number of criticisms were articulated that led to a reappraisal of a number of aspects of this initial formulation and research agendas were developed to begin the process of testing empirically the claims of transnationalism's proponents. Alejandro Portes and associates called for a middle range theory of transnationalism, one that was amenable to quantitative analysis. Rather than investigating the broad subject matter of social fields, this middle range approach called for investigating practices such as travel back and forth to the homeland, remittances, and political, economic, and sociocultural engagements that involve cross-border connections. In the Comparative Immigrant Entrepreneurship Project – which examined Colombians, Dominicans, and Salvadorans in the United States – the researchers found that most immigrants are not engaged in transnational practices, particularly if they are defined in a manner that stresses ongoing routine activities rather than more sporadic involvements. This was true of both political engagements and transnational entrepreneurship, where the percentage of those involved in such activities regularly was in the single digits (Guarnizo, Portes, and Haller 2003; Portes, Haller, and Guarnizo 2002).

Portes and colleagues did not conclude from this finding that transnationalism was necessarily insignificant. On the contrary, they suggested that those engaged in transnational practices might have a substantial impact on both those who remained in the homeland and immigrants not directly involved in transnational activities. They, however, disputed the idea that transnationalism should be viewed as an alternative mode of incorporation to assimilation, contending instead that the two might be capable of coexisting. This rethinking about the relationship between assimilation and transnationalism was but an instance of a more general process of taking stock – of reconsidering and revising what we talk about when we talk about transnationalism. Ewa Morawska considered this author's attempt to represent "immigrant transnationalism as a form of ethnic-path assimilation" to be "the first such attempt in the field" (Morawska 2003: 621; Kivisto 2001). If so, others quickly and independently arrived at a similar conclusion (Levitt, DeWind, and Vertovec 2003; Levitt and Schiller 2004).

The second major revision addressed the issue of the presumed novelty of the phenomenon. Critics pointed out that the past/present distinction was empirically flawed, as one could present abundant evidence to indicate that transnationalism was a common feature of the last migratory wave (Foner 1997;

Morawska 2001; Kivisto 2001). This point was conceded by transnationalism's proponents, though often with the proviso that developments in transportation and communication technologies have made sustained relationships between sending and receiving societies even more likely today. Whether or not this emphasis bleeds into an explanation based on technological determinism is at times an open question, but more problematic is the tendency to overlook the digital divide and the vast gulf between well-off and poor migrants.

Revisions were sometimes made with qualifiers, and as a result instead of a commonly agreed-upon understanding of the parameters of the phenomenon, some use the term in a relatively delimited way while others treat it as quite elastic. Portes can be read as a representative of the former, while Levitt and Schiller can be read as major advocates of the latter stance. This is reflected in their distinction between transnational being and belonging. Whereas they define being as consisting of "actual social relations and practices that individuals engage in," belonging "refers to practices that signal or enact an identity which demonstrates a conscious connection to a particular group." They cite as examples wearing a crucifix or Star of David, stressing that such actions are "not symbolic but concrete visible actions" (Levitt and Schiller 2004: 1010).

Why wearing religious symbols should not be construed as symbolic acts is somewhat puzzling. I suspect that the reason may have to do with the fact that the authors may want to distance themselves from a concept that might be seen as a parallel to Herbert Gans's (1979) idea of "symbolic ethnicity," which predicted the progressive erosion of the ethnic factor in shaping the identities of third and subsequent generations of European-born immigrants in the United States. Symbolic ethnicity referred to a desire to feel ethnic without necessary behavioral consequences. Levitt (2009), for instance, has questioned those who consider transnationalism to be a first-generation phenomenon, destined to largely disappear as the children of immigrants come of age. This is an example of the persistence of the assumption that immigrant transnationalism exists in fairly robust ways and that it is not likely to disappear.

Evidence of immigrant transnationalism past and present abounds. Few would dispute this fact. Thus, the real questions become: how significant a phenomenon is transnationalism and how durable over time and across generations is it likely to be? While Schiller, Levitt, and other proponents are convinced that transnationalism is a singularly significant feature of contemporary immigration and they are inclined to think that it will persist as the second generation comes of age, skeptics question one or both of those assumptions, perhaps nobody quite so insistently as Roger Waldinger (Waldinger and Fitzgerald 2004; Waldinger, 2007, 2008a, 2008b, 2011). Waldinger and coauthor David Fitzgerald (2004: 1182) contend that while the phenomenon exists, it might best be described as "bi-localism," which is meant to describe a more intermittent, uneven, and back-and-forth movement across borders, with local rather than national locations primarily in the minds of migrants. Related to this is Waldinger's emphasis on the ethnic particularism of contemporary immigrants, in contrast to part of the cohort from the Great Migration who, influenced by the idea of international socialism, viewed themselves as workers of the world seeking to forge solidarity with workers regardless of ethnic or national background. Waldinger's third point is that the evidence available at this point indicates that transnational connections are not only quite limited, but also fragile.

But beyond these criticisms, Waldinger is particularly intent on bringing the state back in. He argues that transnational theorists share with assimilation theorists a tendency to offer explanations of social processes they seek to understand without considering the political. Despite lip service to the continuing salience of the state in recent revisions of transnational discourse, he contends that the state has not really been taken seriously. Borders matter and states remain the arbiters determining who has a legitimate right to enter and on what terms, as well as determining who is permitted to become a member of the national community. Succinctly put, "States seek to bound the societies they enclose: they strive to regulate membership in the national collectivity as well as movement across territorial borders, often using illiberal means to fulfill liberal ends" (Waldinger 2007: 343).

Taking issue with the portrayal of a world in which economic and political globalization has resulted in a borderless state when it comes to would-be migrants seeking to improve their lives, Waldinger (2007: 346) points to the fact that states are willing to go to extraordinary lengths to control their borders in the interest of preventing unwanted migrants from "crashing the gates." The immigration policies of all the developed nations remain exclusionary, as states seek to preserve the binary divide between insiders and outsiders.

This leads to his perspective on the role of the state vis-à-vis those on the inside. The overarching state interest remains the same: to maintain control over a population. In the case of those residing within the boundaries of the nation, the state seeks to "cage" that population, "constraining social ties beyond the territorial divide, while reorienting activities toward the interior" (Waldinger 2008a: 9). Viewing migration as first and foremost a political phenomenon, states strive to transform foreigners into nationals. Unlike assimilation, which stresses the decline of the ethnic factor and the entry of newcomers over time into the societal mainstream, Waldinger (2007: 347) describes the transformation as a form of "political resocialization." Being transformed into a national of the receiving country involves acquiring an identity that makes people insiders, a process that simultaneously distinguishes them from outsiders, including citizens of their former homeland. This happens regardless of whether the newcomers end up in the societal mainstream or on the margins (Waldinger 2007: 344).

The internal and external aspects of national identity need not necessarily operate according to the same ideological script. What Waldinger has to say about the United States is, I believe, an accurate account for the world's other liberal democracies: they have become increasingly inclusive internally, while remaining externally exclusive, which is to say that provided that ethnic (or religious) affiliations do not harden into "greedy institutions" that do not allow the individual to be involved in a wide and diverse "web of group affiliations," particularistic allegiances can fit readily into an overarching civic or national identity (Coser 1974; Simmel 1955).

What this suggests is that even if one can speak of the footloose-ness of capital today, the same ease and fluidity of movement is not available to immigrants, and once people do succeed in moving beyond a border and are legitimized there, the state is capable of creating a variety of barriers that can interfere with transnational ties. Although Waldinger sometimes appears to see his position as contrary to that of most transnationalists, I would contend that his state-centered approach is a salutary corrective to much of the literature, offering what might be called a Realpolitik version of transnationalism. At the same time, it is necessary to view reality as more complex than his position would suggest. State actors in democratic societies rarely if ever act without internal tensions and conflicts and the opinions of citizens are also typically divided. Certainly this is the case when it comes to immigration policies.

Perhaps a beginning point for a perspective that takes this into account can derive from an assessment offered by the late historian John Higham (1994: 1289), who, while viewing the nation-state as an entity that "will remain for a long time the strongest politi-cal structure in the world," nevertheless considered it to be "under siege" with "the abounding trust it once enjoyed eroding," the net result being that though strong it is "less capable of dominat-ing the subgroups within its boundaries" than it was earlier. This viewpoint can be read as offering a corrective to Waldinger's thesis insofar as it grants a level of agency to ordinary people – both citizens and immigrants – who have the capacity to question the legitimacy of the state and can therefore potentially undermine, subvert, or resist its ability to "cage." Of course, people can also attempt to avoid, ignore, or otherwise seek to minimize the impact of the state on their everyday lives, cooperating when necessary while seeking out those social spaces where state interference is least felt.

The religions that immigrants bring to a land of settlement confront that state's particular understanding of church–state relations and of the place of religion in the public sphere. This relationship will be addressed in chapter 5, and thus the analysis of religious transnationalism that is taken up in this chapter should be combined with what follows in the next one in order to better place into perspective both the potential impacts of transnational-ism and the possible constraints on that potential as a consequence of state action and the impact of public opinion.

Transnational Religious Connections

With the general overview of immigrant transnationalism pre-sented in the preceding section, we now are in a position to turn to the more specific topic of immigrant *religious* transnational-ism. This section borrows its title from an article coauthored by Robert Wuthnow and Stephen Offutt (2008), who make clear that religious transnationalism is not necessarily or only about immi-gration. Outside of the religious sphere, transnationalism is more than simply the capitalist class from above versus immigrants from below. Rather, besides transnational entrepreneurs (Light 2010), one can speak of transnational nongovernmental agencies, transnational think tanks, transnational social movements, trans-national criminal networks, transnational terrorist networks, and so on. And within the religious sphere, in addition to migration, a number of other types of religious transnationalism are present – and indeed tend to have long histories. The role of missionaries in proselytizing religions has an extremely long history, and in the case of Christianity, missions in the age of colonization played a significant role in shaping and legitimizing the enterprise and in socializing some of the colonized into the ways of the West.

Wuthnow and Offutt do not delve into the dark side of that history, their point being simply that there are a lot of religious workers from one country working in another, often for very lengthy periods of time. They note, for example, that at the begin-ning of the twenty-first century, there were over 40,000 Americans working as full-time missionaries for various Protestant denomi-nations. The number of American Catholics engaged in missionary work is much smaller due to the priest shortage, though at earlier points in the nation's history they, too, were well represented in missionary work. Instead, today the movement of Catholic religious workers has been the other way around, as increasing numbers of priests from developing nations have come to the United States to work, their numbers amounting to 16 percent of all priests in the country by 2005. Wuthnow and Offutt cite research that indicates that 8 percent of religious workers globally work outside of their home countries, with higher percentages in the developing world and lower percentages in the developed world. They go on to observe that although there are no comparable data for the other major world religions, "one estimate counted 141,630 Islamic *da' wah* groups (propagators of the faith) engaged in foreign missions worldwide" (Wuthnow and Offutt 2008: 216–17).

In addition to professional religious workers, many lay people volunteer for short-term projects abroad. Findings from the Global Issues Survey reveal that each year 1.6 million Americans take part in mission trips lasting on average eight days. Whether or not long-lasting connections are formed varies:

> Long term transnational connections may or may not result from short term mission trips. Some medical professionals, for instance, serve in as many parts of the world as possible, and so view a trip to a specific location as a one time event. In other cases, return visits flow out of relationships that form across cultures. For example, a Seattle-based group first visited El Salvador to help build a house and to upgrade a local NGO's computer systems. A year later, one of the team members moved to El Salvador to assist the NGO in different ways. The other team members communicate regularly and visit El Salvador about once a year. (Wuthnow and Offutt 2008: 218–19)

Among the other types of transnational religions connections, Wuthnow and Offutt (2008: 219–23) point to the frequency of congregations and religiously affiliated colleges and universities inviting guest speakers from other countries. The presence of international students on the campuses of the latter is another example. Though no systematic tally of the number of people who engage in religious pilgrimages and religious tourism is available, it is evident that the figure is in the millions (see, for example, Swatos 2006). People traveling internationally for primary reasons other than religion can, nevertheless, also inject a religious message into their visits, as when a businessman who is also an evangelical Christian attempts to "share the good news" with his business associates in another country.

Finally, there is a considerable flow of funding across international borders for religious purposes. This can involve humanitarian aid in response to natural disasters or wars and other conflicts. An example of the latter with longer-term implications occurred when, at the urging of the hierarchy of the Evangelical Lutheran Church in America (ELCA), a number of affiliated colleges invited Namibian students to attend their institutions and paid for all expenses during the Namibian liberation struggle. In yet another way, it can entail people in the developed world providing funding for those in the developed world to build churches, orphanages, hospitals, church-affiliated colleges, and a variety of other church-related institutions. In some cases, long-term relationships are created, with companion parishes engaging in sustained cooperative relationships.

Parenthetically, it is worth noting that much of the work on the forms of activities and connections discussed above that we are broadly calling religious transnationalism are often referred to as manifestations of globalization instead of transnationalism. Such is the case with two books that focus on the Americas. In the first, an edited collection, religious communities defined in ways that transcend national boundaries are treated as crucial resources in addressing a variety of social concerns at the local level, particularly regarding families, citizenship, and the challenges posed by rising levels of immigration (Peterson, Vásquez, and Williams 2001). The second book looks at the varied ways that the sacred has been globalized, focusing on the movement of various religious practices of both Catholics and Protestants across the borders of the nations of the Americas (Vásquez and Marquardt 2003). It is also true of Donald Miller and Tetsunao Yamamori's (2007) study of the globalization of Christian Pentecostalism from its origins in the West to its far-ranging spread, which explored the local forms that these outreach ministries have taken in 20 countries from Africa, Asia, Eastern Europe, and Latin America.

It is within this larger context of transnational religious

connections that the issue of religion for contemporary immigrants needs to be located, for it is clearly part of a larger web of affiliations. As the study of immigrant religion got underway in the 1990s and simultaneously the concept of transnationalism began to achieve traction in immigration studies, the study of religion and transnational migration commenced (Ebaugh 2004). At a relatively early stage in this evolving research agenda, Peggy Levitt (2003) took stock of the state of research, concluding that up to that point most of the research constituted for the most part descriptive snapshots of particular religious groups at specific moments in time. Very little research was longitudinal. She concluded her assessment by noting that, "This article is intentionally short on conclusions and long on calls for more empirical, grounded work" (Levitt 2003: 868).

In a subsequent article, Levitt (2004: 6) focused on the complex interplay of factors contributing to religious identity and practice in migratory settings and to the role of religion in forging and sustaining transnational ties. She offered a provisional typology for understanding the varied ways in which the social construction of a religious presence in a new context takes organizational form. Presenting three organizational types as "heuristic devices rather than static, fixed categories," she distinguishes extended, negotiated, and recreated transnational religious organizations.

The extended type is characteristic of major religions that have succeeded over the centuries in developing a global network of religious institutions. The Catholic Church is the example of this type par excellence. In Levitt's (2004: 2) description, it has such a well-established presence in so many sending and receiving countries that it "allows migrants who choose to do so to move almost seamlessly between sending- and receiving-country parishes and religious movement groups. The Church integrates them into powerful, well-established networks where they can express interests, gain skills, and make claims with respect to their home and host countries." One might suggest that in a somewhat more attenuated way, those Protestant denominations that have remained closest to the Catholic Church – Anglicans and Lutherans – can also be seen as examples of the extended pattern, though in a more limited way. Anglicans, for example, have a network shaped by the British colonial legacy, while Lutherans have developed one since the nineteenth century as a result both of the migration of many Lutherans from the Nordic countries and Germany to North America and elsewhere and of missionary work in the developing world.

Levitt's (2004: 2–3, 8–11) second type, negotiated transnational organizations, applies to religious groups that lack the long histories and the relative size of these three examples. Whether or not there is a central body overseeing work at the local, congregational level, much of the initiative comes from below rather than top-down. There is a far less developed set of routinized policies and procedures, as well as a more flexible and decentralized authority structure. As an illustration of this type, Levitt points to the International Church of the Foursquare Gospel (ICFG), a relatively small American-based congregation founded by the charismatic and controversial fundamentalist preacher Aimee Semple McPherson in 1924, whose Angelos Temple was a forerunner to today's megachurches.

The ICFG's proselytizing work in the developing world has led to substantial growth in a number of countries. In fact, of what are estimated or claimed to be 8 million members worldwide, the vast majority reside outside of the country where the denomination was founded. Levitt's specific case is that of Brazil, where, she reports, there were an estimated 10,000 ICFG churches in 2001 (a large number, and one disputed by the denomination's Brazilian website, which reported 3,988 at that time [http://www.quadrangularbrasil.com/en_estatisticas.htm]). A wave of Brazilian converts has immigrated to the United States, settling chiefly in the Northeast. She has examined one congregation in the Boston area that is ministered to by a Brazilian pastor who, too, is a migrant. Her description of his congregation and its ongoing though loosely structured relationship to the ICFG in Brazil leads her to generalize about the negotiated type, noting that such churches "arise from a set of personal and institutional relationships that emerge organically, in response to the challenges posed by a particular context" (Levitt 2004: 10). In the process of ongoing negotiation with a variety of actors, individual and institutional, both there and here, members of the ICFG congregation in Boston entered into various civic engagements, ranging from signing petitions in opposition to same-sex marriage to volunteering at soup kitchens. They did so with an understanding advanced by their pastor that to be a good Christian required being a good citizen.

The recreated transnational religious group represents an attempt to relocate or transplant a religious tradition in a new national context that is intended to replicate the religious beliefs and practices characteristic of the homeland in the receiving society. Here a premium is placed on "strongly reinforc[ing] members' ties to their home country, often at the expense of receiving-country social integration." To reinforce this organizationally, Levitt (2004: 3) writes that, "Many of these groups are structured like franchises or chapters of sending-country religious organizations." Levitt cites as an example Gujarati Hindus who migrated to the United States, moving from a country where they constitute a sizeable majority of the population to a situation where they are a very small religious minority existing in an institutionally incomplete community (Breton 1964). In contrast to Catholicism, with its hierarchal institutional structure and in the Vatican a clear center of legitimate authority, a defined sacred text, a long history of theological inquiry shaping the contours of the faith, creedal commitments that all the faithful are to embrace, a shared liturgy familiar to all Catholics around the world, and so forth, Hinduism exists at the opposite end of the spectrum. It lacks a central authority and one clearly demarcated institutional structure. The beliefs and practices vary considerably based on a number of factors, including regional and caste differences. Not all agree about what are the religion's sacred texts. Indeed, both within and without Hinduism, some would contend that it is less a religion and more a way of life. Given these profound differences between Catholicism and Hinduism, it is evident why the extended form is not a viable option for the latter.

Examining two groups in the Boston area, the Devotional Associates of Yogeshwar, which is also called the Swadhyaya movement, and the International Swaminarayan Satsang Organization

(ISSO), she describes the reliance of immigrant members of both groups on leadership and guidance from India. Members of the Swadhyaya movement, for example, gather weekly. Part of their gathering is devoted to watching and discussing videotapes of the Indian-based founder of the movement. In addition, leaders in Mumbai continue to play a role in assisting immigrants in their personal lives when financial, marital, or psychological problems arise.

The larger ISSO has state offices and a national office that can intervene at the local level, thereby reducing somewhat the reliance on the Indian operation. For example, within the United States a revolving loan and skill fund is available when members in a particular locale are about to embark on major projects, particularly temple construction. The dependence on *Sadhus* (holy men or teachers) from India who spoke no English and were not only unfamiliar with American customs, but opposed to many, such as interacting with women, meant that they promoted an insular version of religion for the adherents. Despite being a fairly successful group in economic terms, many ISSO members sought to distance themselves and their children from being tainted by many aspects of Western culture and to encourage social relations that were largely confined to their religious community (Levitt 2004: 11–14). In contrast to Foursquare Brazilians, Hindus from these two religious groups exhibited little civic involvement; when they did it was often inadvertent as the general view of most members was that they should focus on family and friends and steer clear of political involvements.

As with her paper from a year earlier, Levitt was both taking stock and seeking to articulate a research agenda for the future, one that addressed issues of identity, connections or networks, and the institutions available or created that seek to make possible religious practice in a transnational idiom. Since then, a growing body of research has been produced, much of it in article form, which often means that although valuable, the publications lack the thick description that more sustained book-length efforts make possible. In what follows, we look more broadly at examples that represent each of Levitt's three types of religious transnationalism.

Catholic Immigrants in the Americas

Roman Catholic immigrants arrived in small numbers during the colonial era, and have been a part of every major migratory wave since. In the era before the Civil War, the Irish constituted by far the largest group of Catholics, with a sizeable German Catholic population joining them, while during the Great Migration, they were confronted by the presence of two other large groups, Italians and Poles – along with a number of smaller groups. And in the post-1965 migration, Mexican Catholics have been by far the largest group, but they were joined by other Latin American immigrants and by Filipinos. All of these different national-origin groups entered a society that contained a majority Protestant population, though over time the percentage of the population that was Roman Catholic rose.

When the Irish arrived in the early nineteenth century, the country was overwhelmingly Protestant. It was also British, which signaled the two intertwined sources of hostility to the Irish presence in the country. Very quickly, the Irish came to dominate the development of Catholicism and it was from their ranks that the large majority of the church's leadership derived. Priests and nuns joined the exodus to America, making possibly the construction of Catholic parishes and parochial schools, the latter seen as a bastion protecting the faithful from Protestantization. The intense anti-Catholic and anti-Irish hostility solidified group boundaries, which were reinforced when Irish nationalist ideology and growing demands for Irish independence began to take hold within sectors of the immigrant community (Dolan 1985). Transnational political involvements proliferated throughout the nineteenth century into the twentieth as Irish nationalism percolated and the republican quest for freeing Ireland from British rule heated up, a fact that the Irish American Catholic leadership was largely opposed to.

The universal character of Roman Catholicism facilitated transnational connections between the Irish American Catholic community and both Irish Catholics and the Vatican. For their part, the clergy of the Irish church were divided about how to respond to emigration, with some priests speaking out against it while others helped to organize groups of would-be migrants and joined them in the move to America. As early as the 1820s, funds were collected to train priests for working with the émigré community, and the Catholic Emigration Society attempted to assist in various ways those about to make the voyage across the Atlantic (Miller 1985: 243). Once they had gained something of a foothold in America, the church hierarchy in America sought to work cooperatively with the church abroad, but pressed the laity to begin the process of Americanization. Their goal was to assist with the incorporation of an immigrant group that confronted serious barriers to inclusion, and at the same time to forge a distinctly American Catholicism.

While transnational activities would persist over time, the emphasis of the church's leadership was on transplanting Catholicism on American soil, nurturing it in an environment that was seen as different insofar as they now resided as a minority religion in the "righteous empire" of American Protestantism (Marty 1970). Moreover, as historian Dennis Clark (1977: 57) has pointed out, a heavily rural population had ended up in urban America, and that dramatically changed the character of religious belief and practice, the new context managing "to all but obliterate the folk religion that the Irish had brought with them to America. The homely compound of simply beliefs, rural rituals, and moral adages was now replaced by a complicated overlay of memorized formulas, rote prayers, stereotyped devotional methods, and arbitrary regulations."

The subsequent arrival of new Catholic immigrants, particularly the two largest groups after 1880 – Italians and Poles – reinforced this pattern. Both groups were forced to deal directly with Irish (and German) dominance of the American Catholic Church. This generated greater conflict with Poles than Italians, leading some of the former to break away and establish the independent Polish Catholic National Church in 1897. Most remained, seeking to find a place for the Polish language and culture in the American church. Both Italians and Poles were at a disadvantage insofar as clergy and nuns from their homelands did not migrate to the extent that Irish religious did. As a consequence, lay members assumed leadership roles to fill the void, in so doing establishing a more influential role for the laity than in Poland (Galush 1977: 87). Moreover, for some time political and cultural (including religious) elites in the homelands were highly critical of emigrants, the former casting them as disloyal to the nation while religious elites were concerned that they would lose control over those departing for distant shores. In some cases, this changed over time as those elites realized that they were not going to be able to stem the tide of emigration.

Mark Choate's *Emigrant Nation* (2008: 50) looks at the shift in response that took place in Italy by the beginning of the twentieth century, after the passage of the 1901 Law of Emigration, which signaled the beginning of a new perspective that treated "emigration as an international expansion instead of an internal hemorrhage." Although his focus is state-centered, he is also attentive to the role of the Italian Catholic Church, which often worked in tandem with the state in efforts to maintain an ongoing relationship with émigré communities in the United States and elsewhere.

While these efforts had an impact in the short term, during the lifetimes of the immigrant generation, they eventually came to an end as the ethnic offspring of that generation came to view themselves as Italian American Catholics sharing more in common with their ethnic counterparts in the United States than with Italian Catholics. To what extent these changes can be attributed to the curtailing of mass immigration in 1924 and to subsequent world events – the Depression and World War II – can be debated, but they certainly loom large in explaining the waning of manifestations of transnationalism, religious and other forms. That being said, through the preservation of certain Italian feast days such as the San Gennaro festival in New York City's Little Italy, they have proven capable of keeping the connections to the ancestral past alive through what might be described as symbolic transnationalism.

The question of historical parallels or divergences is appropriately raised when turning to contemporary Catholic immigrants, chiefly from Mexico, but from other Latin American countries and the Philippines as well, and comparing them to those who arrived earlier. Will the patterns of the past be repeated or will new ones emerge?, a question Robert C. Smith (2003) takes up in his comparative analysis of Mexicans to both Italians and Poles. It is worth noting that Mexicans have been migrating in large numbers off and on since the second decade of the twentieth century. In *A Nation of Emigrants* (2009), David Fitzgerald examines the role of the Mexican state and the Catholic Church in a parallel fashion to Choate's study, and he draws similar conclusions about the role of both institutions in establishing and maintaining connections to Mexicans living abroad. Unlike, for example, their Cuban counterparts, where international politics has impeded transnational ties, world events have not conspired against either the state or the Catholic Church's ability to sustain transnational connections (though Mahler and Hansing 2005 indicate that such ties between Cuba and Miami do exist in attenuated form).

At the same time, the latter finds itself in a position where the American Catholic Church holds ultimate authority over such matters as whether (or when) to encourage ethnic parishes, pan-Latino congregations, or more broadly assimilated ones. The situation for Catholicism in general is increasingly complicated. First, the Evangelical Lutheran Church in America, the largest Lutheran denomination, is increasingly nipping at its heels, seeking to attract Mexicans by redefining Lutheranism through the inclusion of popular Catholicism, such as endorsing the veneration of the Virgin of Guadalupe (Freier 2009). Currently, one of the ten largest congregations in the denomination, located in Irving, Texas, is Iglesia Luterana Santa Maria de Guadalupe. Second, and in terms of numbers far more significant, evangelical Protestantism has grown dramatically in Latin America and many new immigrants from that region have converted either prior to migration or afterwards (Smilde 2007). It is precisely this group that Levitt used as her example of negotiated transnationalism.

Evangelical Protestants from Latin America

Levitt's example of negotiated transnational religious organizations was an American-origin evangelical Protestant organization active in Brazil. There has been a Protestant presence in Latin America since the nineteenth century, a result of both missionary activity and immigration from Europe and North America (d'Epinay 1968). In recent decades, sociologists of religion have pointed to the explosive growth of evangelical Christianity throughout Latin America. David Martin (1990) was one of the earliest scholars to explore the significant inroads of conservative Protestantism into predominantly Catholic societies, with particular attention paid to Pentecostalism. His thesis was that the Protestant challenge should be viewed as a product of a longstanding competition between Anglo and Latino cultures, intertwined with competition in both the economic and political realms. In his view, Catholic religious hegemony is on the decline, and conservative Protestantism is filling a void.

While this may well be true, subsequent scholars such as Smilde (1999) have argued that Martin's thesis oversimplifies a more complex reality. Considerable attention has been paid to assessing factors that have contributed to the appeal of Protestantism. Smilde's (2007) ethnographic research in Venezuela points to the potency of the demands for ascetic self-control of people – particularly men – who have struggled with alcohol, drug abuse, gambling, and criminal activity. Other researchers have also stressed the asceticism of evangelical Protestantism and its role in self-improvement, but rather than focusing on overcoming dysfunctional behavior, the emphasis is on the role that religion plays in economic advancement via individual initiative. These accounts are often explicitly conceived in Weberian terms, with inner-worldly asceticism accounting for an alternative to liberation theology in the form of offering a theological rationale for capitalism as a system and entrepreneurial activities as the central means for achieving individual betterment (Gooren 2002).

A stereotypical portrait of evangelical Christians in Latin America depicts them as highly conservative on social issues such as abortion and gay rights and committed to various right-wing political parties. The former Guatemalan military leader Efrain Rios Montt, accused of genocide committed against the Ixil Maya ethnic minority in that country's dirty war against a Marxist insurgency, is a poster child for this perspective, since he justified his brutal regime by recourse to his fervent evangelical faith. However, as befits a negotiated faith without central authority and shaped by very independent and often charismatic clerics, the reality is more complex. While, as with all stereotypes, there is an element of sociological truth to the above characterization, it does not describe all evangelicals. Some attempt to remain above the fray of politics, their apolitical commitment an expression of a religious value system that urges believers to avoid being tainted by the inherently corrupting nature of politics in particular and "the world" in general.

But the reality on the ground is even more complex since there is evidence that, in some contexts, evangelicals are prepared to support left-wing political causes. Christian Smith and Liesl Ann Haas (1997) relied on 1990 Gallup data from shortly after elections were held in Nicaragua in which the left-wing FSLN was removed from office to analyze the political preferences of evangelical Christians. They discovered that evangelicals were more inclined to support the leftist Sandinistas than were Catholics, despite the impact of liberation theology on the latter. While this is true, in fact more evangelicals voted for the conservative UNO than for the FSLN, and in fact their support for the UNO was almost identical to that of Catholics. When compared to the third category, that of the nonreligious, the differences are starkest, for by over a 2 to 1 margin the nonreligious cast their votes for the FSLN. The conclusion to be drawn is not that in some contexts a majority of evangelicals might embrace leftist ideals and support leftist political parties, but simply that they are not necessarily more conservative than Catholics. But that sets the bar rather low since liberation theology Catholics have always been a minority in the Catholic Church, with a well-funded and powerful conservatism consistently challenging it, as witnessed by the papal regimes of John Paul II and Benedict XVI.

At the end of their article, Smith and Haas (1997: 451) observe a similar pattern in El Salvador, noting that due to the "oppressive atmosphere of El Salvador's civil war, neither Catholics nor Protestants seemed eager to participate politically, and both remained skeptical of the prospects for peace." This atmosphere can be seen not only in this Central American country, but also among the refugee population in the United States that grew substantially during the 1980s, with Los Angeles and Washington, DC becoming the two major destination points. In her ethnographic study of two Catholic and two evangelical congregations in the latter city, Cecilia Menjívar (1999) illustrates how the latter negotiated religious and ethnic identities in a setting away from a war-ravaged homeland. The membership of one of the churches – "God's Light" – is entirely Salvadoran, while the other – Emmanuel's Temple – is composed of a mixed Latino membership, with Salvadorans constituting about half the membership. We look at the former since the pastor at Emmanuel Temple overtly eschews transnational connections, seeking to encourage a break from troubled homelands. Although transnational practices are not absent in this church, they exist by default and are far more attenuated than the connections at God's Light.

Typical of smaller religious bodies that are not as bureaucratic or hierarchal as, for example, the Catholic Church, Menjívar (1999: 594) contends that these organizations "are able to operate more effectively in new religious spaces." At the same time, as with the Laestadians described at the beginning of this chapter, they are subject to schisms. God's Light had within a two-decade period from the early 1980s experienced five schisms. The members were struggling economically and with many of the personal problems and troubled backgrounds described above. Despite their difficult circumstances, members tithed and were willing to attend services three times a week. What they found in this congregation was a transplantation of their homeland, for not only was everyone from El Salvador, but they were from the same communities in the eastern part of the country. Thus, it is not surprising that parishioners would comment that once they entered the church, they felt as if they had left the United States and returned home. Everything about the church reflected the national origins of its members, from the sermon topics to the food served after worship. Members tended to identify themselves, not in panethnic terms, but rather simply as Salvadoran and Christian.

The church was founded in eastern El Salvador, and during the formative years of the refugee churches, the institutional center remained in the homeland. Some of the members of the congregation had been members before departure, while others joined after arriving in the United States. They are part of a network of churches in Maryland, North Carolina, and Virginia, and all of these congregations along with those in El Salvador are in regular contact. In this transnational religious network, a shift occurred as the refugee population grew while those remaining behind declined in numbers. The church's headquarters were relocated to Washington, DC. Three times weekly, God's Light broadcasts a radio program to all of the member churches in both countries. The congregations in El Salvador have become increasingly dependent on members in the United States to assist in financial and other ways. The pastor of God's Light travels to meet with the sister churches in the homeland several times a year, and missionary groups also visit frequently. On the other hand, because of the tenuous legal status of many parishioners, the back-and-forth movement typical of transnational networks is limited.

Whether or not this example of negotiated religious transnationalism will persist into the second generation and beyond is open to question, for the very fact that this is a negotiated form of religious affiliation points to potentially varied consequences. Once the offspring of the refugee generation come of age, the fact that they are more acculturated than their parents and often have citizenship status suggests that they have a variety of options available to them in terms of embracing, redefining, or abandoning their religious identities. For example, they might downplay their Salvadoran identity in favor of a panethnic Latino Christian identity, an American Christian one, or simply define themselves as Christian. They may embrace an altogether different faith community. They may join many of their generational counterparts from the USA in becoming spiritual seekers. Or they may reject religion. The potential for future schisms within the church can undermine the efficacy of the organization or prove to be a source of revitalization. Situational contingencies can push both individuals and institutions in one of a wide variety of possible directions.

Hinduism in America

As with most contemporary immigrant groups in the United States, those originating from the Indian subcontinent can point to small contingents of earlier arrivals who settled in a prior migratory era. Immigrants from India were small in number during the preceding Great Migration, with 6,800 arriving in California from the Punjab in the early twentieth century. A heavily male-dominated migration of agricultural workers, very few of this group were Hindu, though the term Hindu, usually used as a pejorative appellation, was generally employed as a synonym for all Indian migrants. In fact, 85 percent of this group were Sikh and another 10 to 12 percent were Muslim, leaving less than 5 percent who could be classified as Hindu (Kurien 2007: 42).

The post-1965 period has witnessed a much larger number of immigrants from India entering the country, with the numbers picking up substantially near the end of the past century, coinciding to large extent with the rapid expansion of the high tech sector. Their numbers more than doubled between 1980 and 1990, and by the end of the century, they came to constitute one of the largest Asian immigrant groups in the country. Reflecting the religious diversity of India, adherents of the major faiths of India were all represented: Hindus, Sikhs, Jains, Muslims, Christians, and Zoroastrians. Given the fact that in India Hindus constitute approximately 85 percent of the population, and given the findings of the Pew study reported in chapter 1, Hindus, though large in number, are actually underrepresented in this population. Raymond Brady Williams (1998) has argued that two things have happened as Indians from various religious backgrounds have adapted to their new homeland. First, though they come from a country characterized by religious pluralism, they have had to adjust to the specific features of the pluralistic American religious landscape. At the same time, they have taken advantage of communication technologies and the relative ease of long-distance travel to forge transnational linkages with individuals and institutions in India.

Given the sheer diversity of the religions of India, both among the various religions and within the dominant Hindu religion, the manifestations of religious transnationalism are widely varied, with some expressions amounting to voices on the periphery representing small numbers of the overall Indian immigrant population and others capturing something closer to the center. In terms of the former, one can point to the case of the International Society for Krishna Consciousness (ISKCON), more generally known as the Hare Krishnas. It was one of the new religious movements to emerge during the 1960s as part of countercultural seekers' interest in Eastern religions. The Western devotees of the movement actively recruited new members and the initial phase of the movement's history saw substantial growth in numbers. By the 1980s, in a different cultural climate, the movement turned inward. Several scandals – both financial and sexual – undermined the movement and led to a decline in membership. More recently, researchers have discovered a resurgence of interest in ISKCON, now on the part of Indian immigrants who have been actively recruited (Rochford 2007). As a case study of the organization's temple in Chicago revealed, these new immigrant converts have provided both new members and needed resources, doing so by "congregational-level transnational interactions" (Berg and Kniss 2008: 79).

Turning to the mainstream, efforts to create a distinctively American expression of Hinduism were undertaken at precisely the same time that Hindu nationalism was taking hold in India, threatening that country's sometimes tenuous embrace of religious pluralism. In this regard, it is important to note certain distinctive features of Hinduism in the United States. First, Hindu immigrants entered the country as a distinct minority, in stark contrast to Christian immigrants. They departed a country where they constituted a large majority of the population. Second, Hinduism is closely linked to the Indian nation. Hinduism is not a global religion in quite the way that Christianity or Islam are. Not only are its adherents heavily concentrated in India and elsewhere on the Indian subcontinent, but where there are substantial enclaves elsewhere around the world – be it in Fiji, Trinidad, or South Africa – it is due to the fact that those places have become home to members of the Indian diaspora. This leads to the third point, which is that given the close linkage between ethnicity and religion (Kivisto 2007), in the construction of Indian nationalism both during British colonial rule and in the post-independence era, the potential exists for Hinduism to be employed as a resource for nationalist ideology – a potentially problematic resource if it is defined in a manner that denies the legitimacy of religious pluralism in the nation.

The Hindutva movement in India has been criticized for promoting an idea of what it means to be an authentic Indian that shrinks the public sphere. The origins of Hindu nationalism can be traced to the 1920s in reaction to Muslim mobilization that was triggered by opposition to British policies toward Turkey as the Ottoman Empire collapsed. Viewing a growing Muslim militancy in India as a threat contributed to the emergence of its Hindu counterpart. The principal figure associated with Hindutva was Vinayak Damodar Savarkar (1883–1966), whose book gave name to the movement. Savarkar made a distinction between the ancient inhabitants of India versus those who were not. Among the former, in addition to Hindus were those religious traditions whose roots could be traced to Hinduism: Jains, Sikhs, and Buddhists. This meant that Muslims and Christians were viewed as outsiders whose roots were elsewhere (Kurien 2007: 126–7). The ideology took institutional form with the creation of the Rashtriya Swayamsevak Sangh (RSS, the National Volunteer Corps) in 1925, whose second leader was Madhav Sadashiv Golwalkar, a figure who stressed the idea of indigenousness. Both Savarkar and Golwalkar admired Hitler and the latter sought in various ways to pattern the RSS after the Nazi movement.

Critical of Gandhi's ideal of religious pluralism, the RSS was viewed as a threat by the independent nation's first leader, Jawaharlal Nehru, who sought to marginalize the organization in an effort to promote a state that was at once secular and socialist. The latter part of this couplet meant that during the Cold War, without distancing itself too far from the United States, India nonetheless often tilted toward the Soviet Union. By the 1960s Golwalkar would identify three threats to Hindu nationalism: Islam, Christianity, and communism (Kurien 2007: 128). For three decades after independence, Hindu nationalism's fortunes rose and fall, but it was never able to pose a serious electoral challenge to the political mainstream. That would begin to change with the creation of the Bharatiya Janata Party (BJP, the Indian People's Party) in 1980 – at the same time that emigration from India increased.

The transnational dimension of contemporary Hindu nationalism has been a topic raised in several studies (Levitt 2007: 226–7; Biswas 2004; Kamat and Mathew 2003; Mathew and Prashad 2000; Juergensmeyer 1995), but nowhere has it received the sustained attention given to it in Prema Kurien's *A Place at the Multicultural Table: The Development of an American Hinduism* (2007). The product of a long-term study that focuses on both individual religious practices and the role of twelve organizations, Kurien seeks to describe how an American Hinduism has evolved through the interplay of what she categorizes as popular and official Hinduism, the former seen in the lived experiences of ordinary Hindu believers while the latter is articulated in more formal ways by the leadership of major Hindu organizations. This occurs in a context characterized by the potential for considerable variability of religious expression – in contrast to other major religions – insofar as, both in terms of religious doctrine and institutional structure and authority, Hinduism lacks a core. Furthermore, as Rhys Williams (2009: 132) notes, Hinduism tends to be perceived as "the spiritual expression of Indian people."

Kurien's (2007: 40–1) analysis of the transplantation of Hinduism into America begins in agreement with Steven Vertovec's (2000: 8) contention that for Indians outside of India, regardless of the receiving country, religion has served as the primary component of ethnic identity construction. Part of their new identity was that of being a religious minority, in contrast to their majority status in India. Reconfiguring what it means to be Hindu and Indian while simultaneously seeking to become integrated into the receiving society calls for being prepared to rethink aspects of the inherited religious belief system and religious practice, while also revisiting received notions regarding all aspects of social relations, but particularly those related to gender and caste.

Kurien observes that ideas about Hinduism among the American public actually preceded the arrival of Hindu immigrants. Images of Hinduism varied. They included the negative derived from the critical depictions of some Westerners who had spent time in India – including missionaries intent on converting Indians from what they saw as a religion characterized by superstition and idolatry. On the other hand, Swami Vivekananda's speech at the World Parliament of Religions in Chicago near the end of the nineteenth century was an early influential articulation of the ecumenical movement. Complicating the picture was the fact noted earlier, namely that a large majority of the earliest-arriving Indian immigrants were Sikhs, though from the American public's general viewpoint, to say Indian was synonymous with saying "Hindoo."

Hindus arrived in large numbers only in the post-1965 era. In 1970, they accounted for only 70,000 immigrants, but the figure rose significantly near the end of the past century and by 2006 the numbers had grown to 1.5 million, which makes them the fourth largest immigrant group at present. Almost one in five of these immigrants came from somewhere other than India. At present, Indian immigrants are heavily concentrated in five states, with California taking the lead, followed by New Jersey, New York, Texas, and Illinois (Terrazas 2008). Those Indians who sought to find ways to become American Hindus often did so by turning to the study of Hindu history and theology, something that would have been uncharacteristic during their pre-migration lives. But this deepening of religious reflection has not led to a return to a perceived pure expression of Hinduism. On the contrary, transplantation has resulted in far-reaching changes. Kurien (2007: 55) writes in this regard:

> For instance, in keeping with the American ethos, Hindus in the United States tend to offer more individualistic and cultural explanations for success and failure. Gender and caste ideology are also reinterpreted. Moving somewhat away from an orthopraxy tradition, Hinduism in America is becoming more of a theology- and belief-centered religion.

At the same time, a pan-Indian Hinduism is replacing more particularistic practices predicated on factors such as region and caste. Temples, and by the beginning of the twenty-first century there were over 700, have taken on the organizational form of American Christian congregations, including holding religious services (pujas) on weekends, when the largest number of members can be present. Priests from India who have been hired by these temples discover that congregational members have expectations that they not only perform various ceremonies and rituals, but also function in both pastoral and administrative roles that are not expected of them in India.

Popular Hinduism so construed is about the process of integrating into American society, at both the individual and institutional levels. As such, it is about transplantation rather than transnationalism, about finding a new home that over time might become less and less connected to the homeland. However, as Kurien's analysis reveals, at another level transnational connections have been established in which American Hindus are shaping views of both religion and national identity in the homeland. This is occurring at the level of official Hinduism, which has been developed in large part by several umbrella organizations, with one of the most influential early on being the Federation of Hindu Associations (FHA). The FHA and other organizations, whose members tended to be highly educated and economically well-off, proved to be a vital source of funds for the Hindutva movement in India and in various ways promoted its views. Indeed, a second-generation Indian American authored one of the BJP's important statements, "Hindutva: The Great Nationalist Ideology."

Hindu nationalism posed a direct challenge to perceptions of Indian national identity in terms of a secular state and a pluralistic, non-establishment religious landscape. Hinduism was portrayed as a religion of tolerance that had been victimized by adherents of both Christianity and Islam. For example, it was claimed that Muslim invaders had perpetuated a "Hindu holocaust" that was worse than the Jewish holocaust (Kurien 2007: 150). The call, therefore, was to purify Indian national identity by freeing it of elements foreign to its essential character. To accomplish this goal, violence against the enemies of Hindutva was defined as legitimate. In particular, Kurien's detailed account reinforces

Kamat and Mathew's (2003: 4) claim that "a significant segment of the Indian diasporic community" in the United States embraced the "legitimation of violence against Muslims." This is, thus, an example of the dark side of religious transnationalism. The Hindu community in America proved to be instrumental in the electoral success of the BJP, and in turn it was rewarded for its support by the passage of legislation permitting dual citizenship, thereby strengthening the political voice of the expatriate community.

The same leaders of official Hinduism make use of multicultural discourse in claims-making efforts aimed at finding "a place at the multicultural table," which Kurien (2007: 184) depicts as fashioned in a way that seeks to challenge restrictive, Eurocentric versions of American national identity, calling instead for a more pluralistic and expanded definition of what it means to be American. This is, she notes, ironic given their commitment to promoting a more restrictive notion of Indian national identity that if successful would result in a constriction of the public sphere. In staking out these two positions, Hindu nationalists have sought to mask its homeland political involvements from the scrutiny of the American public, an implicit recognition that their endorsement of the politics of recognition in the American context is at odds with their homeland objectives.

Kurien recognizes that Hindutva is embraced by a segment of the Hindu American community, and not by all of it. It is a segment that she contends is well placed and has the financial, human, and social capital to be effective. Moreover, its influence does not appear to be limited to the first generation, but extends to the second. This being said, it is not clear how deep its roots are in the immigrant community, the percentage of immigrants who might be viewed as sympathizers, or what its implications are for Indian immigrants who are not Hindu. Clearly, in Kurien's discussion of student organizations, there are both pro-Hindutva members and those she describes as moderates. She does not identify an anti-Hindutva group. What appears to link these two groups is their shared desire to find ways to integrate into the American mainstream and their sense that race is a critical barrier to inclusion. In this context, one can implicitly assume that Hindu fundamentalism can continue to be promoted as long as it has no significant opposition.

A somewhat different sense of the lay of the land can be found in Levitt's work. She notes that, "Some people see groups like the ISSO, BAPS, and Swadhyaya as fueling this fundamentalist neo-Hindu agenda." But, she goes on, "In general, the people I talked with deeply distrusted politics, whether or not it was accompanied by a stiff dose of religion." Her respondents described the BJP as corrupt and ineffectual and its American supporters as hypocrites since they took little interest in political affairs when they lived in India. More to the point, they thought it best to stay clear of homeland political involvements (Levitt 2007: 141–2).

Two other studies reinforce Levitt's picture of an immigrant community in which most newcomers are intent on steering clear of homeland entanglements: Pawan Dhingra's *Managing Multicultural Lives* (2007) and Caroline B. Brettell and Deborah Reed-Danahay's *Civic Engagements: The Citizenship Practices of Indian and Vietnamese Immigrants* (2012). Both studies were conducted in the Dallas-Fort Worth (DFW) area, and both compared Indian immigrants with one other Asian group, Koreans in the former case and Vietnamese in the latter. The focus of both studies was on the forging of a distinctly Indian American identity, working to reinforce ideas about the model minority when it served to foster acceptance by the receiving society, working to combat racism, and being prepared to think strategically about pan-Asian alliances when they were seen as advantageous. Neither book explicitly addresses the Hindutva movement, which either was not evident to the researchers or was simply not their focus since they are primarily concerned with specifying factors contributing to forging pathways to inclusion.

Dhingra (2007: 216) contends that "Indian Americans tried to walk a fine line between satisfying their communities' interests and appearing divisive." They were prepared to present themselves as Indian, but not too Indian, and likewise with their varied religious identities. In an Indian American youth camp he visited, the emphasis was on a secular, non-sectarian vision of ethnic identity. Seeking to indicate their loyalty to the United States, children held signs in a photo shoot that read "God Bless America" and "USA and India Love Freedom and Democracy," the latter clearly intended to draw a parallel between the two countries based on their presumed shared commitment to democracy. A similar sense is conveyed in Brettell and Reed-Danahay's (2012: 112–13) research findings:

> In DFW, Indians work together through secular organizations for collaborative pan-Indian and transreligious purposes. However, even within the more secular pan-Indian associations, efforts are made not to engage in any activities or make any position statements that might indicate support for either Hindu or Muslim causes in India – that is, choosing between being Indian and being Hindu or Muslim or Christian. Thus, the India Association of North Texas (IANT) acted to raise funds after the earthquake in Gujarat in the early 2000s but made no statement about nor took any action in relation to the Hindu-Muslim confrontations in Gujarat province in February 2002, when Hindu mobs attacked Muslims and burned a mosque and other Islamic facilities in retaliation for the Muslim firebombing of a train that was transporting Hindu activists from Ayodhya, a disputed holy site. Two thousand people died.

These two studies might suggest that those involved in supporting the Hindutva movement that Kurien focused on are, in fact, a very small element in the overall Indian – or to be more exact – Hindu immigrant community. However, in Dhingra's (2012: 158 and 225) more recent study of Indian American motel owners in the United States, dominated by people with the surname Patel, he lent credence to Kurien's conclusion that Hindutva supporters in the United States are something other than a fringe group. In 2005, the Asian American Hotel Owners Association (AAHOA), the trade association of Indian motel owners, invited Narendra Modi, the BJP official serving as the Chief Minister of Gujarat, to be the keynote speaker at their annual meeting.

In a controversy that continues to this writing, Modi has been implicated in the 2002 riots, accused of failing to take actions to stop the killings of Muslims and to have either explicitly behind the scenes or implicitly encouraged the violence. Modi was denied a visa to enter the United States, a State Department decision that was condemned by many members of the AAHOA. Since the organization is quite up front about its lobbying efforts in Washington, DC over an extended period of time on behalf of what its members see as Indian interests, it is clear that transnational ties are well established. That being said, to the extent that these ties are shaped by Hindu fundamentalism, its advocates appear to be aware of the need for discretion, for if conflict between Hindu and Muslim Indian immigrants was to become apparent to the American public, it would work against efforts aimed at incorporation into the societal mainstream.

Transnational Connections / National Incorporation

As these three extended cases of Catholics, evangelical Protestants, and Hindus suggest, religious transnationalism is a varied phenomenon, shaped by the particularities of different religious faiths, the national origins of immigrants, and the religious landscape of receiving societies – which includes the distinctive understandings of church–state relations. Clearly, instances of religious transnationalism abound, and yet, as Thi Thanh Tâm Ngô (2010: 332) contends, the topic "is still rather understudied." And equally clearly, while a typology such as the one Levitt proposed and we made use of herein offers a valuable heuristic in attempting to address the variability and complexity of this phenomenon, a further refining of our theoretical framing is essential. Certainly this is true when considering on the one hand transnational connections and on the other hand national incorporation in the receiving society. Taking seriously Waldinger's injunction to bring the state back into transnational studies, we turn in the following chapter to church–state relations and debates concerning the place of religion in relation to the public sphere.

5

Church–State Relations and the Public Sphere

On November 29, 2009, Swiss voters went to the polls to cast their ballots in a referendum that sought to amend the nation's constitution. The proposal was a very simple one, with voters being asked to vote on an addition to the constitution contained in one short sentence: "The construction of minarets is forbidden." Polls leading up to the election indicated that this initiative, which had been pushed by the Swiss People's Party (SVP), a right-wing populist party whose political fortunes had risen in the years leading up to this ballot initiative, pointed to the likelihood of a decisive defeat of the proposal. The political and cultural establishment had made their opposition to the ban known. This included the leadership of the mainstream political parties, the parliament, and the Federal Council in the political arena and the organization representing Catholic bishops and the representative of the Vatican, the Federation of Jewish Communities, and many other religious and secular civic groups. The mainstream newspapers likewise took editorial stances against the ban.

Nevertheless, when the ballots were counted, the referendum passed with a solid 57.5 percent approval rate, gaining a solid majority in 22 of Switzerland's 26 cantons. The Swiss government reluctantly announced that it would enforce the policy, while seeking to reassure Muslims that they were welcome in the country. Critics were quick to condemn Swiss voters for succumbing to anti-Muslim bigotry and in so doing to violate fundamental values associated with religious freedom. The UN High Commissioner for Human Rights contended that the amendment violated the International Covenant on Civil and Political Rights (ICCPR), and as such would likely end up under the scrutiny of the European Court of Human Rights. A deputy program director for Amnesty International in Europe and Central Asia bemoaned the vote result, stating, "That Switzerland, a country with a long tradition of religious tolerance and the provision of refuge to the persecuted, should accept such a grotesquely discriminatory proposal is shocking" (Cumming-Bruce and Erlanger 2009). This sentiment was echoed by Farhad Afshar, a sociologist at Berne University and head of Coordination of Islamic Organizations in Switzerland, who wrote that, "The result is unworthy of Switzerland's tradition and history" (Traynor 2009). The editorialist for the *Economist* writing under the pseudonym "Charlemagne" warned that if the concern was a lack of integration into Swiss society, the ban would be counterproductive, writing, "It is also clear to me that well-integrated Swiss Muslims can only feel wretchedly isolated by this vote by so many of their compatriots, while radical Islamists must be rejoicing at a cause which they can use to gather support" (*Economist* 2009).

In explaining how the surprising outcome came to pass, commentators pointed to the media campaign waged by proponents of the minaret ban, who did all that they could to ratchet up anxiety levels about the Islamic presence in Switzerland – and, more broadly, in Europe. They were able to build on a context in which, according to a study conducted by Media Tenor International, coverage of Islam on television mainly focused on terrorism and global conflict, with very little attention given to Muslims who are well integrated into Swiss society and even less airtime given to spokespersons for the domestic Islamic community. One widely circulated poster was indicative of the campaigners' efforts to demonize Muslims and to play on fears about a Muslim "invasion" of Switzerland. It depicted a number of black minarets that ominously resembled missiles located close together atop a Swiss flag. In the left foreground of the poster was a women dressed in a niqab, her eyes suggesting anger and militancy.

SVP spokespersons Ulrich Schlüer and Martin Baltisser

articulated the party line in proclaiming that minarets are "symbols of Islamic power" (Traynor 2009). They expressed their belief that Muslims were intent on introducing Sharia law, promoting forced marriages, oppressing women, and condoning honor kill-ings. They depicted the Muslim presence in terms of an invasion, a battle for control of the heart and soul of the nation. That a solid majority of the citizenry endorsed the minaret ban is evi-dence that these claims resonated with large sectors of the public, reflecting, as Justice Minister Eveline Widmer-Schlumpf put it, "fears among the population of Islamic fundamentalist tenden-cies" (Cumming-Bruce and Erlanger 2009). The effort to ban minarets, thus, constitutes a form of symbolic politics that taps into anxieties about perceived threats to national identity. For many on the political right, directing anger at the Islamic enemy is part of a long pattern of depicting good and evil in starkly tribal terms, with one's own ethnic or national group firmly planted on the side of good and the "other" – Jews, the Roma, gays and lesbians, etc. – representing the personification of evil (Wieviorka 2012). Meanwhile, many on the left also appear to have voted for the ban. However, being squeamish about being seen as racist in general or Islamophobic in particular, those on the left opt to criti-cize multiculturalism rather than Muslims directly (Bowen 2012a: 9). It can be accused of being bad for women and for stymieing the integration of immigrants.

Misgivings have been rising since the 1990s about the significance of Muslim immigrants in Europe due to what anti-immigration journalist Christopher Caldwell (2009) describes as a demo-graphic revolution that is undermining European identity and security by introducing an adversarial culture into its midst. That being said, it is still surprising that Swiss citizens voted as they did. The Muslim population in the country registers at about 400,000 in a population of 7.5 million. This means that Muslims represent only 5 percent of the population. There are 1.7 million immigrants overall, and this means that less than one in four immigrants is a Muslim. Moreover, a sizeable majority of Muslims come from the Balkans – Bosnia and Kosovo in particular – and Turkey. The vast majority are not particularly devout. There are around 150 mosques or prayer rooms throughout the country, and of those, only four have minarets (with two additional ones planned at the time of the ban), in Zurich, Geneva, Winterthur, and Wangen bei Olten. The Ahmadiyya Mosque in Zurich was built in 1963, thus having been in existence for nearly a half century before the referendum was held. None of the four issue calls to prayer, thereby eliminating the prospect of challenges on the grounds of noise violations.

Martha Nussbaum observes that although Switzerland is a wealthy nation that ranks high in terms of measures of well-being such as educational quality and life expectancy, there are grounds for anxiety about the future. In no small part, the problems stem from low fertility rates and the challenges associated with an aging population. She writes that "there are reasons to fear for the future, if productivity cannot keep pace, and if new immigrants fail to achieve a level of education necessary for the skilled jobs that move development forward. So worries about immigrants and their assimilation are up to a point highly rational" (Nussbaum 2012: 43–4). However, when the object of fear is transferred to the immigrant "other," that fear becomes irrational. So it was when voters translated their irrational anxiety into a desire to insure that no more minarets would appear on the Swiss landscape. They were seen as emblematic of what Jocelyne Cesari (2005) has described as a very tangible manifestation of the "Islamicisation of European public space."

This chapter makes three shifts from previous chapters. First, it shifts attention from the immigrants themselves to the receiving nations, and in particular to political institutions tasked with framing church–state relations and defining the proper role of religion in the public sphere. Second, the focus will be far more on Europe than the United States, reflecting the fact that many of the issues involved here are being played out most strikingly in Western Europe. A third shift is linked to the second: whereas Islam has received limited attention in preceding chapters, being treated to large extent as one religion among others, in this one it takes center stage.

Religious Bridges and Barriers

The basic outlines of the theses advanced in two widely cited articles that have become frameworks for subsequent comparisons of the United States and Western Europe are germane for what follows. The two articles are Aristide Zolberg and Long Litt Woon's "Why Islam Is Like Spanish: Cultural Incorporation in Europe and the United States" (1999) and Nancy Foner and Richard Alba's "Immigrant Religion in the US and Western Europe: Bridge or Barrier to Inclusion?" (2008). The former begins by noting the simple demographic fact that in the United States Mexicans constitute by far the largest immigrant group, and when other immigrants from Central and South America are added into the mix, over half of contemporary immigrants originate from Spanish-speaking countries. Meanwhile, the Muslim populations in Western Europe, particularly in some of the largest immigrant-receiving nations – France, Germany, Great Britain, and the Netherlands – have come to represent a far larger portion of the immigrant population as a whole and of the country's overall population than is true of the United States. As a consequence, the cultural arenas in which contestation transpires differs, with language being the major fault line in the United States, while religion defines that fault line in Western Europe.

As barriers, language and religion differ. For one thing, in most nations there is a demand for a single official language, one necessary if a person is to function in all facets of public life, whereas religious diversity is an accepted phenomenon. Secondly, individuals are capable of being bi- or multi-lingual, and thus it is not necessarily the case that having an official language means that other languages disappear. At the same time, external pressures – subtle and not so subtle – to conform linguistically often encounter a desire on the part of the second- and third-generation offspring of immigrants to embrace the language of the larger society rather than that of their ancestors. Certainly, the history of American immigration reveals a nation that has proven to be, to large extent and for better or worse, the graveyard of languages other than English. Third, as Zolberg and Woon (1999: 21) point out, "the sphere of language rights is more limited than that of religious rights." They conclude by answering their own question:

> In what sense is Islam in Europe like Spanish in the United States? In that public debates surrounding the emergence of large immigrant groups identified by religion in the one case and language in the other are emblematic of larger issues of inclusion and exclusion, which in the last instance are about identity – of the hosts, of the newcomers, and most important, of the social entities that will result from their prolonged interactions. (Zolberg and Woon 1999: 28)

Following this line of argument, Foner and Alba agree that religion has proven to be a barrier to inclusion in Western Europe, while pointing out that in the United States – as chapter 3 in this book reveals – the conclusion that most scholars have drawn is that religion plays a "positive role in smoothing and facilitating the adaptation process" (Foner and Alba 2008: 360). In attempting to account for why religion would be a barrier to inclusion in one setting and a bridge in the other, they point to three main factors that distinguish the two contexts: (1) the religious composition of the respective immigrant populations differs, with the vast majority of immigrants to the United States being Christian, while a sizeable plurality of the immigrants to Western Europe are Muslims; (2) the level of religiosity is considerably higher in the United States than in Western Europe and being religious is viewed far more positively in the former than in the latter; and (3) different church–state relations, which have deep histories, make religious pluralism easier to accommodate in the United States than in Western Europe (Foner and Alba 2008: 361). In short, the differences are demographic, cultural, and institutional in nature. The first of these needs no further commentary, and thus we turn first to the matter of culture and then to the relationship between the state and religion along with the place of religion in civil society.

The Critics of Muslims and Multiculturalism

How should one read perceptions of the Islamic presence on European soil? If an observer looks at the ways Muslims were generally depicted in the 1980s, the foci of concern were often riveted more on the socioeconomic location and the ethnic or national origins of the immigrants than on religion per se. Writing at that time, political scientist William Safran compared Muslims in the late twentieth century to Jews a century or so earlier. He noted that, unlike Jews, Muslims did not have to contend with the charge of being Christ-killers or with the idea of being a perpetually homeless people. Safran (1986: 106) went on to assert that, "Islam seems too exotic to native Europeans, and the presence of its adherents in Germany and France is too recent, for the majority and for the leaders of the Christian establishment to have developed a distinct theological hostility or a mass paranoia about Islam or Muslims." At the same time, whereas Jews proved to rather quickly improve their economic circumstances, Muslims have had a much more difficult time gaining an economic foothold. The factors contributing to this include discrimination, low educational levels, and the impact of traditionalist ethnic cultures which, for example, encourage large families. It also includes religion, with questions being raised about the compatibility of Islam and modern, largely secular Western societies. Nonetheless, Safran (1986: 106) was convinced that "religion is a far less significant source of tension and hostility for postwar Muslim immigrants than it was for prewar Jewish immigrants."

That assessment was soon to be revisited. Perhaps the turning point was the Rushdie Affair, which can be dated to Iran's Ayatollah Ruhollah Khomeini's issuance of a fatwā in 1989 that called for the murder of Salman Rushdie, the author of *The Satanic Verses,* which had been declared a blasphemous work. The 9/11 attacks in New York and Washington, DC, followed by the terrorist attack on a commuter train in Madrid in 2004, the murder of Theo van Gogh in Amsterdam the same year (Buruma 2006), and both the bombings in London and the Danish cartoon controversy the following year resulted in a reevaluation of the significance of religion as Islam was increasingly perceived to be a threat to security (Kaya 2012). Certainly for many ordinary citizens these events appeared to offer convincing evidence that there was a problem with Islam, an inherent problem that made it incompatible with European liberal values.

That the reality is considerably more complex can be seen in the analysis of Brandeis University Professor Jytte Klausen (born and raised in Denmark) of the last of these events, the publication in the Danish newspaper *Jyllands-Posten* of a dozen cartoons depicting the Prophet Muhammad. The publication resulted in protests by Muslims in Denmark and other European countries against the newspaper and the Danish government, and rioting in numerous Muslim nations resulting in around 250 deaths. While some were quick to see these protests as spontaneous outbursts reflective of the clash of civilizations, Klausen argues that this overlooks the political dimension to the conflict, which involved, among other things, the provocative actions of the Egyptian government (the pre-Arab Spring Mubarak government) as it sought to curry favor with the Muslim Brotherhood and with similar domestic political considerations in several other Muslim nations dictating efforts to encourage conflict (Klausen 2009).

Moving beyond such specific events to factors shaping larger patterns of public opinion regarding newcomers, it is often difficult to disentangle the sources of anti-immigration animus. On the one hand, immigrants *qua* immigrants are often the object of hostility. They can be seen as competitive threats and economic burdens to the receiving society, as well as being in various ways perceived to be culturally "different" in negative terms. Thus, findings from the Eurobarometer in the early years of the twenty-first century found that one in five Europeans in 15 countries surveyed believed that their nation should enact repatriation policies for legal migrants, while four out of ten interviewees expressed opposition to the granting of civil rights to legal migrants (European Monitoring Centre on Racism and Xenophobia 2005). On the other hand, such hostility is typically selectively directed at different ethnic or national-origin groups. The long history of social distance studies, originating with the Chicago School of sociology, seeks to identify group-specific differences in levels of acceptance or rejection. Among the factors that can contribute to where any particular group stands in the social hierarchy is religion.

The difficulty arises when trying to determine the precise impact of economic versus cultural factors. As an illustration, Thomas Pettigrew (1998: 84) noted near the end of the past century that there is "less French prejudice against Asians than North Africans and less Dutch prejudice against Surinamers than Turks." Is this due to the higher human capital levels of Asians versus North Africans and because of the colonial connection with immigrants from Suriname and the lack thereof with Turks? Or is it because Asians and Surinamers are not Muslim, while North Africans and Turks are? Or is there some other reason for these differences?

It is precisely the need to answer these questions that has led to a growing literature on Islamophobia. In an instructive article, Erik Bleich (2011) points to the fact that the term appeared on the scene quite recently, dating it to the late 1990s. Moreover, it was first used by political activists and commentators, and thus was used loosely and often with a polemical edge. He contends that it entered into the realm of a social science concept with a 1997 study funded by the center-left Runnymede Trust on the impact that Islamophobia was having on British race relations. Despite its problematic provenance, he concludes that it is better to maintain the term and shape it into a useful analytical tool rather than, as some have suggested, abandoning it. He does so by defining it as *"indiscriminate negative attitudes or emotions directed at Islam or Muslims"* (Bleich 2011: 1582, italics in the original), thereby making it part of the subset of concepts used to study intolerance (see also Taras 2013).

Reviewing various polling sources in two countries, Britain and France, Bleich (2009) concluded that over a two-decade period running from 1988 to 2008, anti-Muslim prejudice rose in both countries and that, compared to other religious groups, Muslims are viewed with considerable suspicion. They have, in short, moved downward on the ethno-racial hierarchy. However, they have not landed on the bottom, for there are some ethnic groups that fare worse. These include Asians and Arabs, which, given that these ethnic categories overlap considerably with Islam, reveals the dual-edged character of xenophobia. The group that was consistently located at the bottom of the hierarchy is the Roma – which is probably little consolation to Muslims.

During this time period, right-wing extremist groups, such as the English Defence League in Britain and neo-Nazi groups in various continental countries, have proliferated, and radical right political parties have seen their fortunes rise in the polls. Three of the latter stand out for their electoral success: the Austria Freedom Party (FPÖ), the Danish People's Party (DFP), and the Swiss SVP discussed in the introduction to this chapter. Other parties have also gained parliamentary footholds, including the Party for Freedom in the Netherlands and the True Finns. These parties are not alike in all respects. The True Finns, for example, can be described as a right-wing populist party that supports the traditional welfare state while attempting to promote an ethnic versus civic version of national identity (Saukkonen 2013: 288–9). On the other hand, Greece's Golden Dawn is a violence-prone fascist party. In other words, from the perspective of the political mainstream, these parties can be located on a spectrum ranging from the distasteful to the vile. What the radical right parties share in common, according to Cas Mudde (2012: 31), is the way they frame debates over immigration issues in terms of "two main themes: a cultural threat (recently amalgamated as a cultural-religious threat) and a security threat (recently amalgamated as a criminal-terrorist threat). Secondary themes include economic competition and an anti-elite/anti-politics narrative."

These themes are not confined to the radical right. Indeed, the idea that Islamic values and practices are incapable of fitting into modern European culture is a theme that one can find across the political spectrum. Muslims are perceived to be a problem because they are viewed as incapable of becoming truly integrated into Europe. Instead, they are seen as transplanting their worldview onto European soil. Seen in conspiratorial terms, whereby Muslims are engaged in a concerted effort to dominate Europe demographically and culturally, this is depicted as the emergence of "Eurabia." Stressing the paranoid character of such thinking and the parallel to the anti-Semitism of a century earlier, Nasar Meer (2013: 391, 393) dubs this "the protocols of Eurabia," and points to intellectuals such as Orianna Fallaci, Thilo Sarrazin, and Niall Ferguson who have trafficked in these ideas. We turn to one representative example below, Christopher Caldwell, whom John Bowen (2012a: 51) has described as "the most knowledgeable of the recent European-Islamic threat writers."

Islam in Europe

The argument is simply stated: the barrier to the incorporation of new immigrants in contemporary Europe is religion, or to be more precise, Islam. Given the relatively small Muslim population in the United States, it is not surprising that for those who voice concerns about the erosion of a distinct form of American identity, Islam does not loom large from their perspective as a source of the problem. This stands in stark contrast to Western Europe today, as Christopher Caldwell's *Reflections on the Revolution in Europe* (2009) attests. Bowen (2012a: 52) notes that the book's title seeks affiliation with the thought of Edmund Burke, seen in many quarters as the quintessential reasonable conservative, perhaps, as Adam Gopnik (2013: 68) has suggested, because his "doctrines are foggy" and thus open to differing interpretations. Caldwell is an American journalist working for the *Financial Times* and serving as a senior editor at the conservative *Weekly Standard*. His is a far-ranging book that strives hard to appear impartial, but a passage in which he expresses sympathy for the views of Enoch Powell (whose 1968 "rivers of blood" speech voiced concern about an immigrant "invasion" and its violent prospects, while declaring his opposition to pending anti-discrimination legislation) and Norman Tebbit (remembered for his 1990 cricket test of national loyalty) is revealing (Caldwell 2009: 147–8).

While Caldwell's book can be seen as in many respects akin to Samuel Huntington's *Who Are We? The Challenges to America's National Identity* (2004), it operates at a different level of analysis, at the level that Benjamin Nelson (1973) described as "civilizational complexes and intercivilizational encounters." Caldwell is not concerned with Turkish guest workers in Germany per se, nor is he concerned with Algerians in France or Pakistanis in Britain. Rather, he is concerned with Muslims in Christian Europe – with a further qualification that Christian Europe has become an increasingly secular Europe.

That being said, he realizes that Turks were welcomed into Germany in the post-war reconstruction period as guest workers essential to helping the nation by remedying severe labor shortages. The intergovernmental arrangements that defined the German guest worker policies viewed these laborers as temporary sojourners who would, when their services were no longer needed, return home. As such, there was no need to raise issues about integration. Germans had invited Turks in and because they had done so, they had an obligation to be hospitable to their guests. However, the guests have a reciprocal obligation, which is to refuse to transform themselves into Simmel's (1950 [1908]: 402) stranger, the person "who comes today and stays tomorrow." In this regard, Caldwell (2009:71) quotes approvingly Hans Magnus Enzensberger's assertion that, "The guest is sacred, but he may not tarry."

From this perspective, Algerians in France and Pakistanis in Britain are in this regard no different than Turks in Germany. They are simply labor migrants who should have been temporary guest workers but instead became permanent residents. Caldwell elides the fact that unlike Turks in Germany, these particular immigrants constitute the postcolonial subjects of empire, and as such came to the metropole with considerable familiarity respectively with French and British culture and customs. To have addressed this fact would have required considering the varied ways in which the colonists' cultures may have impacted and interpenetrated the cultures of the colonized. But Caldwell's concern is not with relations in the periphery, but in the metropole, relations that are the consequence of mass migration.

Immigration in contemporary Europe is perceived to be a significant problem. In an especially revealing section of the book titled "Civilization and Decadence," Caldwell (2009: 20) warns that "'Advanced' cultures have a long track record of underestimating their vulnerability to 'primitive' ones." Placing the words "advanced" and "primitive" in quotation marks is an indication of an ambivalence running through the text. On the one hand, Caldwell characterizes Islam as the product of a great world civilization, but on the other hand its adherents in Europe are in some unspecified way less developed than their European counterparts and a clear and present danger to the continent.

Part of the book addresses issues of marginalization, self-segregation, poverty, and the social problems associated with ghetto life – or in other words, with issues grounded in social conditions and the habits and mores of people that represent shared behavior, which, to borrow from Nelson (1973: 82) needs "to be differentiated from higher level cultural structures." However, it becomes clear that the crux of the problem does not rest at this level, but precisely at the higher level of cultural structures. Why is Islam a problem? Caldwell argues that it is because taken as either religion or culture, it cannot be squared with the religious tradition and culture of Europe, which has in the contemporary context increasingly been defined in terms of a secular, or one might say post-Christian worldview.

Islam is a "hyper-identity," and in the European context it constitutes an "adversary culture" (Caldwell 2009: 158–62 and 171–3). What this means for Muslim immigrants is that they have two options: to remain a Muslim and thereby an outsider – the perpetual Other – or to abandon Islam in order to become a European. Caldwell is convinced that there is no third way, one in which immigrants become European Muslims in the way that Huntington thought Roman Catholics in the past became American Catholics. Muslims cannot remain Muslims and fit into Europe, and given Caldwell's sense that on the ground Muslims are opting to maintain their inherited culture, the result is that immigration "is not enhancing or validating European culture, it is supplanting it" (Caldwell 2009: 20).

Operating at a civilizational level of analysis, Caldwell shares Huntington's views about the immutability and incommensurability of culture. He ignores the empirical literature on patterns of immigrant adjustment in Europe that would call these views into question. Caldwell appears at times to go beyond Huntington by adding to their shared view of culture a conviction that immigrants are what Harold Garfinkel (1967: 69) termed "cultural dopes," people who, to use a succinct definition of the term offered by Robert Brym and Cynthia Hamlin (2009: 84), "are empty vessels into which society pours a defined assortment of goals, beliefs, symbols, norms, and values," these cultural elements thereby "determin[ing] the actions of individuals." Yet at other times, he hints at the possibility that Muslims could, if they opted to, free themselves from their earlier identity in order to transform themselves into Europeans.

Huntington (2004: 171) did not believe that it was Mexicans alone that constituted the problem. Rather it was the combination of Mexicans and multiculturalism, which he depicts as "an anti-Western ideology." It is likewise the case with Caldwell, for a factor contributing to Muslim resistance to becoming European is that multiculturalism's spokespersons have encouraged them to preserve their cultural heritages while disparaging all that is European. He writes that, "By now it is almost second nature for Westerners to assume that anything familiar, traditional, and Western is to be opposed; and anything discomfort-inducing and foreign to be protected." The result, Caldwell wrote in a subsequent essay, amounts to the Islamic "colonization" of European territory. He describes what he means in the following passage:

> But there is a more important reason [than mere demographic accounts] why "colonization" well describes the influx of the past half-century. It is that the terms governing this transformation are set by the immigrants and not by the natives, who started off not caring, and wound up not daring, to impose too many rules on their new neighbors. (Caldwell 2012: 31)

Here one can see a parallel with Burke. Gopnik (2013: 72) writes that, "Burke overrates the [French] revolutionaries so passionately that one slowly senses the odd message of this and similar paranoias: it is not that the other side has more faults; it is that the other side possesses virtues that we have surrendered." In Caldwell's case, the problem is that Muslims take their culture seriously, while Europeans no longer hold deeply held convictions, especially about religion. In making such claims, Caldwell implicitly raises three questions: (1) what is multiculturalism? (2) have states actually been as ineffectual as his account would suggest in applying existing laws concerning church–state relations to new circumstances? and (3) has there been no success in integrating Muslims into the public sphere and Islam as one of a number of religions in pluralist democracies?

The Multicultural Drama

Critics of multiculturalism abound. Timothy Garton Ash (2012: 33) suggested that, "Painful though this will be to those who have expended their academic careers on multiculturalism, the term should be consigned to the conceptual dustbin of history." Variations on this theme have been voiced for some time in intellectual circles, a part of a larger backlash against multiculturalism (Vertovec and Wessendorf 2010; Alexander 2013). One of the most provocative critiques is contained in the work of Dutch sociologist Paul Scheffer, a former journalist and prominent figure in the Dutch Labour Party. In summarizing his ideas, it is necessary to move from a controversial journalistic essay that appeared in 2000, "The Multicultural Drama," to a scholarly book, *Immigrant Nations* (2011, first published in Dutch in 2007).

The essay begins by asserting that the decision to permit police officers to wear turbans was indicative of "cultural confusion." Scheffer paints a pessimistic portrait of what he concludes are failed efforts at the integration of immigrants, with the result being that even after several generations in the Netherlands, the offspring of immigrants lag behind in terms of socioeconomic success. He also faults his fellow citizens for their "boundless faith in elites" who have convinced the public that resurrecting the old pillarization policies for new times is the answer to the issue of immigrant, and particularly Islamic, integration.

The old scheme, which created separate institutional spheres for Catholics, Protestants, and Social-Democrats, was predicated on the assumption that "the pillars carried the roof," or in other words, each contributed to the national identity and kept the nation whole. The problem with Islam is that it has not liberalized, and in particular resists the idea that religion and politics are separate spheres. The result is that the new instantiation of pillars, now known as multiculturalism, is actually a "house of cards" and an anything goes "cultural of tolerance has now reached its limits" (Scheffer 2012 [2000]: 4–7). The two problematic manifestations of multiculturalism are that the Dutch no longer appear capable of articulating what their national identity actually means and secondly they are content to remain isolated from newcomers, who in turn are frustrated because of their isolation. The consequence is that the "multicultural drama that is taking place is the biggest threat to social peace" (Scheffer 2012 [2000]: 14).

The book – based on his doctoral dissertation – is considerably more nuanced than the article. Moreover, it reveals both a command of the scholarship on immigration and a familiarity with and an ability to compare and contrast immigration a century ago from immigration today. Scheffer (2011: 34) is also less pessimistic than Caldwell, whom he depicts as being too "gloomy." This does not prevent him from advocating more restrictive immigration policies. But he describes immigration incorporation as a long and arduous process, one that takes time and occurs over the course of generational succession. He also appreciates that it is a two-way street insofar as the receiving society has to be prepared to embrace the newcomers and to adjust in some ways to their presence. He understands ambivalence and alienation to be characteristic features of the immigrant experience, and that conflict is both typical and can actually help in the process of inclusion. But he does not share the conclusions drawn by scholars such as Dutch social historian Leo Lucassen (2005) that the evidence to date provides grounds for thinking that immigrant incorporation today is likely to follow the pattern of the past.

As such, he is representative of intellectuals who are concerned about national solidarity (Scheffer 2011: 124–5), which, as David Hollinger (2006: 25) notes, is a reflection of a feeling of deep unease about how to answer the question, "Who are we?" The reasons for Scheffer's particular anxiety were evident in the 2000 essay. On the one hand, he is concerned that Islam is resistant to incorporation into secular cultures and liberal democratic political systems. Here his treatment is more nuanced than in the essay, for he sees Islam as a house divided. There is a minority that wants at all costs to avoid the poisoning influences of the West, seen most pristinely in the impact of the writings of the highly influential Sayyid Qutb, the intellectual progenitor of the Muslim Brotherhood. But there are also reform-minded figures ranging from the complex case of Tariq Ramadan to more overtly liberal figures. Scheffer (2011: 272) portrays a battle over who will define Islam in Europe, voicing his concern that at the moment he thinks the reformers have been less successful than he might have hoped.

On the other hand, the Dutch are accused of creating and perpetuating a "culture of avoidance" (Scheffer 2011: 109–40). They avoid addressing what it means to be Dutch in an increasingly diverse society, and they avoid engaging in social relations – as fellow workers, neighbors, friends, and citizens – with newcomers. In this connection, he qualifies his opposition to multiculturalism, contending that he is a critic of its strong version rather than its moderate variants. However, without indicating how he distinguishes the two, he points to his major complaints: multiculturalism encourages cultural relativism, it is backward looking, and it fails to appreciate the significance of citizenship as a unifying status (Scheffer 2011: 197–203).

Critics of Scheffer have suggested that he operates with a nostalgia about feeling at home that encourages "us" to define what it means to be Dutch so that "they" can be held to account if they fail in the task of becoming Dutch like us (Duyvendak 2011: 100). In an insightful review of the book, Robert van Krieken (2012: 469) convincingly concludes that:

> Rather than seeing the Netherlands as an example of the failure of multiculturalism, it shows how the Netherlands has an imperfect take on what it means to be multicultural. Scheffer's book suggests [unintentionally] that the task is not one of abandoning multiculturalism, but of understanding it better, and engaging it with renewed vigor.

We will revisit multiculturalism and its implications for the incorporation of religious minorities later in the chapter, but it is first necessary to turn to church–state relations and then draw out their implications for immigrant integration.

Church–State Relations

The modern nation-states of Western Europe took form at the moment that Christendom on the continent was fractured by the Protestant Reformation that led to a sustained period of religious wars. Conflict ended, in the oft-recounted account, with the Treaty of Westphalia in 1648. An era of peace was achieved when it was agreed that the religion of any particular state would be determined by the religion of the ruler (*Cujus regio, ejus religio,* the religion of the ruler is the religion of the people). Thus it was that religious pluralism took hold, though a very qualified pluralism. For one thing, the varieties of legitimate religion were limited to Catholicism and Protestantism, and for another, pluralism existed only in a trans-state perspective, not within any particular nation.

But this set the stage for more far-reaching changes in church–state relations and the place of religion in public life. Tariq Modood and Riva Kastoryano (2006: 162) succinctly summarize what transpired, as the idea of a religious monopoly within states was "chipped away at. Not only did toleration come to be seen as equally important but the Enlightenment of the eighteenth century in various ways challenged the Christian faith, the authority of the Church, and the promotion of religion by the state."

This process of political secularization entailed, in somewhat distinctive ways depending on the nation in question, two aspects: (1) the admixture of institutional differentiation whereby religion, state, economy, and civil spheres attained their own relative autonomy; and (2) religious pluralism protected by law and culturally embedded in values supportive of mutual toleration (Maclure and Taylor 2011). But political secularization is only part of the story of the historical trajectory of the Occidental world, for this "secular age" is also characterized by, in Charles Taylor's (2007:

352) words, "the expanding universe of unbelief." While political and cultural secularization are analytically distinct, they interact in complex and context-specific ways, and as such have different implications for varied understandings – both among and within nations – of the proper role of religion vis-à-vis the public sphere.

Focusing specifically on political secularism, Modood (2012) distinguishes between radical and moderate versions. Using different terminology, Ahmet Kuru (2009) offers an insightful comparative account of three different overtly secular political regimes: France, Turkey, and the United States. What Modood refers to as radical, Kuru designates as "assertive" secularism, while he characterizes the moderate variant as "passive." In his view, both France and Turkey are examples of the former, while the United States is an exemplar of the latter. Kuru writes (2009: 11):

> Assertive secularism requires the state to play an "assertive" role to exclude religion from the public sphere and confine it to the private domain. Passive secularism demands that the state play a "passive" role by allowing the public visibility of religion. Assertive secularism is a "comprehensive doctrine," whereas passive secularism mainly prioritizes state neutrality toward such doctrines.

Confining ourselves here to the United States and France, as discussed in chapter 3, the operative concept in the former is disestablishment, derived from the First Amendment's articulation of church–state relations in a formulation that is on the surface remarkably simple: "Congress shall make no law respecting an establishment of religion, or prohibiting the free exercise thereof." That the interpretation of the amendment is not so simple can be seen in the conflicting positions between those who advocate a position that emphasizes the willingness of the state to accommodate to religion versus those who call for a strict wall of separation between religious institutions and the state.

Kuru contends that while the distinction between accommodationists and separatists is to large extent accurate, in fact the competing perspectives are actually more varied than that. He distinguishes the Christian right from other accommodationists, and strict separatists (the new atheists, for example) from their more moderate counterparts. In his view, only the strict separatists want to exclude religion entirely from the public sphere. At the same time, it is only the Christian right that seeks to promote the cultural hegemony of Christianity. When it comes to certain policy preferences, both categories of accommodationists support prayer in public schools and state funding of religious schools, while both categories of separatists reject those policy proposals (Kuru 2009: 54).

It is generally argued that the French policy of *laïcité*, reflecting a history of religious conflict dating to the French Revolution, constitutes a more radical type of secularism than after the American. The history since 1789 was often tumultuous. In the wake of the Revolution, Catholicism was rejected as the state religion but with the Concordat of 1801 it became defined as the hegemonic religion of France. The nineteenth century pitted Catholics and secularists in an ongoing cultural war, seen vividly in the fault lines that characterized the Dreyfus Affair (Fournier 2013: 285–308).

Though the idea of *laïcité* had its origins in the mid-nineteenth century, it was the passage of the Third Republic's 1905 Law on the Separation of the Churches and the State that planted it in the nation's legal system. The law parallels the First Amendment in asserting state neutrality in the religious domain and the freedom of religious expression. One way in which it differs from the United States is a provision of the law defining public powers related to religious institutions. The law was the product of a compromise between Catholics and secularists. In the nineteenth century the state funded four state-proscribed religions: Catholicism, Calvinism, Lutheranism, and Judaism (the last three in combination amounting to less than 2 percent of the French population). The rationale for such funding tended to be articulated in terms of providing compensation for the confiscation of church property in the aftermath of the French Revolution. This practice of direct funding ended with the 1905 law, but a new arrangement was created whereby the state owned worship buildings and thus it assumed responsibility for maintaining them.

Both the American and French versions of church–state relations treat the state as responsible for insuring freedom of religious conscience as part of the larger package of constitutionally guaranteed individual rights. The United States has done so in a context characterized by a history of accommodating diversity and by, in legal scholar Peter Schuck's (2003) phrase, a preference for "keeping government at a safe distance." In contrast, according to Raphaël Liogier (2009: 25) "interference in religion by public authorities is the norm rather than the exception," comparing the French state to sports referees. The state, for example, serves as an arbiter in determining which organizations are bona fide religions and which are "cults," the former achieving the status of legitimate institutions and accruing such benefits as tax-exempt status, whereas the latter are seen as potential threats to public life.

If Americans are anxious about an overreaching state, the French are concerned about the potential challenge to social unity caused by factions. This is a reflection of the difference between the Lockean vision of the Americans versus Rousseau's social contract for the French. Bowen (2006: 15; see also Joppke 2009: 29) summarizes the difference as that of the American commitment to "freedom from the state" versus the French quest for "freedom through the state."

Complicating the picture are nations that are not strictly secular, but instead either make provision for an established state church – with the Anglican Church in Britain constituting the paradigmatic example, but also including Lutheran State churches in Denmark, Iceland, and Norway – and corporatist systems such as Germany and Italy. Freedom of religious expression is protected similarly to the more explicitly political secular states, as is religious diversity. Nevertheless, in these two models, either a single religion is privileged or two or more religions are accorded special status vis-à-vis other religions (Fetzer and Soper 2005). From the point of view of Tariq Modood, an advocate of multiculturalism who is particularly invested in the incorporation of Muslims in Britain, a state church need not necessarily be seen as an impediment to inclusion. Indeed, he thinks that a more pluralistic understanding of the nation's religious landscape is possible, taking comfort in Prince Charles' assertion that as monarch he would seek to be the "Defender of Faith" rather than the "Defender of *the* Faith" (Modood 2005: 145).

Given these different institutional arrangements defining church–state relations, one can expect to find variations in responses to the growing presence of Islam. And at the same time, there is evidence of convergence among pluralist democracies in terms of how their respective legal systems address matters associated with the status of religious organizations. As such, religion is viewed, at least implicitly, as not simply a right of private individuals, but as a collective right possessed by a community of people sharing a religious faith and committed to structuring their life together according to that faith. Differences, however, persist in defining the proper place of those religious communities in relation to the public sphere. We look below at the form that various states' roles have taken in promoting integration, and after that, in a discussion of multiculturalism, we will turn to the content – or in other words, the primary issues provoking controversy and necessitating negotiation.

The State's Role in Muslim Integration

During the initial period of labor migration in the decades after World War II, European governments tended to assume that Muslim migrants were temporary workers, whether or not an official guest worker policy was in place. As a consequence, as Jonathan Laurence (2012) has pointed out, those governments did little to facilitate the integration of these newcomers into the receiving societies. This period was defined by the emergence of what he calls "Embassy Islam," which left the role of addressing the religious needs of Muslims in Europe to third parties. Laurence distinguishes two types of Embassy Islam. The first entails a role played by the main sending countries in seeking to maintain connections in order to bolster a commitment to a national culture as defined by those in power, and in the process stave off the challenges posed by both leftist and Islamist political movements. A state-sanctioned version of Islam was deemed to be a potentially useful antidote to ideological challenges to a regime's legitimacy within its diasporic community. In this regard, the actions of the state and the religious personnel deployed to advance the cause parallel in many respects the past actions of the Italian and Mexican governments, both in a cooperative relationship with the Catholic Church, discussed in chapter 4 (Choate 2008; Fitzgerald 2009).

The second type of Embassy Islam is less strictly nationalistic, but instead part of a quest for a pan-Islamist presence in Europe – with Laurence (2012: 33) pointing to the prominence of both Pakistan and Saudi Arabia, "who fashioned their foreign policy in the guise of heirs to the Caliphate." In this variant, the political goals are more ambitious and more potentially challenging to the European host societies. Laurence (2012: 70–104) completes his account by adding yet one more version of Islam in Europe that is not attached to the policies of sending states, the approach advanced by the proponents of Political Islam. This minority, often well-educated exiles who had run afoul of state authorities in the homeland, found an institutional home early on in organizations such as the Muslim Brotherhood and subsequently in an array of other organizations with similar goals (see also Kepel 2004; Roy 2004). Embassy Islam, especially in its nationalist version, projected itself as an alternative or antidote to Political Islam.

With this contextual backdrop, Laurence (2012: 163–244) chronicles the development since the 1990s of a robust effort on the part of Western European states to actively promote the integration of their Muslim minorities, in part by helping to establish an Islamic institutional presence that contributes to, rather than militates against, the incorporation of Muslims into European society. He refers to this policy shift as one that is intent on the "domestication" of Islam in Europe, which has been undertaken in order "to fashion *national* citizens who are *less* globally interlinked" (Laurence 2012: 11; see also Bowen 2004 and recall Waldinger 2007 on caging).

In pursuing this objective, he contends that the seven countries with the largest Muslim populations in Europe – Belgium, France,

Germany, Italy, the Netherlands, Spain, and the United Kingdom – "have followed remarkably similar pathways to managing their relations with Islam and they display parallel policy developments" (Laurence 2012: 15). Of central importance is the creation of Islam Councils that are intended to shape state–mosque relations and bring both Embassy and Political Islam into the fold, in the process redefining them. Stressing that the outcomes of what has transpired over the two-decade-long efforts aimed at domestication are at best imperfect, Laurence nonetheless concludes that such efforts have contributed to advancing a "broader trend toward greater religious freedom and institutional representation for Islam in Europe" (Laurence 2012: 6).

This view is embraced by Christian Joppke and John Torpey in their recent comparative study of the legal integration of Islam in four countries, the two largest nations in continental Europe – France and Germany – and Canada and the United States in North America. They write that, "the institutional accommodation of Islam in Europe has been more successful than is suggested by [figures such as Zolberg and Woon, and Nussbaum]," and moreover the socioeconomic status of the generational offspring of the immigrants and not Islam is "the root problem" accounting for failures of successful integration (Joppke and Torpey 2013: 11). Contending that their focus is not on the content of Islam, but rather on the responses of liberal states to Islam, they describe themselves as "agnostic" as to whether Islam is a threat to or compatible with liberal principles (Joppke and Torpey 2013: 14). In pointing to liberalism's shortcomings and questioning its capacity to address human diversity, they write from within – to borrow from Ira Katznelson (1996) – "liberalism's crooked circle."

Joppke and Torpey, while agreeing that a convergence along the lines depicted by Laurence is occurring, stress that at the same time nation-specific features remain salient and yield different approaches and outcomes. Comparing France and Germany, they frame the chapter on the former in terms of the "limits of excluding" and the latter in terms of the "limits of including" (see also Kastoryano 2004). Put another way, as they do, France has a problem with religious freedom, while Germany has a problem with religious equality. France, as has been evident from *l'affaire du foulard* (the headscarf debate) in the 1990s to the 2010 prohibition against wearing the burqa in public – which resulted in riots in Trappes in the summer of 2013 as a reaction to enforcing the law (*Economist* 2013) – has claimed that *laïcité* necessitates the exclusion of religion from the public sphere.

Drawing on various understandings of this concept, French policy makers and public intellectuals have justified, in John Bowen's (2011a) phrase, "controlling Muslim bodies." Thus, Patrick Weil (2009: 2709) writes in defense of the headscarf ban that "it is not absurd to think that the majority of Muslim families have felt relieved" because they won't be pressured by the fundamentalists to take up the veil. At the same time, Islam has achieved corporate status in France, placing it in a comparable position to other state-designated religions, and advantageously compared to those organizations designated as cults.

While Germany has not been immune to the issues associated with the veil, it has been less fraught than in France, the most controversial case involving a Muslim teacher (Joppke 2009: 53–80). This is a reflection of the fact that religious freedom is not the central problem in Germany. Indeed, Edward Eberle (2004) has argued that Germany offers greater protection for religious expression than the United States, and a claim that can no doubt be subject to debate. However, the central dilemma concerning liberalism and Islam in this case is less about individual religious rights than about the corporate status of Islam. Having a long-established policy of incorporating Christian denominations, in effect, into the state, to date the state has proven itself to be unwilling to offer Islam similar corporate status. And indeed, it is not simply that Islam has not attained collective parity with the Christian churches, but it finds itself in an inferior position to Judaism. This, at least, is the implication to be drawn from the example Joppke and Torpey (2013: 63–4) cite regarding the Jewish exemption from the provisions of the 1986 Animal Protection Act, which has resulted in Jews being permitted to maintain kosher slaughter practices, while Muslims are prohibited from implementing halal slaughter practices. Subsequent judicial decisions have granted in limited circumstances the right of individuals to obtain meat derived from ritual slaughtering practices, but this has been defined in individual and not corporate terms (Joppke and Torpey 2013: 65–6).

One could expand on the differences in state approaches to the integration of Muslims and of Islam by turning to other case studies in Europe and elsewhere, but the point has been made in the French/German comparison. State approaches will differ depending on the particular interplay of any number of factors, ranging from established legal understandings of church–state relations to the size of the Muslim population, the origins of that population, the prominence of Political Islam, the nation's political landscape (e.g., how significant right-wing political parties are), and public opinion. While considerable attention has been paid to the role played by differing national models (e.g., Kastoryano 2002), Bowen (2012b) has stressed that deeply rooted schemas can coexist in any society, with competing and contradictory schemas in people's minds in ways that allow for dramatic shifts and reversals in normative demands that are historically contingent, and that can result in revisions, rejections, and rehabilitations of policy approaches. In short, an overemphasis on national models projects a perspective that sees policy approaches as more internally uniform and consistent than reality would indicate.

Multiculturalism:
Official Policy and Unofficial Practice

Recall Timothy Garton Ash's call earlier in this chapter for consigning multiculturalism to the conceptual dustbin. He is on firm footing when arguing that the concept has suffered as a consequence of the heated polemics often associated with it, along with its definitional plasticity and thus vagueness. But this is a problem shared by any number of concepts, including what is generally taken to be the antidote to multiculturalism, namely assimilation (Yanasmayan 2011). Others have pointed out that most of the more dispassionate and sophisticated discussions of multiculturalism are framed in terms of normative theory (Bloemraad, Korteweg. and Yurdakul 2008; Koopmans 2013; for an illustrative normative defense, see Bader 2003 and 2007), presumably thereby lessening their potential utility as a tool of sociological analysis.

Despite these challenges to the articulation of a distinctively sociological account of multiculturalism, promising efforts have been made in developing such a concept. Jeffrey Alexander (2006: 425–57) has done so by treating it as one of three pathways to marginalized minority group incorporation into the societal mainstream. Others have done so by focusing on multiculturalism less as a macro-level process and more as a practice entailing claims-making that is amenable to analysis at the micro- or mezzo-levels. Italian theorist Giuseppe Sciortino (2003: 264) offered a succinct definition of multiculturalism as entailing "political claims expressed by actors on behalf of a social category." In a recent article on Islamic religious rights in Western Europe, Sarah Carol and Ruud Koopmans (2013) employ the concept of claims and counterclaims in examining the conflictual engagements of Muslims and their opponents. It is, in short, possible to view multiculturalism sociologically in two reciprocal ways: (1) as a form of claims-making by minority groups; and (2) as a way that the dominant society and its political system accommodate to and manage diversity.

Multiculturalism as Claims-Making

Kivisto has put flesh on the bones of Sciortino's thesis about multiculturalism as claims-making in his article titled "We *Really* Are All Multiculturalists Now" (2012). He begins by pointing out that claims-making occurs within the public spaces of civil society. The claims-makers are the more or less legitimate, contested or uncontested spokespersons for a particular type of social category that he refers to as a "community of fate," with the claims being advanced predicated on concerns about the well-being not only of members of that community, but of the community itself – what he refers to as the fate of the community. This understanding of a community of fate – a term used in widely varied contexts and with no shared systematic definition – is influenced by Michael Dawson's (1994) depiction of the belief in a "linked fate" that informs much of African American politics. Claims may be concerned with redistribution, recognition, or some combination of the two. The two audiences to which claims are directed are the public at large and the state, the latter being crucial when claims call for specific legislative actions, court decisions, or policy initiatives.

Five types of political claims can be distinguished: exemption, accommodation, preservation, redress, and inclusion. All are predicated on the idea that the community of fate has what Avishai Margalit and Moshe Halbertal (1994) describe as a "right to culture." Very briefly, the five types can be defined in the following way. Exemption refers to a demand for differential treatment of the group based on the conviction that such exemption is necessary if certain group practices deemed essential to cultural identity are to be permitted. Differential treatment takes the form of waiving the application of certain laws, rules, and regulations. Accommodation is similar to exemption in its purpose, but it usually does not require waivers. Rather, it entails finding mutually agreeable adjustments, particularly in schools and workplaces that make it possible for individuals to be integrated into the societal mainstream while also being true to their cultural identity.

In both cases, group members themselves are attempting to find ways that they can promote the continuation of their cultural identity and community. Neither calls for the intervention of the state or for actors in the larger society to play an active role in maintaining the viability of the group over time. This is precisely what is called for in the third type, preservation. Here the fear is that without the proactive support of the larger society, the future of the community is doomed. Calls to protect minority languages is a case in point, as sometimes the claims-makers call upon the state to fund school instruction in the native language, to create a bilingual society, and so forth. As with the fourth type, redress, preservation tends to be more controversial than the first two types. Redress claims are based on the conviction that grave injustices have been inflicted on the community of fate in the past, injustices that can only be remedied by compensatory actions. These are claims typically made by indigenous peoples and ethnonational minorities – and not by immigrants. This is a reflection of the argument advanced by Kymlicka (1995) about which sorts of rights are available to which types of minority groups, with Kymlicka contending that immigrant groups are not able to avail themselves of as robust a range of potential rights as are the other two groups.

The final claim – inclusion – is one that should surprise critics insofar as they see multiculturalism as encouraging the balkaniza-tion of societies. But it is precisely this type of claim that most explicitly reveals the incorporative character of multiculturalism, the primary focus of Alexander's (2006) work. Within this type, there are two subtypes. Rainer Bauböck (2008: 3) describes the first as "celebration multiculturalism," which constitutes a public appreciation of diversity in general and of the groups constitut-ing a particular polity. Whereas this type often takes the form of reaching out or appealing to the public rather than making demands, the second type can involve demands, appeals, or both. What is called for here is an expansion of the boundaries of solidarity by finding room within those boundaries for stigmatized minorities without requiring them to become, in effect, clones of those already inside the boundaries.

Inclusion can entail reconfiguring existing definitions of citizen-ship and of who is and who is not capable of becoming a citizen on equal terms with others. The American civil rights movement is perhaps the paradigmatic instance of such a call for inclusion (Alexander 2006). It can also be seen in other arenas of social life. Thus, the perceptual and discursive shift in the middle of the past century from viewing the United States as a Protestant nation to seeing it as a Judeo-Christian one constituted the inclusion of Judaism under the sacred canopy of American religion and in so doing represented an expansion of that canopy. Similar con-temporary calls to find room for Islam under that canopy, often articulated in terms of viewing it as one of the three Abrahamic religions, can be heard not only in the United States (Williams 2011), but in other countries as well.

Multiculturalism as Accommodation and Management

As noted above, the two audiences to which claims-making is directed are the public at large and the state. Within both audiences are those who embrace multiculturalism in one version or another as well as those opposed to multiculturalism either in terms of various particulars or writ large, with many being located on a continuum between the two poles. The public is inevitably and invariably divided and public opinion is subject to change, leading to much social scientific research, the purpose of which is to ascertain the precise breakdown of attitudes in a particular country at a particular point in time, as well as identifying the cultural, demographic, economic, ideological, psychological, and related factors shaping particular attitudes. At issue here are attitudes toward minorities. While the above makes clear that multiculturalism's ambit includes indigenous peoples and ethnonational minorities, our concern here is with immigrants and religion, thereby excluding from consideration not only certain groups of claims-makers, but issues related to topics other than religion, such as language.

At issue are not simply attitudes toward members of minority groups, but also attitudes regarding governmental policies designed to remedy the inequalities and marginalization experienced by various minority groups. Analytically separating attitudes toward minority groups from attitudes about policies such as those located under the rubric "multiculturalism" means that there are four possible variations: (1) negative attitudes toward minorities and opposition to policies; (2) negative attitudes toward minorities, but support for policies; (3) positive attitudes toward minorities, but opposition to policies; and (4) positive attitudes toward minorities and support for policies. The first and the fourth appear to need little by way of explanation since they reflect ideological consistency, the first reflecting an exclusionary and intolerant worldview and the latter an inclusionary and tolerant one. In the first category, antipathy toward Muslims is matched by antipathy toward multiculturalism, while in the fourth support for Muslims is coupled with support for multiculturalism. The second possibility strikes me as a null cell.

The third, however, is a possibility, as Paul Sniderman and Louk Hagendoorn (2009) indicate in their study of attitudes regarding Dutch multiculturalism. Their contention is that most opponents of multiculturalism are, in fact, tolerant and inclusive. Sniderman has previously drawn parallel conclusions about attitudes toward African Americans and affirmative action, contending that this controversial policy actually contributes to anti-black prejudice (Sniderman and Carmines 1997). He and his colleague see a similar dynamic at play in the way the Dutch are responding to Muslims as a result of their dislike of multiculturalism. They contend that an unintended consequence of multicultural policies is that they stoke anti-Muslim animus. This conclusion has elicited criticism, but it is not necessary to go further into this dispute here, the point being that the possibility needs to be taken into consideration in research, be it at the macro-level on "the public" or on what Gary Fine (2012) refers to as the micro-level of "tiny publics."

While there is considerable empirical research on attitudes toward both minorities and multiculturalism – as evident, for example, in the Eurobarometer and European Social Survey – there is considerably less research to date on actions and on patterns of majority–minority interaction. Given the rising tide of right-wing extremism and the concerns about violent reactions to minorities, it is understandable – indeed, appropriate – that the research that is conducted on interaction often focuses on the problems of racism and xenophobia. However, what this means is that the study of mundane patterns of minority–majority relations in everyday life in increasingly diverse societies is in Europe to large extent a field of research that is only in its earliest stages of development.

Far more attention has been directed to the actions of states that are increasingly charged with the task of "managing diversity" (Hasmath 2011; Rodriguez-Garcia 2010). State actors in liberal democracies are guided by a complex interplay of ideological or philosophical political commitments and instrumental or prag-matic objectives in contexts shaped by political party rivalries. It is within this general framework that state actors respond to the challenges posed by heterogeneity and inequality – and react to the claims made by minority group spokespersons for recognition or

redistribution (Faist 2013). While state actors may be motiva...
by concerns for social justice and equity, they also make decisions predicated on their sense of which policy approaches are
most likely to achieve social harmony and equilibrium. One can
reasonably assume that states, when they do subscribe to multiculturalism in some version or another, are doing so because they
have concluded that it is in the interest of their political system as
a whole and is a benefit to their society at large (Kivisto 2002).
Furthermore, one can expect to find different approaches to multiculturalism predicated on the type of church–state configurations
which influence the politics of recognition and differing welfare
regimes that impact the politics of redistribution.

Quotidian Multiculturalism

Critics of multiculturalism such as Christian Joppke (2010, 2012)
insist that it represents a dramatic challenge to liberalism, while
advocates such as Charles Taylor (1992) and Will Kymlicka
(1995) are equally insistent that a liberal multiculturalism is possible and viable. Joppke further is convinced that to speak of
multiculturalism means you are speaking about the state interven-
ing in ways that are designed to protect diversity. He finds the
idea of ordinary people – from both the majority and minority
communities – developing relations of mutuality predicated on
a recognition and respect for difference to be a "harmless thing"
that is somehow beside the point (Joppke 2012: 861). Contrary
to his view, the idea that ethnic and religious diversity can exist
simultaneously with a shared common identity, whether that be
rooted in the nation-state and based on the notion of citizenship,
as Parsons (1971) suggested, or on the more cosmopolitan ideal
of a shared humanity, as Alexander (2006) proposes, points to
the significance of the realm of civil society. Indeed, not all of the
types of claims discussed above necessarily require state action,
but rather can often be adequately addressed within the framework of civic society. This is certainly true of accommodation and
inclusion.

Whether or not the claims-makers seek state intervention, in making claims they are engaged in civil-society discourse that can result in negotiated settlements – adaptations – mutually agreed upon by both the religious minority and the host society. We look in the following section at evidence of such "multicultural" solutions (the quotation marks indicating that what is occurring may be multicultural by the terms of the analysis presented here, but may well be called something else by the parties involved).

Muslim Claims-Making and Negotiated Solutions

The Multiculturalism Policy Index (MPI) is a widely cited source used to compare multicultural policies cross-nationally. Developed by Will Kymlicka and Keith Banting, the eight broad measures used to construct the index are intended to be relevant to indigenous peoples, ethnonational minorities, and immigrants. Reflecting the creators' Canadian emphasis on ethnicity rather than religion, only one of the factors looks at religion (exemptions from dress codes and Sunday closing legislation, and so forth). In contrast, indicative of the centrality of religious issues for multiculturalism in Europe, Ruud Koopmans' (2013) Indicators of Citizenship Rights for Immigrants (ICRI) contains 14 of 23 indicators that directly address religious rights, and as the name suggests focuses solely on immigrants. Actually, it has a more specific focus on Muslim immigrants, as the following list reveals:

- allowance of ritual animal slaughtering;
- allowance of the Islamic call to prayer;
- the number of purpose-built mosques with minarets (calculated per 100,000 Muslims);
- the existence of separate cemeteries or cemetery sections for Muslims;
- allowance of burial without coffin;
- the number of state-funded Islamic schools (calculated per 100,000 Muslims);
- the share of costs of Islamic schools that is covered by the state;
- Islamic religious classes in state schools;

- the right of female teachers to wear a headscarf;
- the right of female students in primary and secondary schools to wear a headscarf;
- Islamic religious programs in public broadcasting;
- imams in the military;
- imams in prisons;
- the existence and prerogatives of recognized Muslim consultative bodies. (Carol and Koopmans 2013: 172)

Koopmans frames these indicators from the point of view of the state and not as claims-making per se, but if examined from the latter perspective, it is clear that none entail the two most controversial types of claims, preservation and redress. Instead, they would appear to fall into the exemption category (e.g., animal slaughter practices and burial without a coffin) or inclusion (e.g., the public call to prayer, building mosques, imams serving as military and prison chaplains). Many of the claims entail achieving parity with established Christian denominations (Carol and Koopmans 2013: 167). The particular type of claim at issue for matters related to education is difficult to determine because countries have different policies regarding such matters as state funding for religious schools and religious instruction in public schools.

In Rosmarie van den Breemer and Marcel Maussen's (2012) comparative analysis of state responses to Muslim claims-making regarding Muslim cemeteries and mosque construction in France and the Netherlands, the authors conclude that despite differing church–state models and differences regarding policies about cemetery ownership, both countries have sought to accommodate Muslim claims. They conclude, quite correctly, that the relevant question is not "whether governments accommodate Muslim demands for recognition, but which demands are accommodated, in what ways, and for what reasons" (van den Breemer and Maussen 2012: 279). The context-specific ways in which claims are made and responded to has been explored in Sarah Carol and Ruud Koopmans' (2013) comparative study of six Western European nations with substantial Muslim populations: France,

Germany, the United Kingdom, the Netherlands, Belgium, and Switzerland.

Using a political opportunity model, they contend that those nations that are the most accommodating will provide the space for minority perspectives within the Muslim community to make more "obtrusive" claims. The Netherlands and the United Kingdom are defined as more accommodating than the remaining four countries, and thus in the mix of claims they hypothesize that these two more accommodating nations will experience a higher level of obtrusive claims. The primary example they cite is that of supporting the use of sharia rights in at least some arenas of social life. While it is true that the percentage of claims in the Netherlands and the United Kingdom is higher than in the others, it is also true that the overall percentages for all six nations is low. Whereas the overall percentage for the six nations is 1.8 percent, it is 4.7 percent for the Netherlands and 6 percent for the United Kingdom. These differences are not that pronounced, given the small percentages in all instances.

At the same time, Carol and Koopmans (2013: 187–8) are no doubt right in concluding that the religious rights of Muslims in the "different countries are likely to settle at diverging equilibria, resulting in a domestication of Islam around nationally specific legal and institutional forms." States react differently depending on their particular understanding of church–state relations, and in turn Muslims adapt to specific national contexts accordingly. Bowen (2011b) has illustrated the differential adaptations based on national context by comparing how Muslim leaders have approached the issue of Muslim women seeking a religious divorce in Britain, France, and the United States.

It should be remembered that however much Islam has been the focus of attention in Western Europe, religious rights issues have been raised by other religions, as well. The case of Hindu cremation practices at the beginning of this chapter is a case in point, as are Sikh demands in the United Kingdom to be exempt from wearing motorcycle helmets to accommodate the turban and to be clean-shaven in work environments involving the handling of food (Parekh 2000: 265). And in all instances, the question of the proper role of religion in the public sphere surfaces. Jürgen Habermas (2006: 9) writes that, "The liberal state must not transform the requisite *institutional* separation of religion and politics into an undue *mental* and *psychological* burden for those of its citizens who follow a faith." At the same time, he contends that people of faith entering into a pluralist public sphere must engage in a process of translation, one that entails a positive "epistemic" stance toward other religions and worldviews, the autonomy of secular knowledge, and the privileging of secular arguments in the public arena (Habermas 2006: 14).

The fear of Islam's critics is that the basic tenets of the religion preclude adopting such an epistemic stance. Taken to extremes, Islamophobia is preoccupied with Islamist terrorism, with a conviction that Islam and democracy do not mix, and that Islam is bad for women. However, when anxieties about legitimate concerns are transformed into fear, occluded from view is the fact that Islam is not monolithic and immigrants identified as Muslim manifest a wide range of attitudes toward the faith – and to faith in general. Fundamentalism – be it Islamic, Christian, Hindu, or other – is an impediment to multicultural incorporation and to the acceptance of religious pluralism. But the religious mainstreams of the major world religions, including Islam, are open to living in a multicultural society. Tariq Modood and Fauzia Ahmad (2007), for example, have written that in the case of Britain's mainstream Muslims, there is compelling evidence of being open to multiculturalism, provided that multiculturalism makes room for faith as one of the acceptable dimensions of difference.

Returning to the Western European–North American contrast captured in Foner and Alba's "bridge or barrier" distinction, it would appear that at present religion is at some level a barrier to inclusion in Europe, but only to a limited extent and, moreover, it does not necessarily have to be. The process of incorporation has evolved to include not only the immigrant generation, but also the second generation who bring greater acculturation to the receiving society with a willingness to be more overtly critical both of their parents' cultures and that of the settlement society (Killian 2007). One significant change underway involves the second generation's separating of the sending society culture from religion, thereby seeking to purify the latter. What precisely this will mean is not entirely clear. David Voas and Fenella Fleischmann (2012: 538) borrow the contrast made by R. Stephen Warner and colleagues in contending that for this generation their religion is like Teflon, in contrast to Catholicism, which is a Velcro religion (see Warner, Martel, and Dugan 2012). If this means that the young adherents to Islam resist a self-reflexive approach to their religion, it can signal a turn to a rigid fundamentalism. And it can mean that they are unprepared for non-Muslims to critically engage their religious beliefs and practices. For those who believe that the participants in the public sphere are to engage in sustained dialogues with other participants about their understanding of the common good, the question arises about whether, in the words of David Hollinger (2013: 199), "religious ideas should . . . be critically engaged or given a pass."

While the situation on the ground is complicated, the preponderance of evidence to date provides grounds for guarded optimism about the future. The vast majority of Muslims who have migrated from majority Muslim societies to receiving societies in which they are and will continue to be a minority religion have proven willing to adapt to living in pluralist democracies. And where multicultural policies and practices have created a climate in which differences are not eliminated, but instead respected, a domesticated Islam is taking root. This conclusion does not overlook the problems within immigrant communities – most related to socioeconomic and civic marginalization, residential segregation, and attendant problems such as high unemployment levels, poverty, and crime, but also including troubling Islamist minorities. Nor does it overlook the hostility that Muslim immigrants confront and the unwillingness of many in the receiving societies to extend a neighborly hand (Lenard 2012).

The future will be determined by which of the multiple social imaginaries shaping the cultural dynamics of modern Western societies will in the end win out. Will it be shaped by an expansive or a constrictive understanding of collective social life (Taylor 2004)?

6

Epilogue

Twice a year, on July 2 and August 16, the Tuscan city of Siena holds a horse race, the Palio. In a well-established selection process, ten of the city's seventeen *contrade* (communes or neighborhoods) take part in the bare-back event, which is held in the seashell-shaped Piazza del Campo. The bricks of the piazza are covered with sand for the event, which is dangerous for riders and horses alike. Intense rivalries among the *contrade* mark the event and lead to a considerable amount of bargaining between and among competing riders intended to enhance the chances of victory or prevent certain riders from winning. At the same time, the event has become the premier tourist attraction for the city, bringing in substantial amounts of income to local businesses and to the municipality.

The race is steeped in tradition. Indeed, its roots go back seven centuries, to around the time that Siena's history as a city-state reached its zenith. In the course of about two centuries, the political life of Siena had changed dramatically. In the twelfth century, it was ruled by the local bishop. During that time, it became an increasingly important city economically, involved in particular in money-lending and the wool trade. Over time, the nobility chafed at theocratic rule and began to press its ecclesiastical rulers to cede power to the aristocracy. This was achieved in 1167. Over the course of the next century, the aristocracy was in turn challenged, some would say by the *popolani,* or common people, but in point of fact more directly and explicitly they were challenged by the rising mercantile class. The entry of that class into the political elite led to the period of republican government known as the rule under the nine, which ran from 1287 to 1355, an era in which the cultural life of Siena flourished (Bowsky 1981). The nine referred to a rotating selection of leaders drawn by lot. The city lost out in the end to the more powerful city-state to its west, Florence. From that point forward over the centuries, one thing remained clear: though the city had broken from theocratic rule, Catholicism was a central feature of the city's identity, and more specifically, the Virgin Mary was of singular significance. When the Sienese prepared for the famous Battle of Montaperti against its Florentine archrivals, the city was dedicated to the Virgin Mary. This would happen again and again during moments of grave crisis, including the dark days of World War II.

Thus, we return to the Palio, which refers not only to the race itself, but to the prize that goes to the victorious commune, a banner awarded to the winning contrada, which is permitted to display it in its meeting house for the following year. Affectionately, the banner is also referred to as *il drappellone* or *il cencio* – the rag. The Municipal Council of Siena appoints a committee to select the artist to design the banner for each of the two races. For most of the Palio's history, the artists were expected to be from Siena. However, that changed in the 1970s, when new selection policies were enacted. Now, the July race's artist is chosen in an international competition, while for the August race, the artist must be an Italian. Interested artists submit preliminary sketches to the committee so that it has an idea of what the final design might look like. Although the artist is given considerable freedom in designing the banner, a number of features must be present in accordance with regulations that went into effect in 1949. First, there must be an image of the Virgin Mary, more specifically one that is faithful to the Madonna of Provenzano, to whom the race is dedicated. The date of the race must be present, along with the municipal black and white flag, two city emblems, crests depicting the three ancient parts of the city, the local government's coat of arms, and depictions of the ten mascots or animals that symbolize each of the ten contradas entered in the race.

The artist selected for the July 2010 race was Ali Hassoun, a Lebanese-born Muslim who immigrated to Italy in 1982, when he was 18 years old. He studied art for a time in Siena, but has long been based in Milan, where he maintains a studio and lives with his wife, an Italian Catholic. Although the mayor of Siena explained that Mr Hassoun had been selected "because his art is traditional, highly figurative, and easy to enjoy," the *New York Times* headline reporting on the race noted with some understatement that "some bristle at the prize" (Pianigiani 2010: A4). His banner depicted the Virgin Mary at the top of the banner, where in the background Arabic calligraphy points to the nineteenth chapter of the *Qur'an*, which is dedicated to the Madonna. She wears a crown on which appear the symbols of the three Abrahamic religions: the Jewish Star of David, the Christian cross, and the crescent symbol of Islam. The central figure of the banner is St. George, slain dragon at his feet. Attired in traditional medieval armor and holding a bow in his right hand, he wears a black-and-white kaffiyeh. St. George appeared on previous banners, but for Hassoun's purposes he was crucial insofar as he is an object of veneration among both Christians and Muslims.

The banner evoked little controversy within Siena itself. After all, it had been vetted by a committee chosen by leading politicians and they could see in the early designs what was coming. The banner, as tradition calls for, was blessed by the local Catholic bishop and placed on display in the cathedral. For their part, the race participants seemed unfazed. One person summed it up by saying, "We don't really care about the painting. For a contrada person, all that matters is to win the rag. Even it if was blank, we'd still cry over it." However, criticism was quickly voiced from some quarters. The newspaper that serves as the voice of the right-wing Northern League bore the headline, "The Hands of Islam on Siena's Palio," while a conservative Vatican official voiced alarm about the banner "from the spiritual and symbolic point of view" (Pianigiani 2010: A4). The vitriol was on display in various anti-Muslim websites with names such as "Jihad Watch," "Winds of Jihad," and "The Gates of Vienna." Wading through these sites, one can find statements such as the following:

- "Italy has the best artists in the world. Why would anyone pick a Lebanese Muslim to soil the banners of Christian traditions that go back many hundred years?"
- "Utterly disgusting!!! And the PC morons who chose the crap that the muslim painted as a winning entry should be removed from its [sic] position of influence."
- "Let a Mohammedan near anything and they insult it just [sic] look at the 9/11 plane crash site memorial in the USA."
- "Italy is being invaded yet again by the Saracens."
- "Creepy creeping sharia."

In contrast to these inflammatory comments in the blogosphere, this is what the artist said about his work. In a phone interview with a journalist from the *New York Times,* he explained his work in the following way: "My Palio talks about spirituality in general, about religions, about the possible encounter among the three monotheistic religions that allows us to transcend our own faith" (Pianigiani 2010: A4). In an interview reported in the *Arab American News,* he went on to say:

> My way of thinking and my way of making art indeed gave me the vision to do the Palio this way. I believe we of the different religions have the same humanity and believe in the same God. I think that artists see things before they happen, they see history for us. It's a way for people to learn more about their vision of humanity and I think that at this moment in our history it is so important to make some new path to be nearer and closer to each other. (Meyer 2010)

Ali Hassoun's Islamophobic critics advocate a constrictive understanding of collective life, a view that is inherently suspicious of newcomers and hostile to their cultures. Theirs is a worldview predicated on a feeling of discomfort with living in a pluralist society. It has been shaped by religious fundamentalists, who in the quest for absolute certainty seek to repudiate other religions by insisting that theirs is the only true path to salvation. Likewise, it has gained expression in the form of quasi-religious right-wing nationalists who define bright boundaries between "us" and "them" (Allievi 2012; Jaspers and Lubbers 2013).

In the predominantly Christian nations of North America and Western Europe, non-Christian immigrants confront a situation in which those in the receiving society that are hostile to their presence tend to concentrate their critiques on their religious identities, treating them as antithetical to the values of the settlement nation. In contrast, Christian immigrants discover that they are condemned, not for their religious beliefs and affiliations, but for an array of other reasons. Nowhere is this more evident than in the United States, where a large majority of undocumented immigrants happen to come from Christian countries (Hagan 2008). Thus, opposition to their presence focuses on legal status, along with claims that they take jobs from citizens, are inclined to criminal activities, and in other ways prove to be "problems." To further complicate matters, fundamentalism is not confined to members of the receiving society, but can be found among immigrants, too, nowhere more clearly than within the Muslim population of Western Europe (Leiken 2011).

It is important to consider the negative impact on immigrant incorporation of anti-immigrant hostility from fundamentalist and radical right groups and from their counterparts in immigrant communities of groups that reject liberal democratic values and resist the idea of embracing pluralism. These opponents of the vision of Ali Hassoun represent serious impediments to a more expansive understanding of a collective social identity. At the same time, these impediments need to be placed into perspective.

The lessons of a quarter of a century of research on immigrants and religion offer grounds for guarded optimism. For those migrants who are adherents of a faith tradition, religion is an important aspect of personal identity and can serve to facilitate the process of adapting and fitting into the receiving society (chapter 2). Just as the vast majority of immigrants are prepared to change, while simultaneously working to preserve what they consider to be vital aspects of their pre-migration sense of self, so, too have they been prepared to revise their religious organizations in ways that promote inclusion into the receiving society's religious mainstream while maintaining the distinctiveness of their religious traditions (chapter 3). In the process, all of the nations in question have become considerably more religiously diverse than was true in the not-too-distant past (chapter 1).

Contrary to some predictions, religious transnationalism – which at least for the first generation is quite evident – does not appear to stifle inclusion into the receiving society but on the contrary encourages it. While the evidence supporting these conclusions derives largely from the North American context, and it appears that in the United States in particular religion serves as a bridge to inclusion, despite differences in church–state relationships, the evidence points to similar trends in Western Europe. This is true even when the religion in question is Islam, which clearly is at present the religion confronting the greatest challenges to inclusion (chapter 4). In this regard, it is worth recalling Joppke and Torpey's (2013: 11) assessment that institutionally accommodating Islam in Europe has proven to be on the whole rather successful. Institutional accommodation is, of course, not the whole story, but it is a crucial part of that story.

Immigrants on both sides of the Atlantic have been prepared to mobilize in their quest for inclusion. In doing so, they have entered into coalitions with actors from the receiving society who are prepared to support their cause – including representatives from labor unions, political parties, a variety of NGOs, and religious institutions (Voss and Bloemraad 2011). Activists in Christian churches have been prepared to lobby on such issues as reforming immigration laws and combatting prejudice and discrimination, to provide various forms of assistance to immigrants, and at times to defy the state by offering sanctuary to the undocumented (Hondagneu-Sotelo 2007). In this, they have engaged in activities that they take to be mandated by their faith's demand for "radical hospitality" toward the stranger (Kivisto and Mahn 2009; Peschke 2009). In so doing, they are part of a larger effort aimed at enlarging their nation's sacred canopy by bringing newcomers and their faith traditions under it as valid expressions of concern about transcendence and what Paul Tillich (1951) called the "ground of being" (chapter 5). This is what Ali Hassoun meant when speaking about creating a new path where people will be united in their diversity.

References

Abramson, Harold. 1975. "The Religioethnic Factor and the American Experience." *Ethnicity*, 2 (July): 165–77.

—1980. "Religion," pp. 869–75 in Stephan Thernstrom, Ann Orlov, and Oscar Handlin (eds.), *Harvard Encyclopedia of American Ethnic Groups*. Cambridge, MA: Harvard University Press.

Akresh, Ilana Redstone. 2011. "Immigrants' Religious Participation in the United States." *Ethnic and Racial Studies*, 34(4): 643–61.

Alba, Richard D. 1990. *Ethnic Identity: The Transformation of White America*. New Haven, CT: Yale University Press.

Alexander, Jeffrey. 2006. *The Civil Sphere*. New York: Oxford University Press.

—2013. "Struggling over the Mode of Incorporation: Backlash against Multiculturalism in Europe." *Ethnic and Racial Studies*, 36(4): 531–56.

Ali, Monica. 2003. *Brick Lane: A Novel*. New York: Scribner.

Alkumal, Antony W. 1999. "Preserving Patriarchy: Assimilation, Gender Norms, and Second-Generation Korean American Evangelicals." *Qualitative Sociology*, 22(2): 127–40.

Allievi, Stefano. 2012. "Reactive Identities and Islamophobia: Muslim Minorities and the Challenges of Religious Pluralism in Europe." *Philosophy and Social Criticism*, 38(4–5): 379–87.

Aranda, Elizabeth M. 2007. *Emotional Bridges to Puerto Rico: Migration, Return Migration, and the Struggles of Incorporation*. Lanham, MD: Rowman and Littlefield.

Archdeacon, Thomas. 1990. "Immigrant Assimilation and Hansen's Thesis," pp. 42–63 in Peter Kivisto and Dag Blanck (eds.), *American Immigrants and Their Generations*. Urbana: University of Illinois Press.

Audi, Tamara. 2012. "US Top Draw for Christians and Buddhists." *Wall Street Journal*, March 9: A3.

Bader, Veit. 2003. "Religious Diversity and Democratic Institutional Pluralism." *Political Theory*, 31(2): 265–94.

175

References

—2007. "Defending Differentiated Policies of Multiculturalism." *National Identities,* 9(3): 197–215.

Bankston, Carl L. III. 1997. "Bayou Lotus: Theravada Buddhism in Southwestern Louisiana." *Sociological Spectrum,* 17(4): 453–72.

Bankston, Carl L. III and Min Zhou. 1995. "Religious Participation, Ethnic Identification, and Adaptation of Vietnamese Adolescents in an Immigrant Community." *The Sociological Quarterly,* 36(3): 523–34.

—1996. "The Ethnic Church, Ethnic Identification, and the Social Adjustment of Vietnamese Adolescents." *Review of Religious Research,* 38(1): 18–37.

—2000. "De Facto Congregationalism and Socioeconomic Mobility in Laotian and Vietnamese Immigrant Communities: A Study of Religious Institutions and Economic Change." *Review of Religious Research,* 41(4): 453–70.

Basch, Linda, Nina Glick Schiller, and Christina Szanton Blanc (eds.). 1994. *Nations Unbound: Transnational Projects, Postcolonial Predicaments, and Deterritorialized Nation-States.* Basel, Switzerland: Gordon and Breach.

Bauböck, Rainer. 2008. "Beyond Culturalism and Statism: Liberal Responses to Diversity." Eurosphere Working Paper Series, Online Working Paper No. 06. http://www.eurospheres.org. Retrieved November 6, 2010.

Bellah, Robert N., Richard Madsen, William M. Sullivan, Ann Swidler, and Steven M. Tipton. 1985. *Habits of the Heart: Individualism and Commitment in American Life.* Berkeley: University of California Press.

Berg, Travis Vande and Fred Kniss. 2008. "ISKCON and Immigrants: The Rise, Decline, and Rise Again of a New Religious Movement." *The Sociological Quarterly,* 49(1): 79–104.

Berger, Peter. 1969. *The Sacred Canopy: Elements of a Sociological Theory of Religion.* Garden City, NY: Anchor.

Berger, Peter, Effie Fokas, and Grace Davie. 2008. *Religious America, Secular Europe? A Theme and Variations.* Burlington, VT: Ashgate Publishing.

Biswas, Bidisha. 2004. "Nationalism by Proxy: A Comparison of Social Movements among Diaspora Sikhs and Hindus." *Nationalism and Ethnic Politics,* 10(2): 269–95.

Bleich, Erik. 2009. "Where Do Muslims Stand on Ethno-Racial Hierarchies in Britain and France? Evidence from Public Opinion Surveys, 1998–2008." *Patterns of Prejudice,* 43(3): 379–400.

—2011. "What Is Islamophobia and How Much Is There? Theorizing and Measuring an Emerging Comparative Concept." *American Behavioral Scientist,* 55(12): 1581–1600.

Bloemraad, Irene, Anna Korteweg, and Görçe Yurdakul. 2008. "Citizenship and Immigration: Multiculturalism, Assimilation, and Challenges to the Nation-State." *Annual Review of Sociology,* 34: 8–27.

Bodnar, John. 1985. *The Transplanted: A History of Immigrants in Urban America.* Bloomington: Indiana University Press.

References

Bourne, Randolph. 1916. "Trans-National America." *Atlantic Monthly*, July: 1916: 86–97.

Bowen, John. 2004. "Does French Islam Have Borders? Dilemmas of Domestication in a Global Religious Field." *American Anthropologist*, 106(1): 43–55.

—2006. *Why the French Don't Like Headscarves*. Princeton, NJ: Princeton University Press.

—2011a. "How the French State Justifies Controlling Muslim Bodies: From Harm-Based to Values-Based Reasoning." *Social Research*, 78(2): 325–48.

—2011b. "Islamic Adaptations to Western Europe and North America: The Importance of Contrastive Analyses." *American Behavioral Scientist*, 55(12): 1601–15.

—2012a. *Blaming Islam*. Cambridge, MA: A Boston Review Book, MIT Press.

—2012b. "Working Schemas and Normative Models in French Governance of Islam." *Comparative European Politics*, 10(3): 354–68.

Bowsky, William M. 1981. *A Medieval Italian Commune: Siena under the Nine, 1287–1355*. Berkeley: University of California Press.

Breton, Raymond. 1964. "Institutional Completeness of Ethnic Communities and the Personal Relations of Immigrants." *American Journal of Sociology*, 70(2): 193–205.

—2012. *Different Gods: Integrating Non-Christian Minorities into a Primarily Christian Society*. Montreal and Kingston: McGill-Queen's University Press.

Brettell, Caroline and Deborah Reed-Danahay. 2012. *Civic Engagements: The Citizenship Practices of Indian and Vietnamese Immigrants*. Stanford, CA: Stanford University Press.

Brubaker, Rogers. 1992. *Citizenship and Nationhood in France and Germany*. Cambridge, MA: Harvard University Press.

—2004. *Ethnicity without Groups*. Cambridge, MA: Harvard University Press.

Brym, Robert and Cynthia Hamlin. 2009. "Suicide Bombers: Beyond Cultural Dopes and Rational Fools," pp. 83–96 in Mohamed Cherkaoui and Peter Hamilton (eds.), *Raymond Boudon: A Life in Sociology*, vol. 2. Oxford: Bardwell Press.

Bursik, Robert. 2006. "Rethinking the Chicago School of Criminology: A New Era of Immigration," pp. 20–35 in Ramiro Martinez, Jr, and Abel Valenzuela, Jr (eds.), *Immigration and Crime: Race, Ethnicity, and Violence*. New York: New York University Press.

Buruma, Ian. 2006. *Murder in Amsterdam: Liberal Europe, Islam, and the Limits of Tolerance*. New York: Penguin Press.

Cadge, Wendy. 2008. "De Facto Congregationalism and the Religious Organizations of Post-1965 Immigrants to the United States: A Revised Approach." *Journal of the American Academy of Religion*, 76(2): 344–74.

Cadge, Wendy and Elaine Howard Ecklund. 2006. "Religious Service Attendance among Immigrants: Evidence from the New Immigrant Survey – Pilot." *American Behavioral Scientist*, 49(11): 1574–95.

—2007. "Immigration and Religion." *Annual Review of Sociology*, 33: 359–79.

Caldwell, Christopher. 2009. *Reflections on the Revolution in Europe: Immigration, Islam, and the West*. New York: Doubleday.

—2012. "Europe's Other Crisis." *The New Republic*, May 24: 29–33.

Carol, Sarah and Ruud Koopmans. 2013. "Dynamics of Contestation over Islamic Religious Rights in Western Europe." *Ethnicities*, 13(2): 165–90.

Casanova, José. 1994. *Public Religion in the Modern World*. Chicago: University of Chicago Press.

Castles, Stephen. 2002. "Migration and Community Formation under Conditions of Globalization." *International Migration Review*, 36(4): 1143–68.

Castles, Stephen and Mark J. Miller. 2009. *The Age of Migration: International Population Movements in the Modern World*, 4th edn. New York: Guilford Press.

Cesari, Jocelyne. 2005. "Mosque Conflicts in European Cities: Introduction." *Journal of Ethnic and Migration Studies*, 31(6): 1015–24.

Chaves, Mark. 2004. *Congregations in America*. Cambridge, MA: Harvard University Press.

—2009. "Congregations' Significance to American Civic Life," pp. 69–81 in Paul Lichterman and C. Brady Potts (eds.), *The Civic Life of American Religion*. Stanford, CA: Stanford University Press.

Chen, Carolyn. 2002. "The Religious Varieties of Ethnic Presence: A Comparison between a Taiwanese Immigrant Buddhist Temple and an Evangelical Church." *Sociology of Religion*, 63(2): 215–38.

—2006. "From Filial Piety to Religious Piety: Evangelical Christianity Reconstructing Taiwanese Immigrant Families in the United States." *International Migration Review*, 40(3): 573–602.

—2008. *Getting Saved in America: Taiwanese Immigration and Religious Experience*. Princeton, NJ: Princeton University Press.

Choate, Mark I. 2008. *Emigrant Nation: The Making of Italy Abroad*. Cambridge, MA: Harvard University Press.

Clark, Dennis J. 1977. "The Irish Catholics: A Postponed Perspective," pp. 48–68 in Randall M. Miller and Thomas D. Marzik (eds.), *Immigrants and Religion in Urban America*. Philadelphia: Temple University Press.

Connor, Phillip Carey. 2008. "Increase or Decrease? The Impact of the International Migratory Event on Immigrant Religious Participation." *Journal for the Scientific Study of Religion*, 47(2): 243–57.

—2010. "A Theory of Immigrant Religious Adaptation: Disruption, Assimilation, and Facilitation." Princeton University. Dissertation Abstracts International, A: The Humanities and Social Sciences, vol. 71, no. 6.

—2011. "Religion as Resource: Religion and Immigrant Economic Incorporation."

References

Social Science Research, 40(5): 1350–61.

—2012. "Balm for the Soul: Immigrant Religion and Emotional Well-Being." *International Migration,* 50(2): 130–57.

Cooley, Charles Horton. 1962 [1909]. *Social Organization.* New York: Schocken Books.

Coser, Lewis A. 1974. *Greedy Institutions: Patterns of Undivided Commitment.* New York: Free Press.

Cumming-Bruce, Nick and Steven Erlanger. 2009. "Swiss Ban Building of Minarets on Mosques." *New York Times,* November 30. www.nytimes.com/2009/11/30/world/europe/30swiss.html. Retrieved July 2, 2013.

Dawson, Michael. 1994. *Behind the Mule: Class, Race, and African American Politics.* Princeton, NJ: Princeton University Press.

Deaux, Kay. 2006. *To Be an Immigrant.* New York: Russell Sage Foundation.

Demerath, N.J. III. 1995. "Cultural Victory and Organizational Defeat in the Paradoxical Decline of Liberal Protestantism." *Journal for the Scientific Study of Religion,* 34(4): 458–69.

d'Epinay, Christian. 1968. "Toward a Typology of Latin American Protestantism." *Review of Religious Research,* 10(1): 4–11.

Dhingra, Pawan. 2004. "'We're Not a Korean American Church Any More': Dilemmas in Constructing a Multi-Racial Church Identity." *Social Compass,* 51(3): 367–79.

—2007. *Managing Multicultural Lives: Asian Professionals and the Challenges of Multiple Identities.* Stanford, CA: Stanford University Press.

—2012. *Life behind the Lobby: Indian American Motel Owners and the American Dream.* Stanford, CA: Stanford University Press.

DiMaggio, Paul and Walter Powell. 1991. "The Iron Cage Revisited: Institutional Isomorphism and Collective Rationality in Organizational Fields," pp. 63–82 in Paul DiMaggio and Walter Powell (eds.), *The New Institutionalism in Organizational Analysis.* Chicago: University of Chicago Press.

Dolan, Jay. 1985. *The American Catholic Experience: A History from Colonial Times to the Present.* Garden City, NY: Doubleday.

Duyvendak, Jan Willem. 2011. *The Politics of Home: Belonging and Nostalgia in Western Europe and the United States.* Basingstoke: Palgrave Macmillan.

Ebaugh, Helen Rose. 2004. "Religion across Borders: Transnational Religious Ties." *Asian Journal of Social Science,* 32(2): 216–31.

Ebaugh, Helen Rose and Janet Saltzman Chafetz. 1999. "Agents for Cultural Reproduction and Structural Change: The Ironic Role of Women in Immigrant Religious Institutions." *Social Forces,* 78(2): 585–613.

—(eds.). 2000. *Religion and the New Immigrants: Continuities and Adaptations in Immigrant Congregations.* Walnut Creek, CA: AltaMira Press.

Eberle, Edward. 2004. "Free Exercise of Religion in Germany and the United States." *Tulane Law Review,* 78: 1023–87.

References

Ecklund, Elaine Howard. 2006. *Korean American Evangelicals: New Models for Civil Life.* New York: Oxford University Press.

Economist. 2007. "From Brick Lane to the Fast Lane: Against All Odds, Britain's Poorest Big Ethnic Group Is Streaking Ahead." October 25: 30–1.

—2009. "The Swiss Minaret Ban." November 30. www.economist.com/blogs/charlemagne/2009/11/_normal_0_false_false_6. Retrieved July 2, 2013.

—2014. "Trouble in Trappes," July 27: 44.

Emerson, Michael O. 2006. *People of the Dream: Multiracial Congregations in the United States,* with Rodney M. Woo. Princeton, NJ: Princeton University Press.

Esping-Andersen, Gosta. 1990. *The Three Worlds of Welfare Capitalism.* Princeton, NJ: Princeton University Press.

European Monitoring Centre on Racism and Xenophobia. 2005. "Majorities' Attitudes towards Migrants and Minorities: Key Findings from the Eurobarometer and the European Social Survey. http://eumc.eu.int. Retrieved March 22, 2010.

Faist, Thomas. 2013. "Multiculturalism: From Heterogeneities to Social (In)equalities," pp. 22–47 in Peter Kivisto and Östen Wahlbeck (eds.), *Debating Multiculturalism in the Nordic Welfare States.* Basingstoke: Palgrave Macmillan.

Faist, Thomas, Margit Fauser, and Eveline Reisenauer. 2013. *Transnational Migration.* Cambridge: Polity.

"Faith on the Move: The Religious Affiliation of International Migrants." 2012. Washington, DC: Pew Research Center.

Fenton, John Y. 1988. *Transplanting Religious Traditions: Asian Indians in America.* New York: Praeger.

Fetzer, Joel S. and J. Christopher Soper. 2005. *Muslims and the State in Britain, France, and Germany.* Cambridge: Cambridge University Press.

Fine, Gary Alan. 2012. *Tiny Publics: A Theory of Group Action and Culture.* New York: Russell Sage Foundation.

Finke, Roger and Rodney Stark. 1992. *The Churching of America, 1776–1850: Winners and Losers in Our Religious Economy.* New Brunswick, NJ: Rutgers University Press.

Fitzgerald, David. 2009. *A Nation of Emigrants: How Mexico Manages Its Migration.* Berkeley: University of California Press.

Foley, Michael W. and Dean R. Hoge. 2007. *Religion and the New Immigrants: How Faith Communities Form Our Newest Citizens.* New York: Oxford University Press.

Foner, Nancy. 1997. "What's New about Transnationalism? New York Immigrants Today and at the Turn of the Century." *Diaspora,* 6(3): 355–76.

Foner, Nancy and Richard Alba. 2008. "Immigrant Religion in the US and Western Europe: Bridge or Barrier to Inclusion?" *International Migration Review,* 42(2): 360–92.

References

Freier, Luisa Feline. 2009 "How Our Lady of Guadalupe Became Lutheran: Latin American Migration and Religious Change." *Migraciones Internacionales,* 5(2): 153–90.

Fournier, Marcel. 2013. *Émile Durkheim: A Biography.* Cambridge: Polity.

"Future of the Global Muslim Population, The." 2011. Washington, DC: Pew Research Center.

Galush, William J. 1977. "Faith and Fatherland: Dimensions of Polish-American Ethnoreligion, 1875–1975," pp. 84–102 in Randall M. Miller and Thomas D. Marzik (eds.), *Immigrants and Religion in Urban America.* Philadelphia: Temple University Press.

Gans, Herbert. 1979. "Symbolic Ethnicity: The Future of Ethnic Groups and Cultures in America." *Ethnic and Racial Studies,* 2(1): 1–20.

Garfinkel, Harold. 1967. *Studies in Ethnomethodology.* Englewood Cliffs, NJ: Prentice-Hall.

Garton, Ash, Timothy. 2012. "Freedom and Diversity: A Liberal Pentagram for Living Together." *New York Review of Books,* November 22: 33–6.

George, Sheba. 1998. "Caroling with the Keralites: The Negotiation of Gendered Space in an Indian Immigrant," pp. 265–94 in R. Stephen Warner and Judith Wittner (eds.), *Gatherings in the Diaspora: Religious Communities and the New Immigration.* Philadelphia: Temple University Press.

—2005. *When Women Come First: Gender and Class in Transnational Migration.* Berkeley: University of California Press.

Gilroy, Paul. 2006. *Postcolonial Melancholia.* New York: Columbia University Press.

Glick Schiller, Nina. 1997. "The Situation of Transnational Studies." *Identities,* 4(2): 155–66.

Gooren, Henri. 2002. "Catholic and Non-Catholic Theologies of Liberation: Poverty, Self-Improvement, and Ethics among Small-Scale Entrepreneurs in Guatemala City." *Journal for the Scientific Study of Religion,* 41(1): 29–45.

Gopnik, Adam. 2013. "The Right Man: Who Owns Edmund Burke?" *New Yorker,* July 29: 68–73.

Granovetter, Mark. 1973. "The Strength of Weak Ties." *American Journal of Sociology,* 78(6): 1360–80.

Guarnizo, Luis, Alejandro Portes, and William Haller. 2003. "Assimilation and Transnationalism: Determinants of Transnational Political Action among Contemporary Migrants." *American Journal of Sociology,* 108(6): 1211–48.

Guglielmo, Thomas A. 2003. *White on Arrival: Italians, Race, Color, and Power in Chicago, 1890–1965.* New York: Oxford University Press.

Habermas, Jürgen. 2006. "Religion in the Public Sphere." *European Journal of Philosophy,* 14(1): 1–25.

Hagan, Jacqueline Maria. 2008. *Migration Miracle: Faith, Hope, and Meaning on the Undocumented Journey.* Cambridge, MA: Harvard University Press.

Hammond, Phillip E. and Kee Warner. 1993. "Religion and Ethnicity in

References

Late-Twentieth-Century America." *Annals of the American Academy of Political and Social Science,* 527(May): 55–66.

Handlin, Oscar. 1951. *The Uprooted.* Boston: Little, Brown.

Harrison, Jim. 2005. *True North.* New York: Grove Press.

Hasmath, Reza (ed.). 2011. *Managing Ethnic Diversity: Meanings and Practices from an International Perspective.* Burlington, VT: Ashgate Publishing.

Herberg, Will. 1955. *Protestant, Catholic, Jew.* Garden City, NY: Doubleday.

Hirschman, Albert O. 1970. *Exit, Voice, and Loyalty: Responses to Decline in Firms, Organizations, and States.* Cambridge, MA: Harvard University Press.

Hirschman, Charles. 2004. "The Role of Religion in the Origins and Adaptation of Immigrant Groups in the United States." *International Migration Review,* 38(3): 1206–33.

Hobsbawm, Eric J. 1964. *Labouring Men: Studies in the History of Labour.* London: Weidenfeld and Nicolson.

—1968. *Industry and Empire.* London: Weidenfeld and Nicolson.

Hollinger, David. 1995. *Post-Ethnic America: Beyond Multiculturalism.* New York: Basic Books.

—2006. "From Identity to Solidarity." *Daedalus,* Fall: 23–31.

—2013. *After Cloven Tongues of Fire: Protestant Liberalism in Modern American History.* Princeton, NJ: Princeton University Press.

Holmio, Armas K. E. 2001[1967]. *History of the Finns in Michigan.* Detroit, MI: Wayne State University Press.

Hondagneu-Sotelo, Pierrette (ed.). 2007. *Religion and Social Justice for Immigrants.* New Brunswick, NJ: Rutgers University Press.

Honneth, Axel. 2007. *Disrespect: The Normative Foundations of Critical Theory.* Cambridge: Polity.

Huntington, Samuel P. 2004. *Who Are We? The Challenges to America's National Identity.* New York: Simon and Schuster.

Iannaccone, Laurence R. 1994. "Why Strict Churches Are Strong." *American Journal of Sociology,* 99(5): 1180–1211.

Jaspers, Eva and Marcel Lubbers. 2013. "Religion as Catalyst or Restraint on Radical Right Voting?" *West European Politics,* 36(5): 946–68.

Jasso, Guillermina, Douglas S. Massey, Mark R. Rosenzweig, and James P. Smith. 2003. "Exploring the Religious Preferences of Recent Immigrants to the United States: Evidence from the New Immigrant Survey Pilot," in Yvonne Yazhede Haddad, Jane I. Smith, and John L. Esposito (eds.), *Religion and Immigration: Christian, Jewish, and Muslim Experiences in the United States.* Walnut Creek, CA: AltaMira Press.

Jeung, Russell. 2005. *Faithful Generations: Race and New Asian American Churches.* New Brunswick, NJ: Rutgers University Press.

Joppke, Christian. 2009. *Veil: Mirror of Identity.* Cambridge: Polity.

—2010. *Citizenship and Immigration.* Cambridge: Polity.

References

—2012. "Rejoinder." *Ethnicities,* 12(6): 859–63.

Joppke, Christian and John Torpey. 2013. *Legal Integration of Islam: A Transatlantic Comparison.* Cambridge, MA: Harvard University Press.

Juergensmeyer, Mark. 1995. "The Debate over Hindu Nationalism." *Contention: Debates in Society, Culture, and Science,* 4(3): 211–21.

—2003. *Terror in the Mind of God: The Global Rise of Religious Violence,* 3rd edn. Berkeley: University of California Press.

Kamat, Sangeeta and Biju Mathew. 2003. "Mapping Political Violence in a Globalized World: The Case of Hindu Nationalism." *Social Justice,* 30(3): 4–16.

Kastoryano, Riva. 2002. *Negotiating Identities: States and Immigrants in France and Germany.* Princeton, NJ: Princeton University Press.

—2004. "Religion and Incorporation: Islam in France and Germany." *International Migration Review,* 38(3): 1234–55.

Katznelson, Ira. 1996. *Liberalism's Crooked Circle: Letters to Adam Michnik.* Princeton, NJ: Princeton University Press.

Kaya, Ayhan. 2012. *Islam, Migration, and Integration: The Age of Securitization.* Basingstoke: Palgrave Macmillan.

Keohane, Robert O. and Joseph S. Nye. 1977. *Power and Interdependence: World Politics in Transition.* Boston: Little, Brown.

Kepel, Gilles. 2004. *The War for Muslim Minds: Islam and the West.* Cambridge, MA: Harvard University Press.

Killian, Caitlin. 2007. "From a Community of Believers to an Islam of the Heart: 'Conspicuous' Symbols, Muslim Practices, and the Privatization of Religion in France." *Sociology of Religion,* 68(3): 305–20.

Kim, Ai Ra. 1996. *Women Struggling for a New Life: The Role of Religion in the Cultural Passage from Korea to America.* Albany: State University of New York Press.

Kim, Jung Ha. 1996. "The Labor of Compassion: Voices of 'Churched' Korean American Women." *Amerasia Journal,* 22(2): 93–105.

Kim, Rebecca. 2004. "Second-Generation Korean American Evangelicals: Ethnic, Multiethnic, or White Campus Ministries?" *Sociology of Religion,* 65(1): 19–34.

—2006. *God's New Whiz Kids? Korean American Evangelicals on Campus.* New York: New York University Press.

Kim, Sharon. 2010. *A Faith of Our Own: Second-Generation Spirituality in Korean American Churches.* New Brunswick, NJ: Rutgers University Press.

Kivisto, Peter. 1990. "The Transplanted Then and Now: From the Chicago School to the New Social History." *Ethnic and Racial Studies,* 13(4): 549–77.

—1992. "Religion and the New Immigrants," pp. 92–108 in William H. Swatos, Jr (ed.), *A Future for Religion? New Paradigms for Social Analysis.* Newbury Park, CA: Sage.

References

—2001. "Theorizing Transnational Immigration: A Critical Review of Current Efforts." *Ethnic and Racial Studies,* 24(4): 549–77.

—2002. *Multiculturalism in a Global Society.* Malden, MA: Blackwell.

—2007. "Rethinking the Relationship between Ethnicity and Religion," pp. 474–94 in James A. Beckford and N. J. Demerath III (eds.), *The Sage Handbook of the Sociology of Religion.* Thousand Oaks, CA: Sage.

—2012. "We *Really* Are All Multiculturalists Now." *The Sociological Quarterly,* 53(1): 1–24.

Kivisto, Peter and Thomas Faist. 2007. *Citizenship: Discourse, Theory, and Transnational Prospects.* Malden, MA: Blackwell.

Kivisto, Peter and Jason Mahn. 2009. "Radical Hospitality: Sociotheological Reflections on Postville, Iowa." *Word and World,* 29(3): 252–61.

Kivisto, Peter and Vanja La Vecchia-Mikkola. 2013. "Immigrant Ambivalence toward the Homeland: The Case of Iraqis in Helsinki and Rome." *Journal of Immigrant and Refugee Studies,* 11(2): 198–216.

—Forthcoming. "Integration as Identity Work: Iraqis in Two European Cities." *Emotion, Space and Society.*

Klausen, Jytte. 2009. *The Cartoons That Shook the World.* New Haven, CT: Yale University Press.

Kleiderman, Alex. 2009. "Can Britain Accept Funeral Pyres?" BBC News. http://www.news.bbc.co.uk/1/hi/uk/7953581.stm. Retrieved June 21, 2013.

Kniss, Fred and Paul D. Numrich. 2007. *Sacred Assemblies and Civic Engagement: How Religion Matters for America's Newest Immigrants.* New Brunswick, NJ: Rutgers University Press.

Koopmans, Ruud. 2013. "Multiculturalism and Immigration: A Contested Field in Cross-National Comparison." *Annual Review of Sociology,* 39: 147–69.

Kurien, Prema A. 1999. "Gendered Ethnicity: Creating a Hindu Indian Identity in the United States." *American Behavioral Scientist,* 42(4): 648–70.

—2001. "Religion, Ethnicity, and Politics: Hindu and Muslim Indian Immigrants in the United States." *Ethnic and Racial Studies,* 24(2): 263–93.

—2007. *A Place at the Multicultural Table: The Development of an American Hinduism.* New Brunswick, NJ: Rutgers University Press.

—2012. "Decoupling Religion and Ethnicity: Second-Generation Indian American Christians." *Qualitative Sociology,* 35(4): 447–68.

Kuru, Ahmet T. 2009. *Secularism and State Policies toward Religion: The United States, France, and Turkey.* Cambridge: Cambridge University Press.

Kymlicka, Will. 1995. *Multicultural Citizenship.* New York: Oxford University Press.

—2010. "Testing the Liberal Multiculturalist Hypothesis: Normative Theories and Social Science Evidence." *Canadian Journal of Political Science,* 43(2): 257–71.

Lal, Barbara Ballis. 1990. *The Romance of Culture in an Urban Civilisation: Robert E. Park on Race and Ethnic Relations in Cities.* London: Routledge.

References

Laurence, Jonathan. 2012. *The Emancipation of Europe's Muslims: The State's Role in Minority Integration*. Princeton, NJ: Princeton University Press.

Leiken, Robert S. 2011. *Europe's Angry Muslims: The Revolt of the Second Generation*. New York: Oxford University Press.

Lenard, Patti Tamara. 2012. "The Reports of Multiculturalism's Death Are Greatly Exaggerated." *Politics,* 32(3): 186–96.

Levitt, Peggy. 2001. *The Transnational Villagers*. Berkeley: University of California Press.

—2003. "'You Know, Abraham Was Really the First Immigrant': Religion and Transnational Migration." *International Migration Review,* 37(3): 847–73.

—2004. "Redefining the Boundaries of Belonging: The Institutional Character of Transnational Religious Life." *Sociology of Religion,* 61(1): 1–18.

—2007. *God Needs No Passport*. New York: The New Press.

—2009. "Roots and Routes: Understanding the Lives of the Second Generation Transnationally." *Journal of Ethnic and Migration Studies,* 35(7): 1225–42.

Levitt, Peggy, Josh DeWind, and Steven Vertovec. 2003. "International Perspectives on Transnationalism Migration." *International Migration Review,* 37(3): 565–75.

Levitt, Peggy and B. Nadya Jaworsky. 2007. "Transnational Migration Studies: Past Developments and Future Trends." *Annual Review of Sociology,* 33: 129–56.

Levitt, Peggy and Nina Glick Schiller. 2004. "Conceptualizing Simultaneity: A Transnational Social Field Perspective on Society." *International Migration Review,* 38(4): 1102–39.

Light, Ivan. 2010. "Transnational Entrepreneurs in an English-Speaking World." *Die Erde,* 141(1–2): 1–16.

Lim, Chaeyoon and Robert D. Putnam. 2010. "Religion, Social Networks, and Life Satisfaction." *American Sociological Review,* 75(6): 914–33.

Liogier, Raphaël. 2009. "*Laïcité* on the Edge in France: Between the Theory of Church–State Separation and the Praxis of State–Church Confusion." *Macquarie Law Journal,* 9: 25–45.

Lorentzen, Lois Ann, with Rosalina Mira. 2005. "El Milagro Está en Casa: Gender and Private/Public Empowerment in a Migrant Pentecostal Church." *Latin American Perspectives,* 140(32): 57–71.

Lucassen, Leo. 2005. *The Immigrant Threat: The Integration of the Old and New Migrants in Western Europe since 1850*. Urbana: University of Illinois Press.

Maclure, Jocelyn and Charles Taylor. 2011. *Secularism and Freedom of Conscience*. Cambridge, MA: Harvard University Press.

Mahalingam, Ramaswami (ed.). 2006. *Cultural Psychology of Immigrants*. Mahwah, NJ: Lawrence Erlbaum Associates.

References

Mahler, Sarah J. and Katrin Hansing. 2005. "Toward a Transnationalism of the Middle: How Transnational Religious Practices Help Bridge the Divides between Cuba and Miami." *Latin American Perspectives*, 32(1): 121–46.

Margalit, Avishai and Moshe Halbertal. 1994. "Liberalism and the Right to Culture." *Social Research*, 61(3): 491–510.

Marotta, Vince. 2012. "Georg Simmel, the Stranger, and the Sociology of Knowledge." *Journal of Intercultural Studies*, 33(6): 675–89.

Marti, Gerardo. 2005. *A Mosaic of Believers: Diversity and Innovation in a Multiethnic Church*. Bloomington: Indiana University Press.

—2012. *Worship across the Racial Divide: Religious Music and the Multiracial Congregation*. New York: Oxford University Press.

Martin, David. 1990. *Tongues of Fire: The Explosion of Protestantism in Latin America*. Oxford: Blackwell Publishing.

Marty, Martin. 1970. *Righteous Empire: The Protestant Experience in America*. New York: Dial Press.

Massey, Douglas S. and Monica Espinoza Higgins. 2011. "The Effect of Immigration on Religious Belief and Practice: A Theologizing or Alienating Experience." *Social Science Research*, 40(5): 1371–89.

Mathew, Biju and Vijay Prashad. 2000. "The Protean Forms of Yankee *Hindutva*." *Ethnic and Racial Studies*, 23(3): 516–34.

Matthews, Fred. 1977. *Quest for an American Sociology: Robert E. Park and the Chicago School*. Montreal: McGill-Queen's University Press.

Meer, Nasar. 2013. "Racialization and Religion: Race, Culture and Difference in the Study of Antisemitism and Islamophobia." *Ethnic and Racial Studies*, 36(3): 385–98.

Menjívar, Cecilia. 1999. "Religious Institutions and Transnationalism: A Case Study of Catholic and Evangelical Salvadoran Immigrants." *International Journal of Politics, Culture, and Society*, 12(4): 589–612.

Meyer, Nick. 2010. "Lebanese Muslim Painter's Artistic Vision: Religious Harmony in Italy." *Arab American News*, July 16. http://www.arabamerican news.com/news/index.php?mod=article&cat=Artamp. Retrieved on May 27, 2012.

Miller, Donald E. and Tetsunao Yamamori. 2007. *Global Pentecostalism: The New Face of Christian Social Engagement*. Berkeley: University of California Press.

Miller, Kerby A. 1985. *Emigrants and Exiles: Ireland and the Irish Exodus to North America*. New York: Oxford University Press.

Min, Pyong Gap. 2010. *Preserving Ethnicity through Religion in America: Korean Protestants and Indian Hindus across Generations*. New York: New York University Press.

Modood, Tariq. 2005. *Multicultural Politics: Racism, Ethnicity, and Muslims in Britain*. Minneapolis: University of Minnesota Press.

References

—2010. "Multicultural Citizenship and Muslim Identity." *Interventions,* 12(2): 157–70.

—2012. "Is There a Crisis of Secularism in Western Europe?" *Sociology of Religion,* 73(2): 130–49.

Modood, Tariq and Riva Kastoryano. 2006. "Secularism and the Accommodation of Muslims in Europe," pp. 162–78 in Tariq Modood, Anna Triandafyllidou, and Ricard Zapata-Barrero (eds.), *Multiculturalism, Muslims, and Citizenship: A European Approach.* London: Routledge.

Modood, Tariq and Fauzia Ahmad. 2007. "British Muslim Perspectives on Multiculturalism." *Theory, Culture, and Society,* 24(2): 187–213.

Mooney, Margarita. 2009. *Faith Makes Us Live: Surviving and Thriving in the Haitian Diaspora.* Berkeley: University of California Press.

Morawska, Ewa. 2001. "Immigrants, Transnationalism, and Ethnicization: A Comparison of This Great Wave and the Last," pp. 175–212 in Gary Gerstle and John Mollenkopf (eds.), *E Pluribus Unum? Contemporary and Historical Perspectives on Immigrant Incorporation.* New York: Russell Sage Foundation.

—2003. "Disciplinary Agendas and Analytic Strategies of Research on Immigrant Transnationalism: Challenges of Interdisciplinary Knowledge." *International Migration Review,* 37(3): 611–40.

Mudde, Cas. 2012. *The Relationship between Immigration and Nativism in Europe and North America.* Washington, DC: Migration Policy Institute.

Mullins, Mark R. 1988. "The Organizational Dilemmas of Ethnic Churches: A Case Study of Japanese Buddhism in Canada." *Sociological Analysis,* 49(3): 217–33.

Nelson, Benjamin. 1973. "Civilizational Complexes and Intercivilizational Encounters." *Sociological Analysis,* 34(2): 79–105.

Ngô, Thi Thanh Tâm. 2010. "Ethnic Transnational Dimensions of Recent Protestant Conversion among the Hmong in Northern Vietnam." *Social Compass,* 57(3): 332–44.

Niebuhr, Gustav. 2007. "All Need Toleration: Some Observations about Recent Differences in the Experiences of Religious Minorities in the United States and Western Europe." *Annals of the American Academy of Political and Social Science,* 612: 172–86.

Niebuhr, H. Richard. 1929. *The Social Sources of Denominationalism.* New York: Henry Holt.

Nussbaum, Martha C. 2012. *The New Religious Intolerance: Overcoming the Politics of Fear in an Anxious Age.* Cambridge, MA: The Belknap Press of Harvard University Press.

Parekh, Bhikhu. 2000. *Rethinking Multiculturalism: Cultural Diversity and Political Theory.* Basingstoke: Macmillan.

Parenti, Michael. 1967. "Introduction to the Torchbooks Edition," pp. vii–xxii

References

in W. I. Thomas, *The Unadjusted Girl: With Cases and Standpoint for Behavior Analysis*. New York: Harper Torchbooks.

Park, Robert Ezra. 1950. *Race and Culture: Essays in the Sociology of Contemporary Man*. New York: Free Press.

Parsons, Talcott. 1971. *The System of Modern Societies*. Englewood Cliffs, NJ: Prentice-Hall.

Persons, Stow. 1987. *Ethnic Studies at Chicago, 1905–45*. Urbana: University of Illinois Press.

Peschke, Doris. 2009. "The Role of Religion for the Integration of Migrants and Institutional Responses in Europe: Some Reflections." *Ecumenical Review*, 61(4): 367–80.

Peterson, Anna L., Manuel A. Vásquez, and Philip J. Williams (eds.). 2001. *Christianity, Social Change, and Globalization in the Americas*. New Brunswick, NJ: Rutgers University Press.

Pettigrew, Thomas. 1998. "Reactions toward the New Minorities of Western Europe." *Annual Review of Sociology*, 24: 77–103.

Pianigiani, Gaia. 2010. "In a Sacred Italian Race, Some Bristle at the Prize." *New York Times*, July 3: A4.

Portes, Alejandro, William Haller, and Luis Guarnizo. 2002. "Transnational Entrepreneurs: An Alternative Form of Immigrant Economic Adaptation." *American Sociological Review*, 67(2): 278–98.

Portes, Alejandro and Rubén Rumbaut. 2006. *Immigrant America: A Portrait*. Berkeley: University of California Press.

Putnam, Robert D. 2000. *Bowling Alone: The Collapse and Revival of American Community*. New York: Simon and Schuster.

Putnam, Robert D. and David E. Campbell. 2010. *American Grace: How Religion Divides and Unites Us*. New York: Simon and Schuster.

Rochford, E. Burke, Jr. 2007. *Hare Krishna Transformed*. New York: New York University Press.

Rodriguez-Garcia, Dan. 2010. "Beyond Assimilation and Multiculturalism: A Critical Review of the Debate on Managing Diversity." *Journal of International Migration and Integration*, 11(3): 251–71.

Roediger, David. 2005. *Working toward Whiteness: How America's Immigrants Became White: The Strange Journey from Ellis Island to the Suburbs*. New York: Basic Books.

Roy, Olivier. 2004. *Globalized Islam: The Search for a New Ummah*. New York: Columbia University Press.

Rustomji, Yezdi. 2000. "The Zoroastrian Center: An Ancient Faith in Diaspora," pp. 243–53 in Helen Rose Ebaugh and Janet S. Chafetz (eds.), *Religion and the New Immigrants: Continuities and Adaptations in Immigrant Congregations*. Walnut Creek, CA: AltaMira Press.

Safran, William. 1986. "Islamization in Western Europe: Political Consequences and Historical Parallels." *Annals of the American Academy of Political and*

References

Social Science, 485: 98–112.

Sassen, Saskia. 1996. *Losing Control? Sovereignty in an Age of Globalization.* New York: Columbia University Press.

Saukkonen, Pasi. 2013. "Multiculturalism and Nationalism: The Politics of Diversity in Finland," pp. 270–94 in Peter Kivisto and Östen Wahlbeck (eds.), *Debating Multiculturalism in the Nordic Welfare States.* Basingstoke: Palgrave Macmillan.

Sayad, Abdelmalek. 2004. *The Suffering of the Immigrant.* Cambridge: Polity.

Scheffer, Paul. 2011. *Immigrant Nations.* Cambridge: Polity.

—2012 [2000]. "The Multicultural Drama." Unpublished English translation of "Het Multiculturele Drama." In *NRC Handelsblad,* 29 January 2000.

Schiller, Nina Glick. 1997. "The Situation of Transnational Studies." *Identities,* 4(2): 155–66.

Schiller, Nina Glick, Linda Basch, and Cristina Szanton Blanc (eds.). 1992. *Toward a Transnational Perspective on Migration.* New York: New York Academy of Sciences.

Schuck, Peter H. 2003. *Diversity in America: Keeping Government at a Safe Distance.* Cambridge, MA: The Belknap Press of Harvard University Press.

Sciortino, Giuseppe. 2003. "From Heterogeneity to Difference? Comparing Multiculturalism as a Description and a Field for Claim-Making." *Comparative Social Research,* 22: 263–85.

Sellin, Thorsten. 1938. *Culture Conflict and Crime.* New York: Social Science Research Council.

Seol, Kyoung Ok and Richard M. Lee. 2012. "The Effects of Religious Socialization and Religious Identity on Psychological Functioning in Korean American Adolescents from Immigrant Families." *Journal of Family Psychology,* 26(3): 371–80.

Shaw, Clifford R. and Henry D. McKay. 1942. *Juvenile Delinquency in Urban Areas.* Chicago: University of Chicago Press.

—1971 [1908]. "The Stranger," pp. 143–9 in Georg Simmel, edited by Donald Levine, *On Individuality and Social Forms.* Chicago: University of Chicago Press.

Simmel, Georg. 1955. *Conflict and the Web of Group-Affiliations.* New York: Free Press.

Sklair, Leslie. 2001. *The Transnational Capitalist Class.* Oxford: Blackwell.

Smelser, Neil. 1998. "The Rational and the Ambivalent in the Social Sciences. *American Sociological Review,* 63(1): 1–16.

Smilde, David. 1999. "El Clamor por Venezuela: Latin American Evangelicalism as a Collective Frame of Action," pp. 125–45 in Christian Smith and Joshua Prokopy (eds.), *Latin American Religion in Motion.* New York: Routledge.

—2007. *Reason to Believe: Cultural Agency in Latin American Evangelicalism.* Berkeley: University of California Press.

Smith, Christian and Liesl Ann Haas. 1997. "Revolutionary Evangelicals in

References

Nicaragua: Political Opportunity, Class Interests, and Religious Identity." *Journal for the Scientific Study of Religion,* 36(3): 440–54.

Smith, Robert C. 2003. "Diasporic Memberships in Historical Perspective: Comparative Insights from the Mexican, Italian, and Polish Cases." *International Migration Review,* 37(3): 724–59.

Smith, Timothy L. 1978. "Religion and Ethnicity in America." *American Historical Review,* 83(5): 1155–85.

Sniderman, Paul M. and Edward G. Carmines. 1997. *Reaching beyond Race.* Cambridge, MA: Harvard University Press.

Sniderman, Paul M. and Louk Hagendoorn. 2007. *When Ways of Life Collide: Multiculturalism and Its Discontents in the Netherlands.* Princeton, NJ: Princeton University Press.

Stepick, Alex, Terry Rey, and Sarah J. Mahler. 2009. *Churches and Charity in the Immigrant City: Religion, Immigration, and Civic Engagement in Miami.* New Brunswick, NJ: Rutgers University Press.

Suárez-Orozco, Carol, Sukhmani Singh, Mona M. Abo-Zena, Dan Du, and Robert W. Roeser. 2012. "The Role of Religion and Worship Communities in the Positive Development of Immigrant Youth," pp. 255–88 in Amy Eva Alberts Warren, Richard M. Lerner, and Erin Phelps (eds.), *Thriving and Spirituality among Youth: Research Perspectives and Future Possibilities.* Hoboken, NJ: John Wiley and Sons.

Sutton, Philip W. and Stephen Vertigans. 2005. *Resurgent Islam:" A Sociological Approach.* Cambridge: Polity.

Swatos, William H., Jr. 2006. *On the Road to Being There: Studies in Pilgrimage and Tourism in Late Modernity.* Leiden, The Netherlands: Brill.

Taras, Raymond. 2013. "'Islamophobia Never Stands Still': Race, Religion, and Culture." *Ethnic and Racial Studies,* 36(3): 417–33.

Taylor, Charles. 1992. *Multiculturalism and the "Politics of Recognition,"* with commentaries by Amy Gutmann, Steven C. Rockefeller, Michael Walzer, and Susan Wolf. Princeton, NJ: Princeton University Press.

—2004. *Modern Social Imaginaries.* Durham, NC: Duke University Press.

—2007. *A Secular Age.* Cambridge, MA: The Belknap Press of Harvard University Press.

Taylor, Jerome. 2009. "The Big Question: Why Do Hindus Want Open-Air Cremation, and Should It Be Allowed?" *Independent,* March 25 (Wednesday). www.independent.co.uk/news/uk/this-britain/the-big-question-why-do-hindus-want-openair-cremation-and-should-it-be-allowed-1653329.html. Retrieved on June 21, 2013.

—2010. "Hindu Healer Wins Funeral Pyre Battle." *Independent,* February 16 (Wednesday). www.independent.co.uk/news/uk/hindu-healer-wins-funeral-pyre-battle-1895116.html. Retrieved on June 21, 2013.

Terrazas, Aaron. 2008. "Indian Immigrants in the United States." Migration

References

Information Source. http://www.migrationinformation.org/isfpcis/print.cfm? ID=687. Retrieved on June 22, 2012.

Thomas, W. I. 1967 [1923]. *The Unadjusted Girl: With Cases and Standpoint for Behavior Analysis*. New York: Harper Torchbooks.

Thomas, W. I. and Florian Znaniecki. 1918/1920. *The Polish Peasant in Europe and America*, 5 vols. Chicago: University of Chicago Press.

Thompson, E. P. 1963. *The Making of the English Working Class*. New York: Vintage Books.

Tillich, Paul. 1951. *Systematic Theology*, vol. 1. Chicago: University of Chicago Press.

Tizon, Orlando. 1999. "Congregation and Family: Changing Filipino Identities," PhD dissertation. Chicago: Loyola University.

—2000. "'Destroying a Marriage to Save a Family': Shifting Filipino American Gender Relations," pp. 381–93 in Peter Kivisto and Georgeanne Rundblad (eds.), *Multiculturalism in the United States: Current Issues, Contemporary Voices*. Thousand Oaks, CA: Pine Forge Press.

Torpey, John. 2012. "Religion and Secularization in the United States and Western Europe," pp. 279–306 in Philip S. Gorski, David Kyuman Kim, John Torpey, and Jonathan VanAntwerpen (eds.), *The Post-Secular in Question: Religion in Contemporary Society*. New York: New York University Press.

Traynor, Ian. 2009. "Swiss Vote to Ban Construction of Minarets on Mosques." *Guardian*, Sunday, November 29. www.guardian.co/uk/world/nov/29/switzerland-bans-mosque-minarets. Retrieved July 2, 2013.

Trzebiatowska, Marta. 2010. "The Advent of the 'EasyJet Priest': Dilemmas of Polish Catholic Integration in the UK." *Sociology*, 44(6): 1055–72.

United Nations, Department of Economic and Social Affairs, Population Division. 2011. International Migration Report 2009: A Global Assessment (United Nations, ST/ESA/SER.A/316).

"US Religious Landscape Survey: Religious Affiliation Diverse and Dynamic." 2008. Washington, DC: Pew Research Center and the Pew Forum on Religion and Public Life.

van den Breemer, Rosmarie and Marcel Maussen. 2012. "On the Viability of State–Church Models: Muslim Burial and Mosque Building in France and the Netherlands." *Journal of Immigrant and Refugee Studies*, 10(2): 279–98.

van Kreiken, Robert. 2012. "We Have Never Been Multicultural." *Contemporary Sociology*, 41(4): 466–9.

van Tubergen, Frank and Jórunn Í Sindradóttir. 2011. "The Religiosity of Immigrants in Europe: A Cross-National Study." *Journal for the Scientific Study of Religion*, 50(2): 272–88.

Vásquez, Manuel A. 2005. "Historicizing and Materializing the Study of Religion: The Contribution of Migration Studies," pp. 219–42 in Karen I. Leonard, Alex Stepick, Manuel A. Vásquez, and Jennifer Holdaway (eds.),

References

Immigrant Faiths: Transforming Religious Life in America. Lanham, MD: AltaMira Press.

Vásquez, Manuel A. and Marie Friedmann Marquardt (eds.). 2003. *Globalizing the Sacred: Religion across the Americas.* New Brunswick, NJ: Rutgers University Press.

Vertovec, Steven. 2000. *The Hindu Diaspora: Comparative Patterns.* London: Routledge.

—2009. *Transnationalism.* London: Routledge.

Vertovec, Steven and Susanne Wessendorf (eds.). 2010. *The Multiculturalism Backlash: European Discourses, Policies and Practices.* London: Routledge.

Voas, David and Fenella Fleischmann. 2012. "Islam Moves West: Religious Change in the First and Second Generations." *Annual Review of Sociology,* 38: 525–45.

Voss, Kim and Irene Bloemraad (eds.). 2011. *Rallying for Immigrant Rights: The Fight for Inclusion in 21st Century America.* Berkeley: University of California Press.

Waldinger, Roger. 2007. "The Bounded Community: Turning Foreigners into Americans in Twenty-first Century Los Angeles." *Ethnic and Racial Studies,* 30(3): 341–74.

—2008a. "Between 'Here' and 'There'": Immigrant Cross-Border Activities and Loyalties." *International Migration Review,* 42(1): 3–29.

—2008b. "Immigrant 'Transnationalism' and the Presence of the Past," pp. 267–85 in Elliott R. Barkan, Hasia Diner, and Alan M. Kraut (eds.), *From Arrival to Incorporation.* New York: New York University Press.

—2011. "Immigrant Transnationalism." *Sociopedia.isa.* www.sagepub.net/isa/resources/pdf/ImmigrantTransnationalism.pdf. Retrieved on January 14, 2012.

Waldinger, Roger and David Fitzgerald. 2004. "Transnationalism in Question." *American Journal of Sociology,* 109(5): 1177–95.

Wang, Yuting and Fenggang Yang. 2006. "More Than Evangelical and Ethnic: The Ecological Factor in Chinese Conversion to Christianity in the United States." *Sociology of Religion,* 67(2): 179–92.

Warner, R. Stephen. 1993. "Work in Progress toward a New Paradigm for the Sociological Study of Religion in the United States." *American Journal of Sociology,* 98(5): 1044–93.

—1994. "The Place of the Congregation in the American Religious Configuration," pp. 54–99 in James P. Wind and James W. Lewis (eds.), *American Congregations,* vol. 2, *New Perspectives in the Study of Congregations.* Chicago: University of Chicago Press.

—1997. "Religion, Boundaries, and Bridges." *Sociology of Religion,* 58(3): 217–38.

—1998a. "Approaching Religious Diversity: Barriers, Byways, and Beginnings." *Sociology of Religion,* 59(3): 193–215.

References

—1998b. "Religion and Migration in the United States." *Social Compass*, 45(1): 123–34.

—2000. "Religion and New (Post-1965) Immigrants: Some Principles Drawn from Field Research." *American Studies*, 41(2/3): 267–86.

—2007. "The Role of Religion in the Process of Segmented Assimilation." *Annals of the American Academy of Political and Social Science*, 612(July): 102–15.

Warner, R. Stephen and Judith Wittner (eds.). 1998. *Gatherings in Diaspora: Religious Communities and the New Immigration.* Philadelphia: Temple University Press.

Warner, R. Stephen, Elise Martel, and Rhonda E. Dugan. 2012. "Islam is to Catholicism as Teflon is to Velcro: Theorizing Ambivalence about Religion and Ethnic Culture among Second Generation Muslim Women and Latina College Students," pp. 46–68 in Carolyn Chen and Russell Jeung (eds.), *Sustaining Faith Traditions in America: Race, Ethnicity, and Religion among the Latino and Asian American Second Generation.* New York: New York University Press.

Waters, Mary. 1990. *Ethnic Options: Choosing Identities in America.* Berkeley: University of California Press.

Weber, Max. 1978. *Economy and Society,* volume 1. Berkeley: University of California Press.

Weil, Patrick. 2009. "Why the French *Laïcité* Is Liberal." *Cardozo Law Review*, 30(6): 2699–714.

Williams, Raymond Brady. 1998. "Asian Indian and Pakistani Religions in the United States." *Annals of the American Academy of Political and Social Science*, 558(July): 178–95.

Williams, Rhys. 2009. "Transnational Religion and the Shaping of Politics, Ethnicity, and Culture." *Contemporary Sociology*, 38(2): 129–33.

—2011. "Creating an American Islam: Thoughts on Religion, Identity, and Place." *Sociology of Religion*, 72(2): 127–53.

Wimmer, Andreas. 2008. "The Making and Unmaking of Ethnic Boundaries: A Multi-Level Process Theory." *American Journal of Sociology*, 113(4): 970–1022.

—2013. *Ethnic Boundary Making: Institutions, Power, and Networks.* New York: Oxford University Press.

Wieviorka, Michel. 2010. *Evil.* Cambridge: Polity.

Wuthnow, Robert. 2005. *America and the Challenges of Religious Diversity.* Princeton, NJ: Princeton University Press.

Wuthnow, Robert and Stephen Offutt. 2008. "Transnational Religious Connections." *Sociology of Religion*, 69(2): 209–32.

Wyman, Mark. 1993. *Round-trip to America: The Immigrants Return to Europe, 1880–1930.* Ithaca, NY: Cornell University Press.

Yang, Fenggang. 1998. "Chinese Conversion to Evangelical Christianity: The

References

Importance of Social and Cultural Contexts." *Sociology of Religion,* 59(3): 237–57.

Yang, Fenggang and Helen Rose Ebaugh. 2001. "Transformations in New Immigrant Religions and Their Global Implications." *American Sociological Review,* 66(2): 269–88.

Yansmayan, Zeynep. 2011, "Concepts of Multiculturalism and Assimilation," pp. 17–27 in Michael Emerson (ed.), *Interculturalism: Europe and Its Muslims in Search of Sound Societal Models.* Brussels: Centre for European Policy Studies.

Zolberg, Aristide and Long Litt Woon. 1999. "Why Islam Is Like Spanish: Cultural Incorporation in Europe and the United States." *Politics and Society,* 27(5): 5–38.

Index

Index

Index

Index

Germany
church–state relations 152
international migrants 14, 15
Lutherans 44
Muslims in 20, 21, 136, 138,
155–6, 166
Nazi 124
Turkish immigrants in 37–8,
143
Ghai, Davender Kumar 62–4
Gilroy, Paul 4
Global Migrant Origin Database
(Sussex University) 12
globalization 105, 109
God's Light 120, 121
Gogh, Theo van 138
Golwalkar, Madhav Sadashiv 124
Gopnick, Alan 142, 145
Granovetter, Mark 44
Greece 20, 141
Greek Orthodox Church 45

Haas, Liesl Ann 119–20
Habermas, Jürgen 167
Hagendoorn, Louk 162
Hague Convention 101
Hamlin, Cynthia 145
Hammond, Phillip 44–6, 50
Handlin, Oscar 54
The Uprooted 34–5, 36–7, 58
Hansen, Marcus Lee 46
Hare Krishnas 123
Harrison, Jim 95
Hasidic Jews 81
Hassoun, Ali 171–2, 173, 174
Herberg, Will 46, 50, 54
Higgins, Monica Espinoza 60–1
Higham, John 106
Hindus
cremation practices 62–5, 166
in the European Union 18
Hindu nationalism 49, 123, 124–5,
127–8
international migrants 12, 13, 15,
16
and Muslims 123, 124, 127–8,
130–1

and recreated transnationalism
112–13
religion and ethnicity 48–9, 50, 80
and gender 52–3
in the USA 122–31
World Hindu Council 79
Hindutva movement 127–9, 130–1
Hirschman, Albert 35, 36
Hirschman, Charles 54
Hitler, Adolf 124
Hogue, Dean 90, 91–2
Hollinger, David 82 84, 147, 168
Holmio, Armas 96
homeland religion 65-6
homophobia 134
Hong Kong Chinese immigrants 15,
26, 84
honor killings 33–4, 134
Huguenot refugees in London 1, 2, 3
human capital 4, 23
humanitarian aid 109
Huntington, Samuel 142, 144–5
Hutterites 41, 42, 44–5

Iceland 152
identity
and Hindu Americans 129–30
and the migratory experience 30–9
Muslims and European identity
134
religion and personal identity 173
multiple identities 40
religious identities 39–54
and congregationalism 66–7
and ethnicity 40–7
and transnational immigrants 105
see also national identity
imams 69–9, 165
immigrant adjustment 54–8, 173
and assimilation 24
experiences of 36–9
function of religion in 7–8, 40
see also organizational adaptation
inclusion 92–4
and immigrant adjustment 36–8,
173
and immigrant mobilization 174

201

Index

inclusion (*cont.*)
  immigrant religions as inclusive 83–90
  inclusion claims 159, 160
  and Islam 94
  religion as a bridge or barrier to 22, 136–7, 142–6, 167, 174
  and transnationalism 101, 174
income
  and religious involvement 24
India 14, 15
  BJP Party 125, 127, 128, 129, 130–1
  Gujarati Hindus 112–13
  Hindu nationalism 49, 123, 124–5, 127–8
  Hindutva movement 127–9, 130–1
  immigrant Christians from Kerala 50, 51–2
  Muslims in 49–50
  religious transnationalism 122–31
  traditional funeral practices in 65
Indian immigrant communities
  gender, ethnicity and religion 52–3
Indicators of Citizenship Rights for Immigrants (ICRI) 164-5
indigenous peoples
  and multiculturalism 161, 164
  redress claims 159–60
individual self-improvement
  and evangelical Protestantism 118
individualism 44
inequalities
  and multiculturalism 159–60, 162–3
  and transnationalism 103
integration
  and assimilation 38
International Church of the Four Square Gospel (ICFSG) 111–12
international migrants 11–22
  destinations 15–16
  in the European Union 16–18
  national origins 11, 14–15, 23
  numbers of 11–12, 17, 22

religious composition of 12–13, 16, 17–18
International Society for Krishna Consciousness (ISKCON) 123
International Swaminarayan Satsang Organization (ISSO) 112–13, 129
Intervarsity 86
Iran 15
Iraqi immigrants 36
Ireland
  Catholic Emigration Society 115
  Muslim population 20, 21
Irish Catholics 43, 45
  immigrants in the Americas 114–15
Irish nationalism 114
Ishpeming, Michigan 95-6
Islamophobia 9–10, 18, 21–2, 133–4, 138–42
  critics of the banner for the Siena Palio 171–2
  and fundamentalism 167, 168, 172
  see also Muslims
isomorphism
  and congregationalism 74
Israel 15
ISSO (International Swaminarayan Satsang Organization) 112–13, 129
Italian Catholics 43, 45
  immigrants to the USA 115–16, 117
Italy
  church–state relations 152, 154
  Muslims in 20, 155
  Siena 169–72
Ivory Coast 15

Jains 13, 85, 122, 124
  and outdoor cremations 64, 65
Janowitz, Morris 67
Japan 15
Japanese Buddhists in Canada 75
Japanese Christians 84
Jasso, Guillermina 59–60

202

Index

Index

see also "Faith on the Move" project

Philippines
Filipino immigrants in the USA 52, 114, 116

pilgrimages 108

pluralism
and anti-immigrant hostility 173
and congregationalism 73
cultural 23, 67
Islam and pluralist democracies 146, 148, 153, 168
and non-Christian immigrant identity 82
religion and the pluralist public sphere 167
religious 59–60, 67, 149, 167
in India 124

Poland 61

Polish Catholics 43, 45
immigrants to the USA 115–16, 117

Political Islam 154, 155, 157

politics
and critics of Islam 138–9, 141–2
and evangelical Christians in Latin America 118–20
Hindu nationalism 49, 123, 124–5, 127–8
and immigrant mobilization 174
the state and Muslim integration 153–7
Swiss ban on minaret construction 132–5
and transnational immigrants 105
see also multiculturalism

Portes, Alejandro 54, 101–2, 103
and Rumbaut, Ruben, *Immigrant America: A Portrait* 7

Portugal 20, 21

postcolonialism 4

Powell, Enoch 142

Powell, Walter 74

preservation claims 159

professional religious workers
and congregationalism 68–9, 71, 75
and religious transnationalism 107–8

proselytizing
and inclusiveness 84–5
and religious transnationalism 107–8, 111–12

Protestants
and congregationalism 67–8, 71, 77
decline of liberal 83
ecumenical and evangelical 82–3, 87, 89–90
Filipino immigrants 52
and inclusiveness 84, 87, 88
Korean Americans 49, 50, 54, 85–7
Latin American 82–3, 88, 117–21, 131
liberal Protestantism and converts 28, 29
Reformation 149
Taiwanese Americans 57
and the theologizing experience thesis 60
transnational religious connections 107, 109, 110–11
see also Lutherans

psychological well-being 54-6

public opinion
and anti-Islamic feelings 138–42
and immigrant identity 38
and multiculturalism 161
on Muslim populations 21–2
on outdoor cremations 63–4
and the Swiss ban on minaret construction 132–5

public sphere 9, 93, 167
and Islam 94, 135, 146, 167, 168
and religious transnationalism 106–7
see also church–state relations

Puerto Ricans 36

Putnam, Robert 54–5, 89–90, 92

Index

quotidian multiculturalism 163–4
Qutb, Sayyid 148

race 5, 23
  and ethnicity 41
  and immigrant identity 40
Ramadan, Tariq 148
Rashtriya Swayamsevak Sangh (RSS) 124-5
Rastafarians 69
recreated transnational organizations 112–13
redress claims 159–60
Reed-Danahay, Deborah 129, 130
refuge
  immigrant adjustment and religion as 54–5, 58
Religion, Ethnicity, and New Immigrant Research (RENIR) 69, 70, 85
religious equality
  and Muslim integration 156–7
religious freedom
  and church–state relations 152
  and Muslim integration 155–6
  and the Swiss ban on minaret construction 132–5
religious symbols, wearing of 103
religious toleration 149
Rey, Terry 92
ritual slaughtering practices 156-7, 164, 165
Roma 43, 134, 141
Roman Catholicism *see* Catholic Church
Rosenzweig, Mark R. 59
Rousseau, Jean-Jacques 152
Rushdie, Salman 138
Russia, international migrants from 14, 15, 18

Safran, William 138
Sami people 96
Sarrazin, Thilo 142
Sassen, Saskia 100
Saudi Arabia 14, 15, 154
Savarkar, Vinayak Damodar 124

Sayad, Abdelmalek
  The Suffering of the Immigrant 35, 36
Scheffer, Paul
  Immigrant Nations 146, 147–8
  "The Multicultural Drama" 146–7
Schengen Agreement (1985) 17
Schiller, Nina Glick 99, 100, 103, 104
Schlüer, Ulrich 133–4
Schuck, Peter 152
Sciortinio, Giuseppe 158
Scottish Presbyterianism 43
second-generation immigrants
  adjustment of 57
  and gender roles in immigrant religious institutions 91
  and inclusiveness 86
  Latin American evangelicals 121
  and multiculturalism 167–8
  religion and ethnicity 81
  and transnationalism 104
secularization
  and church–state relations 149–50
  and congregationalism 67, 73
  and immigrant religions 10
  political 105
  religion and ethnicity 44, 45, 46, 47
segmented assimilation 57
Sellin, Thorsten
  Culture Conflict and Crime 33–4
Seol, Kyoung Ok 55
separatists
  in the United States 150–1
Serbian Orthodox church 43
sexuality issues 89
  and the Laestadian Lutheran Church 98
Shaw, Clifford 34
Siena 169–72
Sikhs
  converts 85
  and Hinduism 124
  immigrants to the USA 122, 126
  and outdoor cremations 63, 64, 65

208